The Kennedy Assassinations

The Kennedy Assassinations

JFK and Bobby Kennedy – Debunking The Conspiracy Theories

Mel Ayton

Pen & Sword

MILITARY

An imprint of
Pen & Sword Books Ltd
Yorkshire – Philadelphia

Pen & Sword
MILITARY

First published in Great Britain in 2022 by
PEN & SWORD MILITARY
An imprint of
Pen & Sword Books Ltd
Yorkshire – Philadelphia

ISBN 978 1 39908 137 5

Typeset in Chennai, India
by Lapiz Digital Services.

Printed and bound by CPI Group (UK) Ltd, Croydon, CR0 4YY

Pen & Sword Books Ltd incorporates the imprints of Pen & Sword
Archaeology, Atlas, Aviation, Battleground, Discovery, Family History, History, Maritime, Military, Naval, Politics, Social History, Transport, True Crime, Claymore Press, Frontline Books, Praetorian Press, Seaforth Publishing and White Owl

For a complete list of Pen & Sword titles please contact

PEN & SWORD BOOKS LTD
47 Church Street, Barnsley, South Yorkshire, S70 2AS, England
E-mail: enquiries@pen-and-sword.co.uk
Website: www.pen-and-sword.co.uk

Or

PEN AND SWORD BOOKS
1950 Lawrence Rd, Havertown, PA 19083, USA
E-mail: Uspen-and-sword@casematepublishers.com
Website: www.penandswordbooks.com

Contents

Praise for articles and essays about the JFK and RFK assassinations written by Mel Ayton:

'Mel Ayton's research on this difficult question: "Who was responsible for the assassination of President John F. Kennedy?" is excellent.' – Colonel Manuel Chavez, Former US Air Force Intelligence Officer assigned to the CIA's office in Miami from 1960–4

'Mel Ayton has a well-deserved reputation for doing the near-impossible: writing about controversial history (including conspiracy theories) in a sober but imaginative way, combining reliable accounts with intellectually stimulating arguments. I highly recommend his work' – Rick Shenkman, publisher, History News Network

'[Mel Ayton] is doing a fabulous job of setting history right' – David Aaronovitch, columnist for *The Times* and author of *Voodoo Histories – The Role of the Conspiracy Theory in Shaping Modern History*

'Mel Ayton [is] one of the few analysts who has fully grasped the crime's Middle East connection. . . . Far from being a "maniacally absurd" crime, as *Newsweek* concluded, the Robert Kennedy assassination was in fact an eminently political act. It was the first "blowback" attack the United States suffered as a result of its Middle East policies' – Stephen Kinzer, 'Shot Heard Round the World', *The Guardian*, 13 June 2008

'The greatest riddle in any of these high-profile assassinations is motive. Thanks to Mel Ayton, the RFK killing can now be removed from that list of mysteries' – Gus Russo, author of *The Outfit and Supermob*

'Mel Ayton has accomplished something that no one writing about the RFK assassination has ever achieved before. By combining a judicious review of the forensic and eyewitness evidence with a firm grasp of the historical context, Ayton has finally made sense of the 1968 killing' – Max Holland, author of *The Kennedy Assassination Tapes* and publisher of *Washington Decoded*

'Mel Ayton presents a compelling examination of the convicted [RFK] assassin's motivations, his state of mind, and the mountain of evidence used to denounce and imprison him' – Craig Hendricks, *The History Teacher*, Vol. 41, No. 2, February 2008

'I have read some of your . . . articles about Sirhan's many conspiracy theories, which demonstrate the wealth of your research as to the RFK murder.' – California Deputy Attorney General Jaime Fuster, 13 December 2011

'Mel Ayton [is] a writer I've found to be a valuable debunker of unwarranted conspiracy theorizing. He reminds us with copious quotations in [his articles] how repeatedly and explicitly Sirhan made clear why he targeted R.F.K.: because Sirhan hated the state of Israel and hated R.F.K.'s support for Israel.' – Ron Rosenbaum, the *New York Observer*, 20 November 2006

'Important and extensively documented. . . . especially pertinent to understanding current lone wolf terrorists, as it discusses leading forensic psychology theories to explain Sirhan's possible mental state and motivations.' – Joshua Sinai, *Perspectives on Terrorism*

'The 1968 assassination of Senator Robert Kennedy by Sirhan Sirhan may well be one of the most transforming events of the last third of the 20th century. . . . Mel Ayton documents the elements that contributed to Sirhan's hatred of anyone or anything associated positively with Israel or Jews.' – Harvard Professor Emeritus Alan Dershowitz, Foreword to the 2019 edition of *The Forgotten Terrorist*

Preface

It is a great assumption in a democratic society that an informed citizenry is preferable to an uninformed one. The notion has been carried down the years. If they are ignorant, facts will enlighten them. If they are ignorant, facts will set them straight.

In fact, as studies have found, facts do not necessarily have the power to change minds. As research has shown time and time again, when misinformed people were exposed to corrected facts in new stories, they rarely changed their minds. So it is with a large percentage of the US public when it comes to an understanding of the JFK and RFK assassinations.

There was always inevitability in the linking of the assassinations to alleged 'conspirators'. The United States is obsessed with conspiracy theories and a large proportion of the population believes there are conspiratorial answers to everything. This has occurred because there is a general psychological tendency for people to think that a major or significant event must have been caused by something similarly major, significant or powerful.

The many bogus revelations, misuse of evidence and uncorroborated allegations of government malfeasance surrounding the assassination of John F. Kennedy were put to rest with the publication of Vincent Bugliosi's 1,600-page book *Reclaiming History* and Professor John McAdams' *JFK Assassination Logic: How to Think About Claims of Conspiracy*. Alas, they are still promoted as fact by many media outlets.

However, notions of CIA involvement in the assassination of President Kennedy have never been proven. Other allegations of Mafia, Cuban or Soviet involvement have also lacked verisimilitude. Year after year, conspiracists have eagerly awaited the next release of JFK assassination government documents hoping to discover the 'smoking gun' that would enable them to claim they were right all along. However, that didn't happen.

Old canards about the RFK assassination were put to rest years ago even though conspiracy advocates still repeat them. The idea that Sirhan had been a hypnotized assassin was proposed by many conspiracy writers but rejected by the American Psychological Association and other professional psychologists such as Professor Graham Wagstaff of the University of Liverpool. Additionally, there is no evidence whatsoever to imply Sirhan had been a 'programmed assassin'.

The 'mysterious' Polka-Dot Girl story, implicating a non-existent human trigger mechanism for the assassin, was rendered false years ago after the discovery by this author of LAPD RFK assassination witness statements.

I was the first author to debunk allegations made by conspiracy writer Shane O'Sullivan that CIA agents had been present at the Los Angeles Ambassador Hotel the night Robert F. Kennedy was killed and insinuated they had been involved in the assassination. And the idea that Sirhan had been programmed to forget the shooting was finally put to rest with the publication of the notes of Sirhan's defence investigator, Michael McCowan, in 2011. The notes, which were made during Sirhan's trial, show clearly and vividly, in Sirhan's own hand, that he did in fact remember the events of 4–5 June 1968. Additionally, other claims about the shooting – RFK was facing the wrong way when Sirhan fired the shots – the RFK autopsy proved Sirhan could not have fired the mortal shot – Sirhan had been firing blanks – have all been addressed and found to be without merit.

Despite these facts, misinformation about the Kennedy assassinations continues to spread throughout the Internet and ideas that flourished only on the fringes of society are now being taken seriously by educated young people.

Conspiracy theorists adopt the trappings of scholarship and engage in endless debates about the tragedies. Rather than build a case from evidence, conspiracists deny the available evidence, maintaining that appearances deceive. Rather than admit to inconvenient facts, they dismiss them as lies, making their own theories irrefutable. Most conspiracists point the finger of guilt at the CIA in full knowledge the agency will never confirm or deny their allegations, thus allowing their readers to consider the possibility they are correct in their assumptions. Another favourite tactic of conspiracists is to make connections where none exist – 'A knows B knows C knows D – therefore A knows D'. Whenever conspiracists are backfooted in online assassination debates they use another form of deception – they change the topic. As Patricia Lambert observed:

> . . . some of the injury (to American society) can, with justice, be attributed to conspiracy theorists who have gone to superhu-man lengths to avoid facing the truth. They have constructed

wildly-implausible scenarios, far-out, fictitious 'conspirators,' and have scandalously maligned the motives of Kennedy's successor, rather than take a hard look at the man who actually did it. They have, ironically, done more to poison American political life than Lee Oswald—with the most terrible of intentions – was able to do.

Challenging the people who needlessly pollute our historical discourse has been no easy task. Following the publication of each of the articles in this book conspiracy advocates have responded with extreme vitriol, no doubt exercized at having their life-long delusions exposed. They never admit defeat when their inferences, guesses and accusations have been debunked and are clearly upset their lifelong toil has amounted to nothing.

As *The Times* columnist David Aaronovitch wrote, 'There are fast tragedies, like seven seconds on Dealey Plaza. And there are slow tragedies like the cost of believing nonsense for five decades.'

Mel Ayton
Durham, England, 2022

This book is a compilation of articles and essays written over a period of twenty years and it is inevitable that particular issues regarding the assassinations of JFK and RFK will be frequently revisited. It is hoped this will not distract from the reader's enjoyment of the book. The original article titles are cited at the start of each chapter and updated commentaries feature throughout.

Acknowledgements

For my research into the assassinations of JFK and RFK I received expert assistance from a number of individuals in the fields of ballistics, intelligence work, investigative reporting and acoustics for which I am eternally grateful:

Larry Sturdivan, an expert on wound ballistics who worked at the US Army's Ballistics Research Laboratory, Aberdeen Proving Ground, Maryland, from 1964 to 1972. In 1964, he observed ballistics tests conducted at the Biophysics Laboratory of Edgewood Arsenal in support of the Warren Commission's investigation into the assassination of President John F. Kennedy. In 1978, as a senior researcher, he was made the US Army's contact in helping the House Select Committee on Assassinations (HSCA) as it re-investigated the JFK assassination.

Philip Harrison worked as a full-time consultant and director for J.P. French Associates, the United Kingdom's longest established independent forensic speech and acoustics laboratory. The company prepares reports for the defence and prosecution in criminal cases on speaker identification, transcription, authentication and enhancement of recordings, acoustic investigation and other related areas, including the analysis of recorded gun shots, and is regularly involved in some of the most important and high-profile cases in the United Kingdom and around the world.

Professor Peter French is the UK's most experienced expert in the field of forensic speech and acoustics and is chairman of J.P. French Associates. He has worked in the field for thirty years and, as well as carrying out research, has been involved in implementing quality regulation and accreditation for forensic speech science.

Steve Barber, whose work was seminal in proving that the Dictabelt recorded by the Dallas Police Department that allegedly contains sounds of the shots in the JFK assassination was actually recorded elsewhere. He worked directly with a panel of the Committee on Ballistic Acoustics (CBA), which included two Nobel Prize-winning physicists, Norman F. Ramsey, chairman of the committee, and the late Luis Alvarez.

David Von Pein, JFK assassination expert and co-author of *Beyond A Reasonable Doubt*.

Michael O'Dell worked as a technical analyst with the Ramsey Panel on its rebuttal of research that attempted to invalidate the panel's criticisms of the HSCA JFK assassination acoustics findings.

Chad R. Zimmerman is an expert in firearms and was part of the Discovery Channel special programme that investigated the 'JFK magic bullet'. In September 2004 he visited the National Archives and viewed the original autopsy photos and X-rays with Larry Sturdivan.

Manuel Chavez was a former air force intelligence officer who was assigned to the CIA's Miami station from 1960 to 1964.

Grayston Lynch was the CIA officer present during the Bay of Pigs invasion and worked from the CIA Miami station.

Luis Rodriguez was an army officer seconded to the CIA Miami station.

Don Bohning was a retired Latin America editor for the *Miami Herald*.

Max Holland, publisher of *Washington Decoded*.

Professor John McAdams, editor of *The Kennedy Assassination*.

Rick Shenkman, founder and former publisher of History News Network.

Gus Russo, JFK assassination expert.

And last, but not least, I thank my friend, investigative journalist Dan Moldea, whose ground-breaking work into the circumstances surrounding the assassination of Robert F. Kennedy was vital to my own research.

My thanks, also, to Martin Mace and John Grehan of Frontline Books, managing director Charles Hewitt and my editor Alison Flowers for shepherding through this project with counsel and dispatch.

Abbreviations

AFT   Bureau of Alcohol, Firearms, Tobacco and Explosives
CIA   Central Intelligence Agency
DA   District Attorney
DEA   Drug Enforcement Agency
FBI   Federal Bureau of Investigation
HSCA House Select Committee on Assassinations
LAPD Los Angeles Police Department
MLK   Martin Luther King Jr
OAS   Organization of Arab Students

Introduction
Conspiracy Thinking

'Conspiracy Thinking and the John F. Kennedy, Robert Kennedy and Martin Luther King Assassinations', first published in John McAdams' e-zine, The Kennedy Assassination, *2006*

A child dies from some unexplained illness; fisherman sail off never to return; random violence takes the life of an innocent bystander. And always behind these tragic events lies the question – Why? But there is a rational answer to such purported mysteries, and it lies in the nature of the human mind which needs to bring order out of chaos; to seek truth where there is no truth. We must invent it because that too is the nature of the human condition. Believing in conspiracies and rejecting coincidences is more comforting than facing up to the fact that some things just happen.

Most conspiracy theorists see little merit in simplicity – to them it suggests feeble-mindedness. They often see the world as a black-and-white entity; enemies are clearly defined and there is a total absence of trust in any individual who works for the government.

Conspiracy advocates were primed from the start. In the 1960s the United States was awash with anti-war and anti-government sentiment and the media had been inundated with speculation about the JFK assassination. Given the mindset of the public during this period it was inevitable Americans would link the RFK and MLK assassinations to suspicions about the JFK murder. As time passed these concerns grew into a popular view that not everything had been explained by the government.

During the past four decades US citizens were presented with a constant stream of books, television documentaries and op-ed newspaper accounts which seemed to suggest that the assassinations of JFK, RFK and MLK had hidden histories; histories that would reveal secret agendas and powerful dark forces that controlled US society. When logical answers were provided to explain some of the anomalies that existed in the assassinations, conspiracy advocates fanned the flames by finding patterns and connections where none existed or connected some parts of the story to speculation about hidden plotters and sinister forces who tried to hide the truth.

The post-Watergate United States became intensely susceptible to conspiracy arguments. Many Americans began to wonder why these murders had happened at all. And because of the chaos and turmoil which followed the shootings it had always been extremely difficult to reconstruct the event in order to make sense of what happened. The assassinations were also criminal acts involving famous people therefore the cases demanded the closest scrutiny by investigative bodies.

The amount of evidence in these cases was therefore voluminous. A less than perfect explanation for the assassinations was inevitable. As a result, the conspiracy minded were always able to uncover one discrepancy after another from the thousands of pages of documented evidence. Thousands of people followed the case and were able, through their collective consciousness, to select many pieces of the murder case puzzles to construct numerous arguments rebutting the official conclusions. As William Buckley wrote, 'If O.J. (Simpson) was found not guilty, why can't everybody be found not guilty?'

The US public also came to believe that conspiracy theories were far more coherent than reality because they leave no room for mistakes, ambiguities and failures which are a prevalent feature in any human system. Allard Lowenstein, one of the first leading proponents of a conspiracy in the murder of Robert F. Kennedy, echoed these sentiments when he said:

> Robert Kennedy's death, like the president's (JFK), was mourned as an extension of the evils of senseless violence . . . a whimsical fate inconveniently interfering in the workings of democracy. What is odd is not that some people thought it was all random, but that so many intelligent people refused to believe that it might be anything else. Nothing can measure more graphically how limited was the general understanding of what is possible in America.[1]

Some answers about the assassinations were never found, many mistakes were made by investigators and there were unrealistic expectations that the public would be presented with 'perfect' criminal cases with orderly, pristine and conclusive evidence.

For example, in the chaos of those crucial moments, many Lorraine Motel, Dealey Plaza and Ambassador Hotel eyewitnesses gave conflicting stories as to what occurred during the shootings. The LAPD did not secure the crime scene very well. The Dallas Police were less than competent in not only securing the physical evidence in the case but also in providing sufficient protection for Lee Harvey Oswald. The area around the MLK murder scene was not secured by Memphis Police in the moments after the shooting.

However, instead of concluding that all bureaucracies are fraught with imperfect methods, conspiracy advocates pointed the finger of suspicion at unknown 'conspirators' and accused the LAPD, the Dallas Police, the Memphis Police and the FBI of deliberate cover-ups.

Reconstructing the JFK, RFK and MLK assassinations was like fitting jigsaw pieces together. Some fell into place immediately while others did not fit quite exactly. There were bad joints here and there in much the same way that eyewitnesses have faulty memories. Human beings are programmed to see patterns and conspiracies and this tendency increases when we see danger. The notion goes back to primitive man who learned to spot danger signs in a bush and thus became programmed to avoid savage animals.

It was not unusual for 'witnesses' to see 'second shooters' in Dealey Plaza, the area around the Lorraine Motel and the pantry of the Ambassador Hotel. In the chaos and confusion that resulted when Oswald, Sirhan and Ray fired their weapons some observers reacted by trying to impose some sense of order. It was like a shooter firing his pistol and then drawing a target around the bullet hole. We give it meaning because it does mean something – but only to us.

It would therefore be surprising had no witnesses come forward to relate the existence of 'second shooters'. If a stream of bullets was ricocheting off Elm Street and bouncing off ceiling tiles in the Ambassador pantry – if the echoes of the shots were reverberating throughout – it would have been a natural inclination, in the periods following the shootings and before the shock of the events had worn off, to believe more than one gunman had been present at each event. In the cases of JFK, RFK and MLK the only 'credible' witnesses to 'second shooters' were later discovered to be not credible at all, but only after researchers spent years investigating their claims.

The truths about 'eyewitness' testimony in the midst of chaos and turmoil was first recognized by the US Army. Many of their reports about battles, based on combat-experienced veterans, have shown that it is extraordinarily difficult to make sense out of a battle until the following day when soldiers have had a chance to get a good night's sleep. Information from 'shell-shocked' soldiers immediately after combat, the army discovered, was notoriously poor. Following an intensely traumatic event the information may still be in the brain but it has not been processed in such a manner that it can be retrieved. Many 'witnesses' in the JFK, RFK and MLK murders who gave reports about the shooting immediately after the event later formulated better 'pictures' of what occurred in subsequent interviews.

Other witnesses discovered their memories of events connected with the assassinations were not as reliable as they initially thought. Some came forward to give detailed information about Sirhan Sirhan's activities in the weeks and months preceding the RFK assassination and of how Sirhan had been accompanied by unidentified accomplices. When asked to state their stories were based on 'positive identification' many balked.

Some witnesses like gun salesman Larry Arnot were eventually given polygraph tests which showed their stories were suspect and not believable. Arnot failed his test and admitted he could not remember selling Sirhan bullets at a time the young Arab visited the gun shop where he worked. Arnot eventually realized he had confused the Sirhan sale with another after the gun-shop owner's wife mentioned to him that Sirhan had been in the shop with others. Gunshop sales assistant Donna Herrick, too, withdrew her story after she said she could not be sure. Mrs Herrick's polygraph test revealed she could not honestly remember the alleged incident.[2]

In the JFK case, Beverly Oliver was typical of how some witnesses promoted themselves through interviews with gullible conspiracy researchers. Oliver's claims that she had seen Jack Ruby, Lee Harvey Oswald and David Ferrie in Ruby's nightclub were investigated by other authors and found to be bogus.[3] She also claimed to have filmed the assassination using a camera that had not been manufactured in 1963. This information did not prevent numerous conspiracy writers from using her tall tales.

Similarly, MLK conspiracy author William Pepper believed in the conspiracy claims made by Memphis restaurant owner Loyd Jowers even after numerous Jowers family relatives and friends came forward to tell the Memphis District Attorney that Jowers had been lying and had invented his stories to 'make some money'.[4] Furthermore, many writers cling on to these witness stories for without them their conspiracy scenarios would collapse.

Conspiracy theorists seized upon numerous anomalies in the investigative reports of the assassinations – they expected all the pieces would fit together exactly, witnesses would give truthful stories and all the evidence collected without any mistakes having been made. Above all, investigations into political assassinations which go beyond the brief of a simple murder require informed judgments about the way police departments and US government investigative agencies work and also the ability to comprehend complex reports about ballistics, forensic pathology and crime scenes. But the public cannot form such judgments. They can glimpse only fragments of the covert picture – and since the world of conspiracy is essentially one of duplicity, carefully selecting evidence and relying on the testimonies of known liars and conmen, they have no way of knowing who is telling the truth or who or what to believe.

Furthermore, how can the government 'disprove' the FBI and the CIA had been involved in the JFK, MLK and RFK assassinations when the public did not believe *any* claims the agencies made? The outcome has been a lethal open season of claim and counter-claim, in which partial out-of-context or otherwise misleadingly presented portions of 'facts' have been put before a bemused public which is in no position to judge their veracity. Thus, a majority of the 'American public' are led into believing there had been conspiratorial involvement in the three assassinations.

In this alternatively constructed world conspiracy advocates claim they are the only people who can be judged to be reliable sources – 'lone assassin' proponents, they allege, are 'tools' of the government. But as the conspiracists probe deeper into the complexities of the cases they also connect together pieces of the puzzle that don't necessarily need to fit or are the result of mere chance. Conspiracy advocates also fail to apply logical and rational answers to many of their conclusions about what really happened. Because the LAPD had made a number of mistakes in the collection and handling of the physical evidence in the RFK shooting and had difficulties in reconstructing the crime (due to the chaotic circumstances of the shooting) it was automatically assumed there were sinister reasons for the anomalies in the collection of the physical evidence – someone had been 'covering up'.

But, as Police Chief Daryl Gates reasoned, conspiracy advocates seek the least plausible explanation. As Gates reasoned, 'In my mind, only one question remains unanswered . . . That is, how could you possibly get the police, the FBI, the Secret Service, prosecutors, courts and special commissions ALL to engage in this cover-up conspiracy?"[5]

The way the LAPD had mishandled particular pieces of evidence was not at all unusual. Expert forensic scientist Michael Baden, who was called in to examine the JFK assassination, said some medical evidence had gone missing – but not because of any sinister motive, Baden insisted. It was simply because people wanted to collect memorabilia. As Baden explained:

> Memorabilia of the famous have a way of vanishing into doctors' private collections. This is what happened to Einstein's brain. In the 1950s, Martin Luther King was treated at Harlem Hospital for a stab wound in the chest.
>
> In 1978, when we tried to get his medical records and X rays for the House Select Committee on Assassinations (HSCA), they were missing. The administrator had put them in a safe, but, somehow, they had disappeared. . . . [Missing evidence] . . . happens all the time; people take x-rays, brain tissue, microscopic slides – almost anything – as collectibles.[6]

JFK, RFK and MLK conspiracy advocates began with the premise that conspirators would organize the assassinations in a certain way. Yet the most basic examination of their 'assassination scenarios' can only leave the reader with the conclusion that the purported 'conspiracy plans' were altogether ridiculous. For example, why would sophisticated conspirators have allowed a 'hypnotized Sirhan' to outspokenly utter contempt for Robert F. Kennedy when the young Palestinian visited the Ambassador Hotel on 2 June and 4 June?

If they had the resources to hypnotize Sirhan to murder then they would surely have been able to make sure the assassin did not act in a way which would bring attention to himself. Behaving in this way is not the modus operandi for conspirators needing to act 'secretively'. Had Ambassador Hotel witnesses Humphrey Cordero and Enrique Rabago, among others, told police about Sirhan's hatred for Kennedy, Sirhan would likely have been detained and searched, thus putting the conspiracy in jeopardy.

Furthermore, it would be entirely irrational had conspirators risked their enterprise by enlisting a 'patsy' who owned an illegal weapon and who could have been arrested at any time in the weeks leading up to the shooting.

Had Sirhan been challenged at the police shooting range he visited on the day of the assassination and asked to show documentation for the weapon the whole conspiracy would have collapsed. And, of course, conspirators could never have been certain they would have been able to avoid being photographed by the dozens of television reporters and photojournalists. Although photographers failed to catch Sirhan on film firing his gun, the possibility of capturing a second assassin on film would always have been a problem.

In the case of Ray, it would have been simply too risky to employ an escaped convict to commit the murder of a famous public figure which would decisively bring all leading law enforcement agencies into play. And, as FBI, DEA and AFT agents and local police departments know too well, in the 1960s hired killers with no direct links to any criminal or extremist group could be bought for as little as $3,000. Furthermore, if Ray had indeed been aided by co-conspirators, they would have spirited him away and placed him in hiding as soon as the murder had been carried out. They would not have allowed him to be exposed so many times during his months on the run. Conspirators would not have put themselves in jeopardy by allowing Ray the opportunity to identify fellow conspirators. And, if Ray had been an unwilling patsy, conspirators could not have been certain that he would flee the scene of the crime. Under these circumstances had Ray stayed put the whole conspiracy would have collapsed. As HSCA Chief Counsel G. Robert Blakey said when questioned about the possibility that conspirators were behind James Earl Ray, 'The fact that Ray is still alive is one of the best arguments against the existence of any sophisticated conspiracy. If the mob, government, or anything like that had been involved, Ray would not have lived for very long after King was murdered.'[7]

These were no sophisticated murders, as conspiracy advocates maintain. JFK was riding in an open limousine and his motorcade route had been well publicized. King was an easy target for any killer bent on eliminating the Civil Rights leader and so was RFK. Both men did not have armed bodyguards; they frequently walked in the midst of crowds; and their travel arrangements were well known in advance.

Conspiracy advocates also expose themselves to central weaknesses in their 'scenarios'. Why would the government, for example, employ so many people in the 'conspiracies' when the risk of 'leakage' would have been so much greater? Had President Johnson wanted to eliminate King all that was required was for him to request the CIA director to arrange a 'contract' and that would have

been the end of it. The government could also have destroyed King by simply arranging for all the 'scandal-filled' surveillance tapes of the Civil Rights
leader to be released and then 'hire' a journalist to publicize them. This would
not have been all that unusual. In the 1960s the CIA enlisted the assistance of
journalists and student groups to promote the government's policies.

In the case of RFK his elimination by the CIA did not require an elaborate plot involving hypnotized assassins and the corruption of the LAPD and
FBI. At any point in such a sophisticated conspiracy a government 'insider'
could have given the game away. Such a purported government agent would
have been endowed with far more credibility than the fantasists quoted by
conspiracy writers.

Conspiracy theorists did not simply use non-linear logic to argue their
theses. They also cleverly misinterpreted statements made by witnesses
in order to create an aura of suspicion. Lisa Pease, for example, quoted
Ambassador Hotel witness Rosy Grier, 'Well, first of all, we were up on the
stage, and they said they was [*sic*] going off to the right of the stage, and at
the last minute . . . Bill Barry decided to change and go a different direction.'[8]
However, Wayne Rogers, Fred Dutton and Bill Barry, close aides or friends
of the Kennedy family, organized the change in RFK's route through the
hotel. It is preposterous to claim they had a hand in the alleged 'conspiracy'.

As the decades passed conspiracy advocates began to insist that Lee
Harvey Oswald, Sirhan Sirhan and James Earl Ray had not fired any of the
fatal shots at all. To 'prove' their claims they managed to bring doubt on the
numerous pieces of circumstantial evidence which pointed the finger of guilt
at the true assassins.

For example, conspiracy writers have attempted to 'prove' James Earl Ray
was innocent of killing Martin Luther King by enlisting bogus 'experts'
to cast doubt on the provenance of the assassin's rifle. They also invented
scenarios in which Ray had been led step by step into the 'conspiracy' unaware he was being used as a 'patsy'. Yet the evidence proving his guilt is
overwhelming.

Every decision and every action taken by James Earl Ray in the year leading up to the assassination was taken by Ray. No credible evidence exists that
would indicate he was used as a 'patsy' or was instructed to participate in the
crime. Ray researched the rifle, the ammunition and the telescopic sight. Ray
bought the Mustang, had it serviced, rented the rooms on his journeys, made
his own telephone calls, bought his own clothes and had them laundered.

Ray was identified as the person who rented Room 5b of the South Main Street rooming house and he was also identified as the lodger who left the rooming house following the shooting. Ray's fingerprints proved that he owned the bundle that was dropped in the doorway of Canipe's amusement store shortly after the shooting.

The bundle contained the rifle used to shoot King. Ray had expressed hatred for African Americans; he was responsible for robberies before and following the assassination and he also applied for his false passport, picked up his passport photographs and collected his travel documents. Incontrovertible and overwhelming evidence exists to prove these facts.

The evidence for James Earl Ray's guilt is clear. He was an avowed racist who expressed his opinions on racial matters numerous times in the years preceding the assassination. His selection of lawyers underscored the racial motive for the crime. He told fellow inmates he was looking for the 'big score', aware that his burglaries, bank robberies and petty crimes had amounted to little. During his time spent in the Missouri State Penitentiary Ray had associated with known racist groups, was known to harbour ideas about a 'bounty' on King's head and evidently believed he could beat any murder case brought against him if he could kill King in the Deep South.

However, the assassin fed the public his own conspiracy line taking every opportunity to build a smokescreen which allowed critics of the government to speculate that the case against Ray was flimsy. Mistakes in the investigation, particularly the rushed autopsy by Dr Jerry Francisco, and the FBI's failure to pursue many leads promoted the idea that the government may have had a hand in King's death. Critics pounced, using mistakes in the investigation to spin tales of an elaborate plot involving the police, the military, the FBI, the Mafia and the CIA. But the Memphis Police Department and the FBI made fewer mistakes in the King case than in a typical murder case.

In most criminal investigations even routine techniques like dusting for fingerprints are frequently overlooked. Moreover, there are very real limits regarding the extent of full investigation and forensics and ballistics testing that can be performed in a case. If the US public demanded 100 per cent certitude in order to convict very few cases would ever come to trial.

Conspiracy advocates similarly claim that anomalies in the RFK murder investigation pointed to Sirhan having been used as a 'patsy'; he was set up to take the blame for the murder of RFK. They allege he had fired blanks and the real killer, security guard Thane Eugene Cesar, who had been standing behind RFK, fired the fatal bullet. However, their thesis is logically flawed. Why would conspirators have Sirhan firing blanks when they could have done a more thorough job by having him fire real bullets? If there had been a conspiracy to kill Robert F. Kennedy, the conspirators would have wanted to draw as little suspicion to themselves as possible.

To that end, having multiple assassins in a crowded room, along with a visible assassin who was shooting blanks, would simply increase the chances that someone would suspect sinister forces at work. And how would the 'team of assassins' have had foreknowledge of RFK's route to the Colonial Room? Conspiracy advocates can only fall back on the theory that either someone in Kennedy's retinue had planned the route with the conspirators or multiple teams of assassins had been stationed at various vantage points in the hotel.

In order for the conspiracy writers to make their 'patsy' arguments plausible they had to rid Sirhan of a motive for the crime. Philosophers reason that any belief can be argued if enough assumptions are present and pertinent facts are forgotten. This is the modus operandi of conspiracy promoters who argued that Sirhan had no motive for killing Kennedy. Philip Melanson's and William Klaber's books are typical examples of how this was accomplished. To prove the assassin did not have a political motive they selected portions of testimony and evidence from police files, and ignored statements made by the many people who knew Sirhan throughout his life. According to Melanson and Klaber, Sirhan had said he heard on the radio that Kennedy had promised to send jet bombers to Israel, '. . . but (RFK's) statements there (at the Zionist club in Beverly Hills) were anything but inflammatory. He spoke mostly about a negotiated settlement between Israel and her Arab neighbours.'[9]

Klaber and Melanson imply that Sirhan did not have any political motive in killing Kennedy as the Senator spoke mostly of peace and only mentioned arms aid in the context of a Soviet build-up in the Middle East. This was important because conspiracy advocates needed to show that a motiveless Sirhan was more likely to have been a pawn in the hands of others. Yet there is a wealth of evidence to show that Sirhan, from a young age, had been fascinated with radical Arab nationalism, left-wing politics and assassination.

There was always an inevitability in the linking of the assassinations to alleged conspirators. The US is obsessed with conspiracy theories and a large proportion of the population believe there are conspiratorial answers to everything. This has occurred because there is a general psychological tendency for people to think that a major or significant event must have been caused by something similarly major, significant or powerful.

As historian Henry Steele Commager observed in the late 1960s:

> There has come in recent years something that might be called a conspiracy psychology: a feeling that great events can't be explained by ordinary processes. We are on the road to a paranoid explanation of things. The conspiracy theory, the conspiracy mentality, will not accept ordinary evidence . . . there's some psychological requirement that forces them to reject the ordinary and find refuge in the extraordinary.[10]

An article in the *American Journal of Psychology* explains this phenomenon as:

> Humans naturally respond[ing] to events or situations which have had an emotional impact upon them by trying to make sense of those events, typically in values-laden spiritual, moral or political terms, though occasionally in scientific terms. Events which resist such interpretation—for example, because they are, in fact, senseless—can provoke the inquirer to have recourse to ever more extreme speculations, until one is reached that is capable of offering the inquirer the required emotional satisfaction. Once cognized, confirmation bias and avoidance of cognitive dissonance may reinforce the belief. In a context where conspiracy theory has become popular within a social group, communal reinforcement may equally play a part. As sociological historian Holger Herwig found in studying German explanations of World War, those events that are most important are hardest to understand, because they attract the greatest attention from mythmakers and charlatans.[11]

Dr Patrick Leman of the Royal Holloway University of London also conducted research into the phenomenon. Leman said that conspiracy theories flower because people feel distanced from institutions of power so are more likely to distrust official accounts. Furthermore, he observed, the rise of the Internet allows new theories to spread quickly and widely.[12]

The idea that the US government covered up the truth about the three assassinations has gained powerful political currency in the United States. Conspiracy theories have been given respectability by the electronic and print media and the most powerful arbiter of cultural consensus – Hollywood. The level of debate is not enhanced when Hollywood celebrities, many of whom do not know their way around the vast volumes of evidence, side with the conspiracy theorists. Actor Mike Farrell joined with others in calling for a re-investigation of King's murder, putting his name to a press release that stated: 'There are buried truths in our history which continue to insist themselves back into light, perhaps because they hold within them the nearly dead embers of what we were once intended to be as a nation.'[13]

In the late 1990s Oliver Stone, whose 1991 movie *JFK* convinced millions of people that a conspiracy was responsible for the death of President Kennedy, told reporters he wanted to make a movie about King's assassination. Stone said, 'Johnson was a bastard, man. The King thing may have come from the top. I think it had to. Because I don't think military people, who I believe are involved, would do something of that nature unless they had a hierarchical OK.'[14]

More unsettling has been the response of African Americans to the official government investigations of the King murder. The conspiracy idea among African Americans is traceable to dynamics rather than the merits of the case against James Earl Ray. From the start African Americans believed that King was the victim of the white establishment. Statements by Coretta Scott King and Martin Luther King's aides fuelled this idea.

The Memphis prosecutors had contacted Coretta King for her approval of the plea bargain they had worked out with Ray's lawyers, to which she agreed. However, after Ray had been sentenced to a ninety-nine-year term in prison Coretta King released a statement calling on the government to do all it could to find anyone who may have conspired with Ray. She did not believe that Ray had acted alone.

The majority of African Americans, according to polls taken over the past thirty years, have indicated a strong belief that the state may have conspired to kill King. This, of course, is entirely consistent with the role African Americans have played in the short history of the United States. African American distrust in the state has historical roots centred around their existence as second-class citizens for most of the past 300 years. African Americans were victims of a government who, for the most part, conspired to 'keep them in their place'.

Conspiracy ideas emerged to explain why African Americans could still not attain social and economic equality in spite of new legislation. As the existing order did not make African Americans truly equal with white Americans, theories flourished that sought to lay the blame on powerful forces outside the democratic/political structure.

From the idea that the US government *must* have had a hand in the deaths of black leaders like Malcolm X and Martin Luther King theories spread that perhaps other sinister plots against African American communities existed. African American leaders across the United States began to promote these malicious ideas, including the notion that African Americans were being used as medical guinea pigs, the US government was behind the AIDS epidemic and African American communities were being deliberately sabotaged. Jesse Jackson, for example, endorsed the idea that the CIA had conspired to flood African American communities with crack cocaine in order to suppress the African American population. His allegations were supported by polls that stated that 60 per cent of African Americans believed that it was possible that crack cocaine had been deliberately introduced into their communities by the CIA.

However, despite the repeated allegations that the murders of John F. Kennedy, Robert F. Kennedy and Martin Luther King Jr were the results of conspiracies, a residue of optimism remains. As Daniel Pipes observed, 'I am more optimistic, trusting the stability of a mature democracy and noting that Americans have survived previous conspiracist bouts without much damage. But nonsensical, ugly, and pernicious ideas do not fail of their own accord; they need to be fought against and rendered marginal. The task starts with recognizing that they exist, then arguing against them.'[15]

Part I
JFK

Chapter 1

Who Killed JFK?

'The Warren Commission Report: 40 Years Later It Still Stands Up', first published by History News Network, 2004

President Lyndon B. Johnson's commission to investigate his predecessor's assassination eventually published the results of its ten-month inquiry. The Warren Commission, named after its chairman, Supreme Court Chief Justice Earl Warren, concluded that President Kennedy had been killed by a lone assassin, Lee Harvey Oswald, and there was no evidence of conspiracy. The findings were accepted by a majority of the US public. However, a significant minority greeted the findings with instant scepticism. A public opinion poll immediately afterwards revealed that only a slight majority, 56 per cent, accepted the commission's conclusions. And within a year of the report's release two US best-sellers, Mark Lane's *Rush to Judgment* and Edward J. Epstein's *Inquest*, created enough doubt about the Warren Commission's conclusions to persuade a majority of Americans that the president's panel had gotten it wrong.

By the beginning of the new century scepticism had turned to incredulity. Opinion polls now showed that around 90 per cent of Americans believed that Lee Harvey Oswald was innocent, or, at most, he merely assisted in a conspiracy to kill the president.

As the decades progressed the purported plots became labyrinthine in their complexity. The Mafia, the CIA, the military industrial complex, Texas oilmen, pro-Castro Cubans, anti-Castro Cubans, the KGB, J. Edgar Hoover and the FBI, Lyndon Johnson, southern racists and the Joint Chiefs of Staff all came under suspicion.

So how did we arrive at this position?

The assassination of JFK had a profound effect on the US public. Before 22 November 1963, Americans held the view that the optimism that JFK engendered would take the United States into a brighter future. After that time many began to question the direction the country was taking, and their fears would shortly be realized as the political turmoil of the 60s set in. Even today the effects of the assassination are still imbedded in the national consciousness. More than forty years on many historians acknowledge the assassination was the beginning of the end of US innocence. Furthermore, as the idea of conspiracy grew, the US people began to distrust what their leaders were telling them. A new cynicism took root in the US psyche.

From the start, the fact that a crazed psychotic could have changed the world in a single moment staggered belief. The US public simply could not believe that such a monumental crime could be committed by such a pathetic individual. The probable cause – Oswald was a self-appointed champion of Castro, as the Warren Commission discovered – seemed so disproportionate to the consequences.

Another answer lies in how the investigation of Kennedy's murder was handled by the US government. In the hours following the assassination US leaders feared that a public hysteria would demand revenge for the death of the president. At the very least their hopes for detente with the Soviet Union would be dashed. Some believed a world war would be imminent if evidence had been found that the Soviets or Cubans were behind the murder. Although intelligence agencies, using sophisticated methods, confirmed that Khrushchev and Castro were not involved, President Johnson was fearful suspicions alone could lead to conflict. The government therefore decided they must convince the public that the president's death was the work of a lone madman, not of some vast communist conspiracy. In the context of the time this strategy was well intentioned, but many leads were ignored or swept under the carpet.

The actions of succeeding US administrations can also explain why the US public became open to persuasion by conspiracy advocates. The US people faced a litany of lies, distortions and half-truths by government agencies during the administrations of Johnson (Vietnam War), Nixon (Watergate) and Reagan (Iran-contra), therefore allegations of a cover-up did not appear unusual or outrageous.

The start of the assassination myths, however, began with the release of the Warren Commission's 888-page summary report. Although the investigation was large in scope, too many areas of concern were not properly dealt with. Had the commission carried out a more thorough investigation and demanded complete cooperation from the FBI and CIA, questions about

Oswald and his nefarious activities in the weeks leading up to the assassination may have been immediately answered.

An opportunity arose to address these charges when Congress re-investigated the assassination in the mid-1970s. If the FBI and CIA had been more forthcoming with the HSCA some of the mysteries about Oswald's connections to government agencies would have been cleared up. Had a full accounting of the information the CIA and Army Intelligence held on Oswald been released to investigatory bodies there would have been little room left for the conspiracy theorists to manoeuvre.

One of the most important failures of the Warren Commission was in not investigating the possible links between the CIA's plots to kill Castro and the assassination of the president. Former CIA director Allen Dulles, a Warren Commission member, failed to tell his colleagues on the commission or staff investigators about the Castro plots. This knowledge could have given investigators an important lead on Oswald's time in Mexico City in the short period before the assassination. Commission members Richard Russell and Gerald Ford also knew about the CIA's attempts to kill the Cuban leader. However, if no link existed between Oswald and the Soviet or Cuban governments, they reasoned, there was no reason to inform the staff investigators who wrote the commission's report.

The CIA had its reasons for withholding files from the Warren Commission and the HSCA. During the Cold War information concerning the electronic bugging and surveillance of the Russian and Cuban embassies in Mexico City was deemed sensitive (as it is to this day). The National Security Agency's capabilities and the methodology of its electronic intercepts are the most highly guarded of secrets. Information gleaned from bugging is protected on the grounds that it may inevitably lead to the discovery of intelligence-gathering methodology or the placement of undercover agents. Even though the CIA files were (and are) central to proving that Oswald was not the agent of a foreign power (or an agent of the CIA, for that matter) they remained partially classified for these reasons.

Blame for the way suspicions were engendered can be shared. The Dallas Police was careless with Oswald; its carelessness led to the assassin's murder by Jack Ruby. But the police were not conspiratorially involved. The FBI failed in its duty to protect the president and failed to keep Oswald under observation during the presidential visit. They had a file on Oswald which traced his movements back to his time in the Soviet Union. Two weeks before the assassination Oswald marched into the local FBI office in Dallas and created a scene, complaining about the harassment his wife was receiving from its agents who were trying to keep track of the ex–Marine Russian defector.

In this sense the 'cover-up' is an historical truth.

The US media can also bear some responsibility for fanning the flames of conspiracy thinking. Following the assassination, every witness, no matter how remote from first-hand knowledge, became a 'news-maker'. Being in the national spotlight confused many of them – seldom did any respond with a 'don't know' answer to media questions. The result was a flood of distortion and misinformation. As Patricia Lambert wrote:

> . . . may have played a greater role in turning the majority of Americans away from the conclusions of the Warren Report than any book written. In those days most of the country still relied heavily on the print media for its news. LIFE was . . . an honoured part of the American scene. For an institution as conservative and important to endorse such an idea seemed, in itself, to validate the notion of conspiracy.[1]

Thousands of new documents, released following the enactment of the JFK Records Act in 1992, also show how the Kennedys may have inadvertently fed the conspiracy machine. Jacqueline Kennedy and the president's brother, Robert F. Kennedy, asked many of those present at the autopsy to promise not to talk about the procedure for twenty-five years. They feared JFK's health problems, which he lied about to get elected, may have been revealed. Conspiracy theorists pointed to this wall of silence as 'proof' of a continuing cover-up, when in fact the doctors and staff were merely adhering to the wishes of the family. Beyond the autopsy, Robert F. Kennedy may have worried that the Warren Commission might stumble onto the government's plots to kill Castro. He did not want the Warren Commission investigating Cuba even though the plots had nothing to do with the assassination.

Conspiracies, imagined or otherwise, have endured to a degree because they are part of the culture of US society. Far reaching and complex conspiracy themes have been the staple diet of Hollywood with movies like *The Manchurian Candidate, Conspiracy Theory, The Parallax View, Total Recall* and *JFK*. Even television and the Internet have joined forces to promote sinister and anti-libertarian motives of the US government. And the enduring popularity of conspiracies makes them a highly lucrative enterprise and vested interests keep the myths alive. As many as 6 million people a year visit the JFK assassination site where 'researchers' peddle books, autopsy pictures and signed 'grassy knoll witness' photos. The visitor can experience a virtual Disneyland of assassination themes from limousine rides which trace JFK's route from Love Field to Dealey Plaza to bus trips which follow Oswald's escape route. It is a multi-million-dollar industry promoting books, videos, CD-ROMs, T-shirts and even board games. Conspiracy theories have brought the assassination into the world of entertainment.

Conspiracy theories have also taken root because they are part of the US experience and they have been promoted by ideologues left and right alike. During the 1950s and 1960s conspiracy theorists were generally right-wingers like Joseph McCarthy, who saw a United States subverted by communists. From the late 60s to the present it has been the idealists of the left who tended to see the United States subverted by right-wing conspiracies.

JFK conspiracies have undergone a similar shift. Early targets were the Russians or the Cubans. By the late 1960s it had become popular to suggest that the president's death was the result of clandestine groups or agencies that had a natural right-wing bias like the CIA, the Pentagon or right-wing Texas oilmen. While the Soviet Union and Castro's Cuba were busy subverting democracies in Latin America, conspiracy theorists in the United States began to look inward to the subversion of democratic institutions by faceless and powerful groups dedicated to the advancement of US corporations and the military industrial complex that President Eisenhower spoke of. These ideas, as intelligence expert Christopher Andrew and author Max Holland were to discover in the 1990s, were propagated by the Soviet Union's KGB as part of a strategy to bring about disaffection in the West.

The methodology of the conspiracists has ensured the durability of their preposterous claims. When named individuals were discovered to have been innocent, conspiracy theorists have fallen back on the idea that the government was to blame. The suggested scenarios have been impossible to discredit – a very powerful group of individuals inside officialdom killed the president, a group powerful enough to engage vast legions of workers to cover up the conspiracy. These allegations led Professor Jacob Cohen to criticize 'the platoons of conspiracists [who] concertedly scavenged the record, floating their appalling and thrilling "might-have-beens" unfazed by the contradictions and absurdities in their own wantonly selective accounts, often consciously, cunningly deceitful'.[2]

Even though assassination conspiracy theories have been successfully challenged time after time, and found to be without merit, they have remained very appealing.[3] Conspiracy theories are powerfully seductive, offering mystery and intrigue to the reader. Additionally, a conspiracy with a valid aim suggests control; the psychotic actions of a lone individual suggest chaos. And people are always looking for simple and straightforward answers. Furthermore, conspiracy theories are like the legendary Hydra – cut off one of its heads and a score of others will replace it.

Scientific research, which was not available to the Warren Commission, together with the release of government files, has now established the true circumstances surrounding the assassination, despite the protestations of the conspiracy minded. All the major issues of the case, which centre around the existence of single or multiple assassins, have been successfully addressed by the leading scientific and legal experts in the US.

Even though conspiracy advocates continue to insist that a conspiracy killed JFK, the evidence does not support their arguments. No smoking gun from the JFK assassination files has been unearthed. Sophisticated re-enactments of the assassination using state-of-the-art technology (computer models and laser-assisted weaponry) have shown that three shots were fired, all from the direction of the sixth floor of the Texas School Book Depository where eyewitness Howard Brennan placed Oswald at the time of the shooting. The rifle and the pistol were traced directly to Oswald. Spectrographic analysis of photographs purporting to show gunmen on the grassy knoll reveal only light and shadows. Neutron-activation analyses of bullet fragments support the single–bullet theory which was central to the single–assassin conclusion. A computer enhanced version of the Zapruder film (which became the most important visual record of the assassination) has confirmed that Oswald could have fired the shots in the time sequence required. Ballistics experts have testified that Oswald's rifle was more than adequate for the job. Forensic pathologists and physicists have proven that the backward snap of Kennedy's head is consistent with a shot from the rear.[4]

Incontrovertible evidence links Oswald with the murder weapon. And credible eyewitness testimony and circumstantial evidence establishes that Lee Harvey Oswald fired the shots that killed President Kennedy. His fleeing the scene of the crime established his consciousness of guilt. Incontrovertible evidence proves that Lee Harvey Oswald murdered Police Officer Tippit within an hour of shooting President Kennedy.

Researcher Don Thomas' acoustics research, published in 2001, alleging that more than three shots had been fired, has now been proven to be flawed. Reports of Oswald's alleged contacts with anti-Castro Cubans, KGB agents, rogue elements of the CIA and Castro's intelligence agents have been researched fully and found to be the product of guilt by association and gross speculation. The Jim Garrison investigation, made famous by Oliver Stone's movie *JFK*, in which the New Orleans District Attorney claimed to uncover the conspiracy behind the assassination, was found to be politically inspired and bogus when his files were opened for scrutiny by the Assassination Records Review Board, which reported the results of its five-year investigation of government files in 1998.

Books by Gerald Posner and Patricia Lambert revealed how conspiracy advocates, fuelled by a public hooked on conspiracy theories, have continually abused the evidential record. The authors have shown how conspiracy theorists misrepresented the facts of the case through a selective use of witnesses, a presentation of crude scientific opinion about the physical evidence and a steady stream of accusations against government officials that are baseless. Furthermore, over a period of forty years, documents connected to the case have been proven to be forged (including a fake document forged by the KGB), 'conspiracy witnesses' have provided no corroborative evidence and conspiracy authors have accused innocent individuals of involvement in the crime.

Conspiracy advocates have never been able to address many logical aspects of the crime which decisively argue against conspiracy. For example, how could a conspiracy, which would have to involve hundreds if not thousands of people, remain a secret in an age when whistle-blowers have succeeded in revealing everything from corruption in government to initiating the impeachment of presidents.

Confusion about motive was at the heart of the Kennedy murder. The Warren Commission failed to decisively conclude that Oswald was anything but a deranged assassin, which left open many avenues for speculation. Yet there was definitely a political motive for Oswald's actions. He had spent his adolescence and early manhood pursuing a communist dream and searching for some kind of involvement in revolutionary activities. Disillusioned with his time spent in the Soviet Union, the young Oswald returned home searching for a new cause. He found it in his hero, Fidel Castro, and began planning a way to help the revolution. As his wife Marina said, 'I only know that his basic desire was to get to Cuba by any means and all the rest of it was window dressing for that purpose.'[5] His friend Michael Paine said Oswald wanted to be an active guerrilla in the effort to bring about a new world order.[6]

During the time Oswald spent in New Orleans he set himself up as an agent provocateur for the cause and imagined himself as a hero of the revolution. In New Orleans it was common knowledge that anti-Castro exiles had been planning another invasion of Cuba and had also been attempting to kill Castro with the assistance of the CIA. As an avid reader of political magazines and newspapers Oswald could not have failed to see a September 1963 New Orleans newspaper article in which Castro threatened retaliation for attempts on his life. It is plausible Oswald had been inspired by this article.

Oswald's political ideals remained with him up to the moment of his death at the hands of a Dallas self-appointed vigilante, Jack Ruby. It was inevitable that someone as politically motivated as Oswald would wish to reveal his political sympathies to the world following his arrest for the murder of the president and a Dallas Police officer. However, he did not accomplish this by confessing but instead paraded around the Dallas Police Station giving a clenched fist salute. Most conspiracy advocates had assumed Oswald had been merely showing his manacled hands to reporters. But two photographs taken that tragic weekend clearly show Oswald's left-wing salute. His actions were confirmed by Dallas Police officer Billy Combest, who accompanied Oswald in the ambulance as he lay dying. According to Combest, Oswald 'made a definite clenched-fist salute'.[7]

However, conspiracy advocates continue to muddy the waters with the release of new books to coincide with the fortieth anniversary of the assassination and the fortieth anniversary of the release of the Warren Commission's Report. Engaging in indiscriminate presentations of 'fact' and applying a fractured logic they continue to construct false theories. The end result is a narrative of half-truths and speculation 'proving' President Johnson and a mixed bag of intelligence agents, military officers, gangsters and police officials conspired to eliminate a supposedly dangerous president. Even the most erudite reader would have to spend a considerable amount of time filtering the information they present, eventually becoming overwhelmed by the masses of esoteric and highly technical data, most of it the work of self-proclaimed experts, who have been ridiculed by the scientific community. Conspiracists are, however, at an advantage in that their use of facts and evidence, which purportedly support their theories, are not easily verifiable.

On the other hand, books that rightly reject the conspiracy solution to the Kennedy assassination have been relatively unsuccessful because there are no new and real dramatic discoveries.

The true facts cannot now be established with absolute precision. Too many false leads have been sown, too many witnesses have died and the volume of material pertaining to the case can be misinterpreted by anyone who wishes to construct a false story. And time has a way of eroding the truth. However, after forty years of speculation we can now say, for the purposes of historical accuracy, that the fundamental conclusions of the Warren Commission were essentially correct, and no evidence has been forthcoming that could decisively point a conspiratorial finger. Nor has any evidence negated the Warren Commission's argument in establishing Oswald's guilt.

* * *

Mel Ayton, review of John McAdams, JFK Assassination Logic: How to Think about Claims of Conspiracy *(Potomac Books, 2011), first published by* History News Network, *21 November 2011*

Every now and then a JFK assassination book comes along that bristles with erudition and common sense, providing the reader with rational answers to anomalous pieces of evidence in the case that have been exaggerated beyond belief by bogus historians cashing in on the public's desire for drama and intrigue.

In the 1970s, Priscilla Johnson McMillan's *Marina and Lee*, a book that could be characterized as 'Marina Oswald's Memoirs', gave the US public an insight into the mind and character of JFK's assassin, Lee Harvey Oswald, an enigmatic young man who had remained a puzzle to the US people since the November 1963 assassination.

In the 1980s, Jean Davison's *Oswald's Game* gave readers a logical explanation for the assassination: Oswald, a hero-worshipper of Fidel Castro and a wannabe revolutionary, had political motives and he likely acted out of a distorted sense of political idealism.

In the 1990s, Gerald Posner's *Case Closed*, a well-written account of the assassination that debunked numerous conspiracy scenarios, provided a refreshing antidote to Oliver Stone's movie about the assassination, *JFK*. Stone's largely fictional drama had been released in cinemas in the early 1990s. Its central character was Jim Garrison, the New Orleans District Attorney who accused the CIA of Kennedy's murder. His false history of the assassination had a corrosive effect on a new generation's ability to understand this important event in US history. Fortunately, another corrective to the movie came in 1998 with the publication of Patricia Lambert's excellent book *False Witness*, which firmly exposed Garrison as a charlatan and a fraud.

In recent years Vincent Bugliosi's *Reclaiming History*, a mammoth 1,600-page book, examined *every* theory and *every* conspiracy claim. The former Los Angeles lawyer, who became famous for his prosecution of hippie killer Charles Manson, took the debate about conspiracy allegations a step further by providing a devastating no-nonsense approach to the ridiculous assassination scenarios constructed by conspiracy authors, *all* of whom, as his book ably demonstrates, deliberately skewed the evidence in the case. His book was a masterwork that decisively marginalized JFK conspiracists.

So, at the end of the first decade of the new century the matter appeared to be settled. I, among many JFK assassination researchers, would have thought there was nothing more to say on the subject. The above authors provided all the answers to conspiracy allegations to the satisfaction of history.

I was wrong. John McAdams has added to the sum of knowledge about this case and other famous conspiracy theories by writing a book which will help many who have fallen victim to the vast conspiracy literature on the market. His 'how to' book challenges readers to look at how conspiracy writers have interpreted the evidence using seriously flawed methods.

McAdams has provided a blueprint for understanding how conspiracy theories arise and how anyone interested in conspiracies should judge the mass of contradictory evidence in the case. Having studied the JFK assassination for the past two decades he has developed a sharp intellectual ability at pointing out the illogical nature of virtually all conspiracy theories and helps the reader to separate the wheat from the chaff in Kennedy assassination literature.

The author's intent is not to persuade the reader that there is no credible evidence to prove that JFK was assassinated as the result of a conspiracy. Instead, McAdams concentrates on advising the reader how to *think* about conspiracy theories, especially the JFK assassination. By addressing the logical weaknesses in conspiracy books, he has been able to demonstrate how not to be duped about this important event in US history. For example, McAdams asks the reader to think logically; to stick to the evidence; to stick to common sense. He teaches you how to reach a rational, compelling conclusion based on evidence and reason, not on emotion or conjecture. His work is based not on theory, speculation, rumour, third-hand hearsay or secondary evidence or opinion (save those of scientifically qualified experts). Instead, he advises the reader to reach a conclusion based on reflecting on the notion of 'coincidence', selectivity in the use of evidence, making an informed choice between contradictory pieces of evidence and to search for evidence that fits a coherent theory. This advice is central to his didacticism.

Many of the assassination's elements have become part of US folklore – the so-called 'Magic Bullet' (the subject of a recent National Geographic Channel documentary, *The Lost Bullet*), the grassy knoll shooter, the ballistics and medical evidence and the alleged mysterious deaths. McAdams immerses the reader in the fine points of each element then demonstrates to the reader how illogical the conspiracist interpretation really is.

Three of the more interesting expositions in the book address the alleged conspiracy remarks made by the FBI director, J. Edgar Hoover, the alleged involvement of the CIA in the president's murder and the repeated and wrongful use of Jack Ruby's statements to the press and the Warren Commission.

As McAdams demonstrates, Hoover was 'clueless' in the first weeks after the assassination. The FBI director had been kept informed about the direction of the FBI's investigation by his agents on the ground. Inevitably, investigating agents were confronted by contradictory statements made by witnesses at the scene of the assassination and the doctors who attended the president and Governor Connally. The 'less than coherent' data that agents collected in the frenetic circumstances of the time was utilized by Hoover when the director passed information about the investigation to President Johnson, Bobby Kennedy and other government leaders.

The FBI eventually cleared up the false data, false leads and false witness statements, and its completed report on the assassination became central to the Warren Commission's own investigation. However, conspiracists simply ignored its contents and instead concentrated on Hoover's wrong-headed comments as proof of a conspiracy, instead of putting Hoover's remarks in context as the act of a confused person attempting to grasp what exactly had happened in the hours and days following the assassination.

McAdams also challenges those who believe the FBI was part of a conspiracy by asking, 'So just how does somebody who is so confused on so many points direct a cover-up?' In a similar vein, McAdams debunks allegations of CIA involvement in the assassination by demonstrating how the agency mishandled their investigation into Oswald's nefarious political activities. In telling the story of the CIA's involvement in Jim Garrison's 1967/1968 New Orleans investigation, McAdams allows the reader to come to the logical conclusion that bureaucratic bungling, rather than conspiratorial malfeasance, lay at the heart of their efforts.

McAdams, in his chapter 'Bogus Quoting: Stripping Context, Misleading Readers', shows how conspiracy writers have abused the evidence by taking quotes and statements out of context. He demonstrates this no better than by making reference to the countless times conspiracists have used Jack Ruby's published statements to the press and the Warren Commission which allude to a 'conspiracy'. For example, the conspiracist par excellence Mark Lane wrote:

> Ruby made it plain that if the commission took him from the Dallas jail and permitted him to testify in Washington, he could tell more there; it was impossible for him to tell the whole truth so long as he was in the jail in Dallas . . . [Ruby said] 'I would like to request that I go to Washington and . . . take all the tests that I have to take. It is very important . . . Gentlemen, unless you get me to Washington, you can't get a fair shake out of me.'

However, it is clear from Ruby's Warren Commission testimony that he simply wanted to inform the commissioners of a conspiracy to murder Jews. Earl Warren, the commission's chairman, said:

> I went down and took Jack Ruby's testimony myself – he wouldn't talk to anybody but me. And he wanted the FBI to give him a lie detector test, and I think the FBI did, and he cleared it all right. I was satisfied myself that he didn't know Oswald, never had heard of him. But the fellow was clearly delusional when I talked to him. He took me aside and he said, 'Hear those voices, hear those voices?' He thought they were Jewish children and Jewish women who were being put to death in the building there.

Ruby told Earl Warren, Gerald Ford and others, 'I am as innocent regarding any conspiracy as any of you gentlemen in the room.' Ruby was actually begging the commission to take him back to Washington so that he could take a polygraph examination and prove that he was telling the truth when he denied any role in a conspiracy.

McAdams divides his book into further chapters dealing with how eye-witnesses and ear witnesses behave, how over-reliance on witness testimony weakens any crime investigation, the use of photographic evidence and how bureaucracies behave. He allows the reader to become a detective who tries to solve an intriguing puzzle. The solution, in each case, involves using intellectual tools and skills.

If those wishing to learn the truth about the JFK assassination (and other bogus conspiratorial hauntings of the US psyche) follow his step-by-step approach in understanding conspiracy claims there may well be a time when a new generation of Americans will be able to once more take control of their own history.

In the opinion of this reviewer John McAdams' book is the final nail in the coffin of conspiracy theorists who have grabbed the attention of the mainstream media for far too long – mainly because the media understands all too well how the public loves a mystery. If John McAdams' book is read in conjunction with the excellent books mentioned earlier in this review the JFK assassination will be no mystery at all.

Commentary 2022

Philip Shenon's international best-seller *A Cruel and Shocking Act: The Secret History of the Kennedy Assassination*, acclaimed by the *New York Times* and published in 2013, supports the essential conclusions I had previously made, that the failings of the Warren Commission Report helped to guarantee the flourishing of a conspiracy culture, but no credible evidence exists that JFK was killed other than by a lone assassin – Lee Harvey Oswald. Shenon's judgment is that the Warren Commission was flawed from the start, but not because the commissioners or the staff themselves were part of a conspiracy to bury the truth.

Rather, Shenon makes a case for information being buried out of selfish bureaucratic indulgence by the top echelons of the FBI and CIA; men like FBI director J. Edgar Hoover and CIA chief of the counterintelligence staff James Jesus Angleton, who put pride and reputation of themselves, their colleagues and the then undiminished reputations of their agencies above full disclosure.

None of the information buried was indicative of the FBI or CIA being any part of the assassination, but rather their knowledge of Oswald beforehand and their dereliction in ensuring the information was properly disseminated to other agencies (i.e. the infamous destruction of a note delivered by Oswald to the Dallas FBI in November 1963 or information the CIA held in its possession regarding Oswald rubbing shoulders in Mexico City with Cuban embassy personnel or Cuban intelligence are notable examples of information suppressed by these agencies when confronted by the commission).

This knowledge did not prevent film director Oliver Stone from doubling down on his 'CIA-did-it' theory. In his 2021 JFK assassination documentary he claimed that President Kennedy was murdered by the CIA, backed by the military industrial complex. 'Do you believe that the CIA killed JFK?' Pulitzer Prize winner Tim Weiner asked. 'Millions of Americans suspect so.' He wrote:

Let me ask you, then: *Why* do they believe it? The tale can be traced to a Russian disinformation operation. It came from the same arsenal of culture warfare that convinced half the world that the U.S. Army created AIDS. The one that monkey-wrenched the 2016 election for Donald Trump. The one now flooding the internet with deadly lies about the coronavirus and vaccines. The goals of these campaigns were one and the same: to divide Americans, to pour salt in our self-inflicted wounds, and ultimately to convince you that there is no truth. That crackpot fantasies are cold hard realities. . . . that conspiracy theories are now conspiracy facts . . .[8]

Chapter 2

The Rosetta Stone – The Life of Lee Harvey Oswald

'Lee Harvey Oswald's Motives', first published in John McAdams' e-zine, The Kennedy Assassination, *2005*

After nearly forty years the question remains: Why? What kind of rage, pain or pathology could have provoked Lee Harvey Oswald to such a dark deed?

The explanation of Oswald's motive for killing President Kennedy was buried with him. But I believe the mystery can be solved by penetrating Oswald's personal life, his ideological beliefs and his increasingly disturbed behaviour in the months leading up to the assassination.

Oswald's State of Mind

Most crime does not happen in a vacuum. It does not happen by blind chance – something causes it. Sometimes the reasons are social, sometimes psychological, most often both. The real answer as to why President Kennedy was killed centres around how Lee Harvey Oswald grew up as a misfit, having no real control or moral guidance with which to exist in, and poorly equipped to meet the demands of, society. Answers also lie in the way Oswald embraced a radical ideology in order to compensate for his lack of education and to enhance his self-image.

I believe there are telling references relevant to an understanding of Oswald's frame of mind in an article published in *The American Journal of Psychiatry* (July 1960).[1] The article was used as a reference point by Truman Capote in his book *In Cold Blood* as a way of understanding the psychological make-up of the mind of a murderer. Written by Dr Joseph Satten in collaboration with three colleagues, Karl Menninger, Irwin Rosen and Martin Mayman, the article is chilling in its delineation of a criminally intentioned mind:

In attempting to assess the criminal responsibility of murderers, the law tries to divide them (as it does all offenders) into two groups, the 'sane' and the 'insane'. The 'sane' murderer is thought of as acting upon rational motives that can be understood, though condemned, and the 'insane' one as being driven by irrational senseless motives. When rational motives are conspicuous (for example, when a man kills for personal gain) or when the irrational motives are accompanied by delusions or hallucinations (for example, a paranoid patient who kills his fantasied persecutor), the situation presents little problem to the psychiatrist.

But murderers who seem rational, coherent, and controlled and yet whose homicidal acts have a bizarre apparently senseless quality, pose a difficult problem, if courtroom disagreements and contradictory reports about the same offender are an index. It is our thesis that the psychopathology of such murderers forms at least one specific syndrome which we shall describe. In general, these individuals are pre-disposed to severe lapses in ego-control which makes possible the open expression of primitive violence born out of previous, and now unconscious, traumatic experiences.

The authors had examined four men convicted of seemingly unmotivated murders. All had been found 'sane'. The doctors' description of how the murderers behaved provides a template for Lee Harvey Oswald's personality:

- 'The most uniform and perhaps the most significant, historical finding was a long-standing, sometimes lifelong, history of erratic control over aggressive impulses . . . during moments of actual violence, they often felt separated or isolated from themselves, as if they were watching someone else . . .' – Oswald's friend, Ruth Paine: '[At the Dallas jail] he seemed utterly "apart" from the situation he was in.'
- 'In all these cases, there was evidence of severe emotional deprivation in early life . . .' –Lee Harvey Oswald's brother, Robert Oswald: 'The idea even crossed [my] mind that [my] mother might want to put [me] and John up for adoption; anything to be rid of the burden.'

- 'This deprivation may have involved prolonged or recurrent absence of one or both parents, a chaotic family life in which the parents were unknown, or an outright rejection of the child by one or both parents with the child being raised by others . . .' – Robert Oswald: 'We learned very early that we were a burden . . . she wanted to be free of responsibility'.

- 'Most typically the men displayed a tendency not to experience anger or rage in association with violent aggressive action. None reported feelings of rage in connection with the murders, nor did they experience anger in any strong or pronounced way, although each of them was capable of enormous and brutal aggression . . .' – Lee Harvey Oswald, following his attempt to kill Major General Edwin A. Walker: 'Americans are so spoiled . . . They chased a car. And here I am sitting here . . . What fools . . .' – Oswald, following his attempt to kill Major General Edwin A. Walker. Dallas Police Detective James Leavelle: 'He [Oswald] was a cool character.' New Orleans anti-Castro militant Carlos Bringuier: 'He [Oswald] was really cold-blooded . . . he was not nervous . . .'.

- 'Their relationships with others were of a shallow, cold nature, lending a quality of loneliness and isolation to these men . . .' – Oswald's friend, William Wulf: 'We were 16 . . . he seemed to me a boy that was looking for something to belong to. I don't think anybody was looking for him to belong to them.'

- 'People were scarcely real to them, in the sense of being warmly or positively . . . or even angrily . . . felt about . . .' – Oswald's friend, Michael Paine: 'People were like cardboard [to him]'.

- 'The 3 men under sentence of death had shallow emotions regarding their own fate and that of their victims . . .' – Oswald, following the murder of Dallas Police Officer J.D. Tippit: 'Poor dumb cop.'

- 'Guilt, depression, and remorse were strikingly absent . . .' – Marina Oswald: 'Lee had no moral sense at all . . . only egotism, anger at others on account of his failures'.

- 'The murderous potential can become activated, especially if some disequilibrium is already present, when the victim-to-be is unconsciously perceived as a key figure in some past traumatic configuration. The behaviour, or even the mere presence of this figure adds a stress to the unstable balance of forces that results in a sudden extreme discharge of violence . . .' – Lee learned of a past boyfriend of Marina's – he bore a startling resemblance to JFK.

Psychologically, Oswald had always been a loner and an outsider. He had always been attracted to things that would provide enhanced self-esteem, becoming a Marine, learning Russian, defecting to Russia, inventing a fictitious chapter of a radical political organization.

But it was the attacks on his psyche in childhood – his father dying, his experiencing only sporadic and detached associations with his mother's boyfriends, his relationship with an angry, unstable and domineering mother – that helped turn Lee in adulthood into an embittered, angry misfit. Psychologists believe that a child who lives an isolated life, as Oswald did, and who is brought up by a mother who refused to subordinate herself for her children's welfare, often sees the world as an adversary.

A fatherless upbringing and lack of a meaningful male role model had a crucial effect on the young Oswald, moulding and forming a personality that hid some of his darkest impulses. The young Oswald, whose real father died in a car accident when he was a baby, had only shallow relationships with his mother's many boyfriends whose personalities were often weaker than the domineering and unstable Marguerite's. He was unable to connect with a father, to learn his emotionality and the unique way of how to compete and to channel aggression effectively. Oswald was denied a nurturing system which was male-driven, in which discipline, morality teaching and emotional sustenance were provided by males for males.

Without moral grounding and direct parental guidance the child is unable to recognize moral prerequisites for living in an adult world. Without the attention only a mother can give, the child is denied the necessary socialization. The angry and embittered Marguerite Oswald was unable to provide that background. This was recognized by Lee's brother Robert when he said that mother and son's world view were alike in many ways. They both saw themselves as victims, isolated and surrounded by people and government agencies who failed to understand their special place in the scheme of things. As Norman Mailer wrote, '. . . it seems certain at the least that every malformation, or just about, of Lee Harvey Oswald's character had its roots in her'.[2]

Oswald's Violent Tendencies

Within the literature of the JFK assassination there are telling pieces of evidence which point to Oswald's willingness to commit violent acts to further his own ends.

In the mid-1950s Oswald had spoken about shooting a US president. Palmer McBride testified to the Warren Commission that, in 1956, he befriended Oswald and they often discussed politics. McBride said that one central theme in their discussions was the 'exploitation of the working class' and on one occasion, after they began discussing President Eisenhower, Oswald made a statement to the effect that he would like to kill the president because he was exploiting the working class. McBride said that the statement was not made in jest.[3]

There is also clear evidence that Oswald had a history of wife-battering. Oswald's treatment of his wife is documented in the numerous statements made by the Russian émigré community in Dallas and by his wife Marina. According to Ruth Paine, Marina was worried about Lee's 'mental state'. Marina Oswald testified that her husband was given to fits of 'unreasonable rage'.[4]

In the 1960s domestic violence did not have the high profile that it does today. In the 1995 criminal trial and the 1997 civil trial, evidence of O.J. Simpson's wife-battering was indeed relevant in supporting the prosecution's case for Simpson's guilt. Similarly, Oswald's treatment of his wife is pertinent to an understanding of his propensity for violence. At one stage Oswald tried to strangle his wife. There were incidents when Oswald hit Marina and she ended up with bruises on her body. At one time during the final year of their lives together some members of the émigré community 'rescued' Marina, but she returned to her husband after a two-week separation.

Mahlon Tobias recalled a time when a neighbour of the Oswalds complained to him about the couple's violent arguments. The neighbour reported, 'I think he's really hurt her this time . . . I think that man over there is going to kill that girl'. Michael Paine was shocked that Lee treated his wife like a vassal and he believed Marina was a person who acted as though she were in bondage and servitude.[5]

These kinds of abusive behaviours are all about control of the victim. A variety of seemingly unconnected events are part of that strategy to maintain that control – methods like telling her who she can be friends with, how much she can spend, what kind of clothes she can wear, belittling her, demeaning her. All of these things accomplish the end objective – control. The ultimate act of control is violence – the classic pattern that reflected Oswald's behaviour.

Oswald's Personal Motives

Lee Harvey Oswald lived most of his adult life hiding behind a mask of normality. His mask was convincing to many except those who knew him well. What lay beneath the surface was Oswald's fatally crippled personality, a dark side, a defensive and surly character that no one could penetrate, not even his wife Marina.

Oswald was a bitter and angry young man. As a youth his mother had little or no control over him and, indeed, conspired with him in his rebellion. He was determined to get what he wanted. Prison files are full of case histories like his. He learned very early in life to hate the world, learned early that he had to sink or swim on his own resources. He also learned that he had to develop his life unsupported by a mother who could never give true maternal warmth.

Lee Oswald's lifelong isolation left him without the resources for the kind of role-modelling and parental guidance most of us take for granted. People who are close to others turn to them in moments of stress and doubt to interpret the meaning of an event or a social interaction. As an adult, Lee Oswald was unable to accomplish this with the only person who was truly close to him – his wife Marina. He was too domineering and insistent she follow his 'commands'. He could not ask her if his thoughts and actions were consistent with the world around him, seeking out meaning, exchanging ideas. To Lee, Marina had to follow and admire.

To those who knew him well Oswald was secretive, aggressive and arrogant – to a degree almost paranoid. His brother Robert said Lee liked to create drama and mystery around himself. As a child Lee became fascinated with television programmes about espionage and subversive activities.

Lee Harvey Oswald believed he was an important man and his wife often ridiculed him for this 'unfounded' belief. To a disturbed man like Oswald, his wife's scornful attitude likely acted as a catalyst, fuelling

Oswald's anger and resentment. The evening prior to the assassination he tried to make up with his wife after a series of bitter disagreements about their lives together. She rejected his advances. It must have been a terrible blow to his ego.

Oswald not only saw himself as an unappreciated revolutionary but a person who was superior to his contemporaries. This is borne out by the many people who crossed Oswald's path, especially in the years after his return from the Soviet Union. Although psychologists have long believed that low self-esteem causes aggression and other pathologies, the concept of unfounded high self-esteem has not really been considered until recent years.

High self-esteem that is unjustified and unstable, as in Oswald's case, has led in many instances to violence. Like Oswald, many narcissists are supersensitive to criticism or slights, because deep down they suspect their feelings of superiority are bogus. Because his grandiosity was challenged (Marina laughed at his notion that he would eventually become a statesman-like leader) he reacted violently. Oswald's inflated self-esteem had a powerful effect on his aggression. When the real world failed to recognize his 'superior gifts' he exploded. 'At least his imagination,' Marina said, 'his fantasy, which was quite unfounded, as to the fact that he was an outstanding man. [I] always tried to point out to him that he was a man like any others who were around us. But he simply could not understand that.'[6]

In many ways Oswald's actions in killing Kennedy were a protest – undoubtedly the result of his feelings toward authority and a society that had relegated him to a menial position in life. His need to protest festered as he strove to gain recognition. So much of what he did was egocentric, ego-satisfying. What he did, especially in his political world, wasn't done in order to help others but to draw attention to himself; to satisfy his narcissistic tendencies. Oswald desperately wanted to become famous and successful. His brothers and his wife have testified to the many occasions when they sensed a bitter disappointment in Oswald when he failed to draw attention to himself.

Oswald's Political Motives

Oswald's upbringing bears directly on his actions as a young man. Poor parenting from a single, unstable mother and a fatherless home life affected Oswald greatly, warping his sense of right and wrong and creating an individual who was continually frustrated in his relationships with others. In response to these frustrations Oswald transferred his emotional attachments to his inadequate and poorly thought-out political philosophy.

Oswald turned to radical politics for the purpose of ego-building. Marina believed that learning Russian gave Lee a reputation for being intelligent, making up for the fact that he had a reading disability which gave him feelings of inadequacy. He got from his politics something he couldn't get from individuals. It shows the poverty of Oswald's emotional relationship with people which is a psychopathic trait.

Oswald's belief in the socialist ideal has been confirmed by numerous sources who knew him. As an 18-year-old Oswald espoused his political principles to Palmer McBride and William Wulf. McBride told the FBI:

> During the period I knew Oswald he resided with his mother in the Senator Hotel or a rooming house next door . . . I went with him to his room on one occasion, and he showed me copies of *Das Kapital* and the *Communist Manifesto*. Oswald stated he had received these books from the public library, and he seemed quite proud to have them.[7]

Aline Mosby, a reporter, interviewed Oswald in Moscow after his defection and this interview gives a 'clue' to the way Oswald acted out his political dramas. Oswald told her he became interested in communist ideology when 'an old lady handed me a pamphlet about saving the Rosenbergs'.[8]

The pamphlet led Oswald to change the direction of his life for it was from this period he became enamoured with left-wing politics. The memory of the Rosenberg case, I believe, lasted until his incarceration in the Dallas Police Jail; the Rosenbergs were tried as Soviet spies in a case that fascinated Oswald as a boy. Oswald had made repeated requests the weekend of the assassination for John Abt to defend him. Abt was a left-wing New York lawyer who had defended communists and a newspaper story about Abt had appeared on the same page as the president's visit to Dallas. In attempting to contact Abt Oswald was revealing something about himself – he was already preparing for his appearance on the political stage, emulating the Rosenbergs by becoming a cause célèbre.

Oswald had a desperate desire to act in a political way to further the cause of his commitment to communism and to the Cuban Revolution and in so doing elevate himself as an important 'revolutionary'. He needed a cause to belong to; to inflate his self-image and sustain it. Oswald said that nothing kept him in the United States, and he would lose nothing by returning to the Soviet Union. His real destination, of course, was Cuba. Cuba was a country that embodied the political principles to which he had been committed since he was an adolescent.

To Oswald, Cuba was the last gambit – his last chance to fulfil his political fantasies. As Marina testified to the Warren Commission, 'I only know that his basic desire was to get to Cuba by any means and all the rest of it was window dressing for that purpose'.[9] He hatched a plan to hijack a plane to Cuba and wanted Marina to help. When she refused, he abandoned his plans.

Marina has testified to Oswald's view of Castro as a 'hero' and said Lee had wanted to call their second child 'Fidel' if it had been a boy. Michael Paine told PBS researchers that Lee 'wanted to be an active guerrilla in the effort to bring about the new world order'.[10] Nelson Delgado, Oswald's friend in the Marine Corps, said that Oswald's hero was William Morgan, a former sergeant in the US Army who became a major in Castro's army.

In August 1959 Morgan received considerable press coverage when he lured some anti-Castro rebels into a trap by pretending to be a counter-revolutionary. This may explain Oswald's 'counter-revolutionary' activities in New Orleans when he visited anti-Castroite Carlos Bringuier. Oswald wanted to emulate Morgan.[11]

An incident from Oswald's time in the Marine Corps testifies to Oswald's revolutionary fervour. Fellow Marine, Kerry Thornley, testified to the Warren Commission about an incident 'which grew out of a combination of Oswald's known Marxist sympathies and George Orwell's book *1984*'. After Thornley finished reading the book they took part in a parade. While waiting for the parade to start they talked briefly about *1984* even though Oswald 'seemed to be lost in his own thoughts'. Oswald remarked on the stupidity of the parade and on how angry it made him, to which Thornley replied, 'Well, come the revolution you will change all that.' Thornley said:

> At which time he looked at me like a betrayed Caesar and screamed, screamed definitely, 'Not you, too, Thornley.' And I remember his voice cracked as he said this. He was definitely disturbed at what I had said and I didn't really think I had said that much . . . I never said anything to him again and he never said anything to me again.[12]

Oswald's political ideals remained with him up to the moment of his death and there is convincing evidence to support this. It was inevitable that someone as politically motivated as Oswald would eventually reveal his political self that tragic weekend. A man like Oswald needed a stage to show the world he was a true revolutionary. But he did not do this by confessing. Instead, he showed his commitment to his ideals by a clenched fist salute, a symbol of left-wing radicalism, as he was paraded around the Dallas Police Station. There are at least two published photos of Oswald giving this gesture. The most famous photograph showing Oswald's clenched fist salute was first identified by Jean Davison in her excellent book about Oswald's motives, *Oswald's Game* (1983). The photo was taken by an Associated Press photographer.[13]

The second photo has been overlooked by most researchers and appeared in the UPI/American Heritage book *Four Days* (1964). The caption for the UPI photo reads, 'Oswald shakes his fist at reporters inside police headquarters', an unlikely description of Oswald's actions.[14]

Most JFK conspiracy advocates have assumed that Oswald was merely showing the photographers his manacled hands. But there is a definite clenched fist salute portrayed on both occasions. He repeated this gesture as he lay dying in the ambulance. According to Dallas policeman Billy Combest, he made a 'definite clenched fist'.[15] Some conspiracists have dismissed this vital piece of evidence claiming that a clenched fist salute did not come into vogue until the late 1960s. However, communists and left-wing militant groups have used the salute since the 1930s – in the political elections in Germany in 1930 and in Spain during that period.

Oswald was influenced in his beliefs and his desire to act them out by a number of politically motivated people and political literature during the last year of his life.

The periodicals that Oswald subscribed to may have had an impact on his actions. As the Warren Report pointed out, 'The October 7th., 1963, issue of the *Militant* reported Castro as saying Cuba could not accept a situation where at the same time the United States was trying to ease world tensions it also was increasing its efforts to "tighten the noose around Cuba".'[16]

Castro's opposition to President Kennedy's attempt to deal with Cuba was also reported in the October 1, 1963, issue of the *Worker*, to which Oswald also subscribed. Oswald spoke to Michael Paine about the *Worker* saying, 'you could tell what they wanted you to do . . . by reading between the lines, reading the thing and doing a little reading between the lines'.[17]

In the month before the assassination Oswald may have entered into his revolutionary fantasies while watching television. A Secret Service interview with Marina was first recognized by Jean Davison as a telling indication of Oswald's state of mind. Marina told agents that on Friday, 18 October, Oswald had watched two movies on television, and he had been 'greatly excited'.

The first movie was *Suddenly*, in which Frank Sinatra played an ex-soldier who planned to shoot a US president. Sinatra's character was to shoot the president with a high-powered rifle from the window of a house overlooking a railway station.

The second movie, *We Were Strangers*, was based on the overthrow of Cuba's Machado regime in 1933. John Garfield had played an American who had gone to Cuba to help a group of rebels assassinate the Cuba leader. Oswald's reactions to these movies made a strong impression on his wife according to the Secret Service report.[18]

Given Oswald's orientation to violence as evidenced by his willingness to take General Walker's life, his treatment of his wife and his belief in revolutionary violence the movies are vital to an understanding of his frame of mind. As the movie plots suggested, Oswald could see a way in which he could strike out against a government he detested and support a government he admired.

It is also feasible that Oswald could have had more direct knowledge about CIA plots to assassinate Castro. On 9 September 1963, the *New Orleans–Times Picayune* published a story about Castro's warning about assassination plots against him. Castro declared that US leaders would be in danger if they aided anti-Castro terrorist plans to assassinate Cuban leaders. It is possible that Oswald's 'revolutionary' heroic actions in killing Kennedy were a response to these plots. Although the US people as a whole did not learn of CIA plots to murder Castro until the 1970s, it would have been easy for newspaper readers in New Orleans to 'read between the lines' because it was common knowledge that anti-Castro exiles were engaged in efforts to topple the Castro regime.

Oswald's first reply to a police officer when he was arrested inside the Texas Theatre was, 'I haven't anything to be ashamed of'. He did not say, 'I didn't shoot anyone'. He was obviously giving himself time to think of an answer to the inevitable questions he would be asked when interrogated. His answer, 'I haven't anything to be ashamed of' is a natural response for a true believer in revolutionary action. He may have committed murder – but within the confines of his own reasoning Oswald's crime was 'an act of war' which put him outside the norms of lawful behaviour and moral culpability.

In his revolutionary state of mind, Oswald needed only a catalyst to spur him on. And it came in the form of an aristocratic member of the Dallas émigré community, George Serguis de Mohrenschildt. De Mohrenschildt had an important influence on Oswald in the year before the assassination. He befriended the Oswalds and the older man became Lee's mentor. Unlike the other members of the community, de Mohrenschildt had a soft spot for Oswald and sympathized with his left-wing views. In reality, de Mohrenschildt thought Oswald was a pathetic individual who saw himself as a pretentious intellectual and revolutionary.

It is possible that de Mohrenschildt's statements had influenced Oswald in his decision to assassinate the right-wing firebrand General Walker. Oswald's 'mentor' referred to General Walker as the 'Hitler of tomorrow' and Oswald, according to Marina, often repeated unoriginal things which she believed may have come from de Mohrenschildt. One of Oswald's oft-repeated sayings was that if Hitler had been assassinated it would have benefitted the world. It is therefore possible that the anti-fascist de Mohrenschildt unintentionally provoked Oswald to kill General Walker. Oswald may have wanted to impress his 'surrogate father'.

According to Samuel Ballen, who was de Mohrenschildt's close friend, in the latter's conversations with Lee, 'his unconventional, shocking, humorous and irreverent ideas would have been coming out of George all the time'. Ballen stated that he thought de Mohrenschildt could have influenced Oswald to kill General Walker.[19]

The contempt Lee Harvey Oswald showed for authority and to those who disagreed with his vision of the world, the simple ideological answers he embraced in the face of complex issues he spoke of, generally are expressions of self-aggrandizement and a 'narcissistic tendency'. Until 1963 this side of Oswald had been in hiding. When he began to see himself as 'the commander', the learned revolutionary who was given only menial jobs, the gifted politician who headed an imaginary chapter of the Fair Play For Cuba Committee, 'the hunter of the right wing fascists' – the grandiose side was revealing itself. If Lee Oswald had not assassinated President

Kennedy, he would inevitably have committed a different kind of violent political act.

Oswald's struggle was to get what he wanted – to be considered an important political figure. He achieved a modicum of recognition when he appeared on television and radio in New Orleans in summer 1963, when his Fair Play for Cuba activities were noticed. However, his esteem was damaged when television presenter Bill Stuckey ambushed Oswald with statements about his defection to Russia which took away Oswald's status as an objective spokesman for Castro's communist regime.

Oswald hated the US way of life. Years earlier he had come to detest his beloved Russia. And now his entry to his brave new world was barred. Failure seemed to follow him everywhere. He had nowhere to turn except inwards to his embittered and disillusioned self.

Now and then, in the final year of his life, Oswald would show his normal side, seeking work and interacting with others. But the rare occasion he gathered with friends was tempered by the realization that when the social-izing ended he would eventually return to his life of despair, psychological isolation and unfulfilled political fantasies.

Lee Harvey Oswald's failure as a man, a husband, a worker, a son, a soldier began shortly after his birth. And Oswald's embrace of communism, his strong belief in Castro and the Cuban Revolution and a desire to be recog-nized as an important person provoked him to kill President Kennedy.

* * *

Commentary 2022

In writing the above article, I concluded that Oswald had personal and political motives in killing John F. Kennedy and the story of Oswald's life is the real key to understanding the circumstances surrounding the tragedy. In recent years journalist Peter Savodnik adopted this thesis in his book *The Interloper* (2013).

Savodnik documented Oswald's stay in the former USSR, particularly Moscow where the journalist was based. He delivered a genuine biography that emphasizes the nearly three years Oswald spent in the Soviet Union and addressed the oft-neglected question of why he wanted to kill the president.

Additionally, as the years passed, other writers added to the importance of Oswald's background, suggesting it was his personality and character that underpinned the JFK assassination.

Chapter 3

Jack Ruby and the Mafia

Jack Ruby and the Mafia, 'Why Jack Ruby Killed Lee Harvey Oswald', first published in Crime Magazine, *2009*

In March 1964, 52-year-old Jack Ruby was found guilty of the murder of John F. Kennedy's assassin, Lee Harvey Oswald, and sentenced to die.

For thirty-two months, since the time he shot Oswald, Ruby had been locked in a windowless cell on the Dallas County Jail's corridor 6-M. A 'suicide watch' guard looked in on him around the clock – a single exposed light bulb glared over his bed. Several times Ruby would make attempts on his own life.

Ruby could not tell night from day. He read every newspaper he could lay his hands on, eagerly sifting them for his name. He read dozens of books, including Perry Mason novels and the Warren Report, played cards with his guards, did physical exercises – and seemed out of his mind most of the time, according to jail staff.

Ruby was clearly tipping over the edge in his psychosis and paranoia. He rammed his head against the plaster walls and raved over and over about the suffering Jews who were being killed as revenge for his crime. Near the end, Ruby screamed that his prison guards were piping mustard gas into his cell. Later, when his doctors discovered that he was suffering from brain tumours and adenocarcinoma – a cancer that had spread swiftly through most of the cavities, ducts and glands of his body, Ruby accused them of injecting him with the disease – a medical impossibility.

On 5 October 1966, the Texas Criminal Court of Appeals granted Ruby a new trial on the grounds that his statements to Dallas policemen immediately after the shooting should not have been allowed as evidence against him and that the original court should have granted a change of venue to another jurisdiction because a fair trial was all but impossible in Dallas.

By 5 December the same year, Wichita Falls had been selected as the new venue for the trial. When the sheriff of Wichita Falls arrived a couple of days later to transfer Ruby to Wichita Falls, he noticed that Ruby was ill and refused to take him away. The Dallas County Jail had been treating him with Pepto-Bismol for a stomach problem. He was taken to Parkland Hospital on 9 December 1966 and the doctors treated him for pneumonia. A day later they realized he had cancer in his liver, brain and lungs, and had probably been suffering from it for fifteen months.

Almost from the time he arrived at the hospital, Ruby's condition was considered hopeless. He died on 3 January 1967.

Who Was Jack Ruby?

According to the Warren Commission Report, Jack Ruby was born in 1912 to a Russian immigrant, a quiet, gentle woman who was intimidated by her husband and who spent some months in her later years in an Illinois mental home as a result of her alcoholism. She died in an asylum for the insane in Chicago. His father was a drunk and was treated for psychiatric disorders. A brother and a sister had psychiatric treatment.

Ruby and his brothers and sisters spent much of their childhood in a series of foster homes while their parents were separated. By the time Ruby was 8 or 9 years old, he was making money selling shopping bags in the Chicago streets at Christmas time. In his teens he started selling pennants and earned money by parking cars. At age 23 he went to California to sell tip sheets at a racetrack. When that didn't work, he sold subscriptions for Hearst newspapers.

Until he was drafted into military service in 1943, he continued with these types of petty jobs. He worked as a union organizer, travelled through the Eastern states selling punchboards, then opened what he called a legitimate mail-order business.

Ruby was inducted into the US Army Air Force on 21 May 1943. He spent most of his service at military bases in the South. Two people who recalled Ruby's military service said he was extremely sensitive to insulting remarks about Jews. Ruby attacked a sergeant who had called him a 'Jew bastard'. He expressed to some soldiers his high regard for Franklin D. Roosevelt and cried when he was informed of Roosevelt's death in April 1945.

Ruby attained the rank of private first class and received the good conduct medal. His character and efficiency ratings were classed as excellent.

Following his honourable discharge from the Army Air Force he returned to Chicago. With his sister, Eva Grant, now residing in Dallas, Ruby moved there, and through her got involved in the nightclub business there.

In 1952 a Dallas club he ran failed badly and, depressed about it, he went to a Dallas hotel and considered suicide. He changed his mind and decided to re-enter the club business. Ruby explained:

> I was doing some things on the side. I made a trip to New York to promote a little coloured boy who could sing and dance. Then I became a distributor for pizza pie and for some medicine. I built some log cabins for a man named Gimble, but we didn't do well. I took over a private club in 1960 but I didn't make a go of it with all the credits involved so I changed it to the Carousel Club in 1961.[1]

The Carousel was a sleazy striptease nightclub near the Adolphus and Baker hotels in Dallas.

Ruby's medical history gives some insight into the origins of his mental instability and his impulsive and aggressive behaviour throughout his adult life. The records show a series of head injuries. In 1928 when he was selling tickets outside Soldiers Field in Chicago, two plainclothes policemen beat him on the head with their pistols. In 1941, in some sort of brawl, he suffered a concussion. In 1955, while he was running the Silver Spur nightclub in Dallas, he got in a fight with three customers and a woman ended it by hitting him over the head with a half-gallon jug of wine.

He had a long history of violent, antisocial behaviour, and when it was over he wouldn't remember what he had done. A stripper named Penny Dollar, who once worked at Ruby's Carousel Club, testified at Ruby's trial in 1964. She told the jury that she had seen Ruby throw a man downstairs and beat his head repeatedly on the pavement, then rise in bewilderment and say, 'Did I do this? Did I do this?'

Ruby's autopsy revealed '15 brain tumours', according to Ruby's lawyer, Joe Tonahill.[2]

Ruby had a habit of carrying a gun and assaulting patrons who wouldn't pay or who bothered women at his clubs. He acquired the nickname 'Sparky' because of his quick temper. And he loved to play the big shot, bragging of his friends in the Mafia, cultivating friends among the Dallas Police, and pestering reporters for publicity. Friends and acquaintances have testified that Ruby wanted to appear as a big shot by dropping names and appearing to be an insider with the Dallas Police.

Many friends spoke of Ruby's yearning for class. He wanted a clean image for his clubs and always thought he would eventually own a 'high class joint'. Ruby's efforts to attain class were frequently humorous. He was a Mr Malaprop in his use of language, once telling one of his girlfriends, 'You make me feel very irascible', or 'it's been a lovely precarious evening'.

Conspiracy advocates have often alleged that Ruby may have been homosexual but there is no evidence to support their claims. The rumours may have started because Ruby was a bachelor and he shared an apartment with his friend, George Senator.[3]

Ruby had a long-standing relationship with Alice Reaves Nichols, who helped him manage his club. When asked why they hadn't married Ruby told a friend she had too much 'class' for him. Nichols said she never seriously considered marrying Ruby because he had a gambling habit. Ruby also had intimate relationships with a number of women who worked for him, but they were only fleeting affairs as he was enamoured with Alice.

Ruby's nightclub dancers spoke of his frequent acts of kindness, giving them money when they got into debt and paying their children's medical bills. Many of his staff thought Ruby was a kind and generous person but he was also a man who displayed frequent outbursts of anger towards his staff. Afterwards, he was invariably remorseful but instead of apologizing he would leave the club and return with food snacks as a way of saying sorry. He had a hands-on approach to the running of his clubs and whenever a dispute with patrons arose, he would angrily confront whoever had been responsible, sometimes beating up a customer who got out of hand. Yet he had strong feelings for the underdog, frequently buying a meal for people who were down on their luck. And he was also an emotional man often reacting violently to any slights about the Jewish faith.[4]

Rabbi Silverman, who had known Ruby for ten years, said that one day in 1963 Ruby suddenly appeared on his doorstep with half a dozen dogs. Ruby was crying and said that he was unmarried but, pointing to one dog, described it as 'his wife'. He then pointed to the other dogs and described them as 'his children'. According to Rabbi Silverman, Ruby was sobbing and crying and seemed to be 'a very emotional, unstable, erratic man'.[5]

At the moment President Kennedy was assassinated on the afternoon of Friday, 22 November 1963, Ruby had been at the offices of the *Dallas*

Morning News, placing advertisements for his two clubs, the Carousel and Vegas, which would appear in the newspaper. When word reached the building that Kennedy had been shot Ruby was clearly upset at the news.

The next evening Ruby visited his sister, Eva. They talked about the assassination and Ruby's feelings came pouring out. He was remorseful of what the assassination had done to Dallas and of how the Jews had lost a great friend in the president. Ruby was highly strung and obviously disturbed. Later that evening he went to the Dallas Police Station and observed Oswald's midnight press conference. Ruby was enraged that Oswald was smirking at the police officers who surrounded the alleged assassin. Close friends who met Ruby that evening spoke of Ruby's anger, revulsion and hatred for Oswald.

At his last stop that night, at the Southland Hotel's coffee shop, he told his friend George Senator of his anger at an anti-Kennedy advertisement which had been placed in Friday's *Dallas Morning News*. He was especially upset because the advertisement had been placed by someone who had a 'Jewish sounding name' which he believed would bring discredit on the Jews.[6]

Ruby slept until 9 a.m. Sunday morning. He watched television for a while and then made breakfast. When he left the apartment at 11 a.m. he took his pet dachshund with him. Into his jacket pocket he slipped his .38 calibre revolver. Ruby usually carried the weapon in his car or, if he was holding cash receipts from the clubs, in his jacket. Bob Larkin, a doorman at Ruby's Carousel nightclub said, 'He carried a lot of money . . . that's why he kept a gun in the bank bag . . . whenever he was carrying money, he kept his piece handy'.[7]

Ruby drove downtown past the Texas School Book Depository and parked his car not far from his destination, the Western Union Telegraph office where he was to telegraph some money for one of his dancers. He left his dog Sheba in the car, a telling act that would later convince a number of Ruby's friends the nightclub owner had not planned on killing Oswald.

At 11.17 a.m. the Western Union clerk gave Ruby a receipt for his money order. Ruby walked out the door and headed down Main Street toward the police station. He was four minutes away from his historic role in the tragic events of that weekend – the slaying of the president's alleged assassin before a television audience of millions.

Detectives L.C. Graves and James Leavelle led Oswald to the basement of the Dallas Police Station. As they were going down in the lift Leavelle said to Oswald, 'If anybody shoots at you, I hope they're as good a shot as you are.' Leavelle was handcuffed to Oswald's right arm and Graves held his other arm.

The armoured car that was to take Oswald to the County Jail could not manoeuvre down into the basement so a police car was assigned for the job. As Oswald came through the swing doors Ruby had just positioned himself in a group of television and newspaper reporters. Camera lights flashed and blinded the detectives and police officers who were guarding the basement.

As Oswald was escorted out the swing doors to the basement garage, 10 to 15ft away from the escort car, Ruby angled himself directly in front of Oswald's path. Ruby then rushed forward and fired a single shot into Oswald's abdomen, the bullet striking vital organs. Leavelle grabbed Ruby by the shoulder and pushed down on him. Graves had the hammer of the pistol locked with his thumb while Ruby was trying to pull the trigger again. Detectives L.D. Montgomery and Blackie Harrison grabbed Ruby from the back and got him to the ground. Ruby responded with, 'I'm Jack Ruby. You all know me.' As he was taken to a third-floor interrogation room, Ruby said, 'I hope I killed the son of a bitch. It will save you guys a lot of trouble.'[8]

After Ruby was subdued, Oswald was carried back into the jail office and given artificial respiration. The ambulance arrived in a matter of minutes and Oswald was taken to Parkland Hospital. One of his escorts, Detective Billy Combest, said Oswald made a 'definite clenched-fist salute' during the journey to the hospital. Oswald was pronounced dead at Parkland Hospital at 1.07 p.m., about an hour and a half after he was shot.

Ruby and the Mob

It was Ruby's relationships with unsavoury mob-linked characters throughout his life that led to a great deal of speculation that he was controlled by organized crime. The Warren Commission's investigation into his background failed to dispel this notion because the commission – which basically relied on hundreds of FBI interviews of Ruby's known associates – did not fully investigate his alleged Mafia connections and his trips to Cuba.

One of the most intriguing questions surrounding Oswald's assassin concerned Ruby's 1959 trip to Cuba. The 1976–9 HSCA investigation determined that he had made at least three trips to Havana that summer and that he had visited a safe deposit box in Dallas in the meantime.[9]

However, the trips had nothing to do with the Mafia, as Ruby's lawyer Melvin Belli explained:

It came out in one of our earliest interviews that he had tried to arrange some sort of deal with Cuba soon after Fidel Castro over-threw the Batista regime. But that, Ruby would insist, was when Castro was considered something of a hero in the United States. Now Castro was considered a Russian-supported Communist, and Ruby was mortified to think that anyone might get the wrong impression of the deal.

'When Castro first came in he was considered a hero,' Ruby said, 'and I thought maybe I could make a deal in selling jeeps to Cuba. He was still a hero at the time; his brother was the first one to turn. Steve Allen and Jack Parr (television entertainers) and Jake Arvey's son were all interested then in making deals with him. I had been associated with a very high type of person, but a gambler, Mack Willie, who ran a club in Cuba, so I went there for eight or 10 days.'

People would say he had planned to give guns to Cuba, Ruby fretted; they would think he wasn't a good American. He insisted that we telephone all over the place to try to set the record straight on this, although I got the impression, frankly, that the deal had been primarily the figment of his imagination.[10]

That same year, according to the HSCA, the FBI contacted Ruby eight times trying to recruit him as an informant. But J. Edgar Hoover, head of the FBI, withheld the information from the Warren Commission. Later it was disclosed that Ruby, because of his advantageous position as a Dallas night-club owner, had given FBI agent Charles Flynn information about thefts and similar offences in the Dallas area.

In November of 1959 Flynn recommended that no further attempt be made to develop Ruby as a PCI (Potential Criminal Informant), since his information was useless. Ruby had been trying to dish the dirt on his night-club competitors.

Hugh Aynesworth, a *Times Herald* reporter who knew Ruby well, said:

In 1959 the FBI tried eight times to recruit Jack Ruby. They wanted him as an informer on drugs, gambling, and organized crime, but every time they contacted him, Ruby tried to get his competitors in trouble. 'Ol' Abe over at the Colony Club is cheating on his income tax . . . Ol' Barney at the Theatre Lounge is selling booze after hours.' After a while the FBI gave up on the idea.[11]

As the years passed following Ruby's death, discoveries about his activities provided more material for sensationalist speculation by conspiracy advocates. During the 1970s the public learned that the CIA failed to disclose a report that Ruby may have visited Santo Trafficante, mob boss of Florida, during the time Trafficante was in a Cuban jail. The HSCA later investigated these reports but did not place any credence upon them.[12]

Ruby's telephone records have been the subject of numerous investigations and some conspiracists have alleged they provide proof of Mafia involvement in the assassination of President Kennedy. While it is true that Ruby made many telephone calls to his underworld contacts in the months before the Kennedy assassination, the calls had nothing to do with any arrangements to kill the president. There is no evidence the calls were conspiratorial in nature. In fact, the calls centred around the fact that Ruby had wanted assistance from the strippers' labour union to dissuade rival clubs from using amateur talent.

Furthermore, most of the calls were made before the president's trip to Dallas was even announced, much less before the motorcade route was set. Journalist Seth Kantor speculated that Ruby borrowed money from the mob and that the mob later called in the debt by asking him to silence Oswald. However, he provides no evidence it was anything but speculation.[13]

Conspiracy advocates rightly point to Ruby's association with Dallas mob bosses Joe Civello and Joe Campisi as evidence that Ruby was mob-linked but they fail to put the connection in the right context. Ruby's world consisted of nightclubs and socializing with people who were in the same business. As the McClellan Committee recognized in the 1950s, no city in the United States was immune to Mafia control of off-track betting, gambling and nightclub entertainment.

It was the milieu in which Ruby operated. Ruby also entertained many Dallas Police officers at his club. None of them testified to any sinister connection with the Dallas bosses. One police officer, Joe Cody, said that Ruby was often seen with Joe and Sam Campisi because they were part of Ruby's social scene. Ruby ate at the Egyptian Lounge and Cody often joined Ruby and the Campisi brothers. Cody said there were no criminal reasons for the meetings.[14]

It was inevitable that Ruby would associate with characters who could be linked in some way with the underworld. But it is illogical to assume mob involvement in Ruby's actions that tragic weekend. The evidence indicates otherwise.

Tony Zoppi, a close friend of Ruby's, told author Gerald Posner:

> It is so ludicrous to believe that Ruby was part of the mob. The conspiracy theorists want to believe everybody but those who really knew him. People in Dallas, in those circles, knew Ruby was a snitch. The word on the street was that you couldn't trust him because he was telling the cops everything. He was a real talker, a fellow who would talk your ear off if he had the chance. You have to be crazy to think anyone would have trusted Ruby to be part of the mob. He couldn't keep a secret for five minutes. He was just a hanger on, somebody who would have liked some of the action but was never going to get any.[15]

Former Dallas Assistant District Attorney Bill Alexander said:

> It's hard to believe . . . that I, who prosecuted Ruby for killing Oswald, am almost in the position of defending his honour. Ruby was not in the Mafia. He was not a gangster. We knew who the criminals were in Dallas back then, and to say Ruby was part of organized crime is just bullshit. There's no way he was connected. It's guilt by association, that A knew B, and Ruby knew B back in 1950, so he must have known A, and that must be the link to the conspiracy. It's crap written by people who don't know the facts.[16]

Conspiracy advocates have alleged that Ruby had been involved in the nightclub business in Chicago and was sent to Dallas by the Chicago Mafia. However, many years later Ruby's brother Earl said: 'That's absolutely false. I worked with Jack during that time, and he never had anything to do with nightclubs in Chicago. When you were actually there and know what went on, it drives you crazy to hear charges like that, which are just completely wrong.'[17] Bill Roemer, the FBI agent in charge of investigating the Chicago Mafia in the 1960s, agrees:

Ruby was absolutely nothing in terms of the Chicago mob. We had thousands of hours of tape recordings of the top mobsters in Chicago, including Sam Giancana (the Chicago godfather), and Ruby just didn't exist as far as they were concerned. We talked to every hoodlum in Chicago after the assassination and some of the top guys in the mob, my informants, I had a close relationship with them – they didn't know who Ruby was. He was not a front for them in Dallas.[18]

Roemer knew how the Mafia operated. He arrested many members of the Mafia and bugged the Armory Lounge, Giancana's headquarters. Roemer was convinced that if the Mafia hired anyone for a hit they would choose someone who had a track record of killing and who would remain 'tight lipped'. None of these traits applied to Ruby.

Ruby certainly knew many people who had police records. Bill Alexander said:

It was the nature of his business. Running those types of nightclubs, he came across plenty of unsavoury characters. The police had a pretty good idea of what happened at Ruby's club, and there was no dope and he certainly didn't allow any of the girls to do anything illegal from the club, because that would have cost him his license. Ruby was a small-time operator on the fringe of everything, but he never crossed over to breaking the law big time.[19]

Jack Ruby and the Conspiracy Theorists

Despite attempts by conspiracy writers to prove Ruby was part of a conspiracy to kill JFK, there are compelling and persuasive reasons that Ruby was acting alone when he shot Oswald. Despite some claims to the contrary, there is no evidence to suggest Ruby had been hired by the Mafia to silence Oswald. Allegations that Ruby acquiesced to the Mafia's demands because he knew he had cancer have made the rounds for years – and continue to do so – but are spurious.

There are no medical records or statements from his brothers and sister to say that Ruby knew he had cancer prior to killing Oswald. Ruby certainly never claimed he had cancer prior to killing Oswald. It would not be until

1966 that Ruby, suffering from paranoia and delusions, would claim that he was being injected with cancer cells. The doctors at Parkland Hospital, who began treating Ruby for cancer in December 1966, estimated he'd had the disease for only the previous fifteen months.

Mark Lane in his conspiracy book *Rush to Judgment* (1966), Oliver Stone in his movie *JFK* (1991) and Henry Hurt in his book *Reasonable Doubt* (1986) examined Ruby's 1964 testimony to the Warren Commission and concluded it indicated Ruby's involvement in a conspiracy.

After Ruby had been convicted of Oswald's murder and sentenced to death, Warren Commission members Earl Warren and Gerald Ford questioned him at the Dallas County Jail. For many months there had been rumours that Ruby was a hit man whose job had been to silence Oswald. In the opinion of Lane and Stone, Ruby seemed eager to disclose his part in a conspiracy. According to Lane:

> Ruby made it plain that if the commission took him from the Dallas jail and permitted him to testify in Washington, he could tell more there; it was impossible for him to tell the whole truth so long as he was in the jail in Dallas . . . [Ruby said] 'I would like to request that I go to Washington and . . . take all the tests that I have to take. It is very important . . . Gentlemen, unless you get me to Washington, you can't get a fair shake out of me'.

However, it is clear from Ruby's Warren Commission testimony that he simply wanted to inform the commissioners of a conspiracy to murder Jews. Earl Warren, the commission's chairman, said:

> I went down and took Jack Ruby's testimony myself – he wouldn't talk to anybody but me. And he wanted the FBI to give him a lie detector test, and I think the FBI did, and he cleared it all right. I was satisfied myself that he didn't know Oswald, never had heard of him. But the fellow was clearly delusional when I talked to him. He took me aside and he said, 'Hear those voices, hear those voices?' He thought they were Jewish children and Jewish women who were being put to death in the building there.

He told Warren, Gerald Ford and others, 'I am as innocent regarding any conspiracy as any of you gentlemen in the room'. Ruby was actually begging the commission to take him back to Washington so that he could take a polygraph examination and prove that he was telling the truth when he denied any role in a conspiracy.[20]

After his arrest, Ruby had been diagnosed as a psychotic depressive. His testimony to the Warren Commission indicates that he believed he was a victim of a political conspiracy by right-wing forces in Dallas. He suggested that the John Birch Society was spreading the falsehood that he, a Jew, was implicated in the president's death in order to create anti-Jewish hysteria.

Ruby insisted:

> The Jewish people are being exterminated at this moment. Consequently, a whole new form of government is going to take over our country . . . No subversive organization gave me any idea. No underworld person made any effort to contact me. It all happened one Sunday morning . . . If you don't get me back to Washington tonight to give me a chance to prove to the President that I am not guilty, then you will see the most tragic thing that will ever happen . . . All I want is a lie detector test . . . All I want to do is tell the truth, and that is all. There was no conspiracy.

A letter Ruby sent to his brother, Earl, clearly reveals Ruby's mental state. In it he wrote:

> You must believe what I've been telling you for the past two and a half years. If you only would have believed me all along you would have found some way to check out what I said. You would have saved Israel, but now they are doomed, because they think the U.S. are for them, but they are wrong because [President] Johnson wants to see them slaughtered and tortured. Egypt is making believe they are an ally of Russia, that is only to fool Russia and the U.S. It's too late now to do anything, and we are all doomed. They are torturing children here.
>
> If you only would believe what I'm telling you . . . Earl, they are going to torture you to death, and you will witness your own family being put to death. Forgive me for all this terrible tragedy

I've caused. I know you won't listen to me Earl, but if you go to a public phone booth, they may be watching you, pretend that you are going to a department store or a movie, and then give them the slip.[21]

Another primary claim that conspiracy theorists make is the Dallas Police conspired with Ruby to take out Oswald. Oswald was scheduled to be transferred from the Dallas Police Jail to the County Jail at 10 a.m. on Sunday, 24 November. Before the transfer of Oswald to the County Jail, the alleged assassin was due a further interrogation by Captain Will Fritz and representatives of the Secret Service and FBI. Oswald's interrogation on Sunday morning lasted longer than originally planned because Postal Inspector Harry D. Holmes arrived. Holmes had helped the FBI trace the money order that Oswald used to buy the Mannlicher-Carcano rifle. Holmes had also helped the FBI trace the ownership of the post-office box number to which Oswald's rifle and pistol were sent.

The arrival of Holmes delayed the transfer of Oswald. In his testimony to the Warren Commission Holmes said:

> I actually started to church with my wife. I got to church and I said, 'You get out, I am going down to see if I can do something for Captain Fritz. I imagine he is as sleepy as I am.' So I drove directly on down to the police station and walked in, and as I did, Captain Fritz motioned to me and said, 'We are getting ready to have a last interrogation with Oswald before we transfer him to the county jail. Would you like to join us?' I said I would.[22]

Secret Service agents and an FBI agent interrogated Oswald after Fritz. Unexpectedly, Fritz then turned to Holmes and asked whether he wanted to interrogate Oswald. Holmes accepted.

It was for this reason the interrogation continued for another half hour or so.

Ruby shot Oswald approximately 5 minutes after Ruby left the Western Union office. If Inspector Holmes had continued on to church with his wife that morning, the length of interrogation would have been shortened and Jack Ruby would never have had the opportunity to kill Oswald. David Scheim in his book *Contract On America* (1988) ignores this vital piece of evidence surrounding the transfer of Oswald. Scheim took part of Ruby's testimony out of context in order to present evidence that Ruby had had assistance in the murder of Oswald: 'Who else could have timed it so perfectly by seconds. If it were timed that way, then someone in the police department is guilty of giving the information as to when Lee Harvey Oswald was coming down.' Exactly the same conspiratorial statement, taken out of its proper context, was used ten years later by Noel Twyman in his book *Bloody Treason* (1997).[23]

This 'conspiratorial' statement contradicts Ruby's actual testimony. What Ruby really said was:

> . . . but I know in my right mind, because I know my motive for doing it, and certainly to gain publicity to take a chance of being mortally wounded, as I said before, and who else could have timed it so perfectly by seconds. If it were timed that way, then someone in the police department is guilty of giving the information as to when Lee Harvey Oswald was coming down. I never made a statement. I never inquired from the television man what time is Lee Harvey Oswald coming down. Because really a man in his right mind would never ask that question. I never made the statement 'I wanted to get three more off. Someone had to do it. You wouldn't do it.' I never made those statements . . . Anything I said was with emotional feeling of I didn't want Mrs. Kennedy to come back to trial.[24]

Some conspiracists have alleged that the Dallas Police allowed Ruby to enter the Dallas Police basement through an unlocked door instead of entering by a ramp. However, they ignore an important witness who actually saw Ruby descend the ramp. The witness was an ex-Dallas Police officer named Napoleon Daniels who had observed Ruby go down the ramp when the police officer guarding the entrance, Roy Vaughn, was distracted by a car trying to manoeuvre into the basement entrance. Vaughn had to walk into the middle of the street to divert the car. Daniels thought the man entering the basement was a police detective and did not tell Vaughn. He did, however, notice a bulge at the person's waist that he believed to be a holstered handgun. The Dallas Police tried to discredit Daniel's testimony possibly because he was black but also because his testimony revealed the incompetence of the Dallas Police Department.[25]

Another authoritative source has gone on record as late as March 1997 which confirms that Ruby, in the confusion that surrounded the police station that Sunday morning, did not have any assistance in entering the basement. Paul McCaghren, a retired police lieutenant who was not present at the time but later investigated the shooting of Oswald, said that Ruby's access to the basement was just lucky timing on his part. He said that in hindsight things should have been done differently but it was a situation that had never occurred before.[26]

According to the report filed by the Dallas Police Department investigating Oswald's shooting, an armoured truck was to be used to transport Oswald to the County Jail from the Dallas Police Jail. According to the report, police decided that 'an unmarked police car would be better from the standpoint of both speed and deception . . . Such a car, bearing Oswald, should follow the armoured truck.'[27]

But the police lieutenant driving the squad car was forced to go the wrong way on a ramp at police headquarters to pull in front of the armoured car because the exit was blocked. Another police officer, guarding the area, the report said, was surprised when the lieutenant pulled in and blasted his car horn to hold the pedestrian traffic. McCaghren said this is when Ruby slipped into the basement, went immediately down the ramp and shot Oswald.[28]

Jim Ewell, a former reporter with the *Dallas Morning News*, maintains that the idea that the Dallas Police Department had a hand in assisting Ruby is not true and that Dallas Police Department officials would have done things differently in the transfer of Oswald but top city officials over-ruled them. He believes the police would have made the media stand in the street had they been given their way. The city officials wanted to make sure the world knew that Oswald was not being mistreated. Furthermore, during the transfer of Oswald, many officers were blinded by the high-intensity television lights which accounted for the fact that Ruby was able to move among them without being challenged.[29]

Conspiracy advocates raise all kinds of similar conspiratorial questions about Ruby in their attempts to prove he was part of a plot. As David Belin first noted in *Full Disclosure* (1988), nearly every conspiracy theorist ignores the testimony of Ruby's rabbi, Hillel Silverman. Rabbi Silverman had visited Ruby in prison frequently. Rabbi Silverman is convinced Ruby was not part of a conspiracy.

According to Silverman, at his first meeting with Ruby on the day after the shooting of Oswald, Ruby told him that, 'Had I intended to kill him [at a press conference on the Friday evening], I could have pulled my trigger on the spot, because the gun was in my pocket'. The truth of Ruby's explanation is confirmed by Lonnie Hudkins, a newspaper reporter, in an interview with PBS Frontline researchers: 'I asked him if he was packing a pistol at that midnight press conference,' Hudkins said, 'and he said "Yes". I asked him, "Why didn't you plug him then?" and he said "I was frightened of hitting one of you guys."'[30] These circumstances are vital to an understanding of Ruby's actions because the time to shoot Oswald would have been the Friday night press conference. It was pure coincidence that Ruby had an opportunity to kill Oswald on the Sunday morning.

The final words by Ruby about the allegations that federal agents or the Dallas Police were instrumental in allowing Ruby to enter the basement of the Dallas Police Station were uttered shortly before he died. Ruby made a deathbed statement using a tape recorder, secreted in an attaché case, which was smuggled into his hospital room by his brother, Earl Ruby. Ruby was questioned by his lawyers. The tape recording was later incorporated in an LP record entitled *The Controversy* (1967). The interview lasted 12 minutes but was edited down to 3 minutes for the recording.

Ruby said that it was pure chance in meeting Oswald at the Dallas Police Station:

> The ironic part of this is I had made an illegal turn behind a bus to the parking lot. Had I gone the way I was supposed to go, straight down Main Street, I would never have met this fate, because the difference in meeting this fate was 30 seconds one way or the other . . . All I did is walk down there, down to the bottom of the ramp and that's when the incident happened – at the bottom of the ramp.

In the final recording of Ruby's voice, he was asked if he knew the time Oswald was supposed to have been moved. Ruby replied, 'He was supposed to be moved at 10 o'clock'. Ruby explained he always carried a gun because he often had large sums of money.[31]

Furthermore, it is logical to assume that no conspiracy could profit by silencing Oswald in a public fashion. There would be no point in eliminating one suspect while simultaneously handing the police another. And, if it were

Oswald's intention to 'talk', he could have done so in the two days he was incarcerated in the Dallas Police Station.

Ruby denied that he knew Oswald and said Oswald had never been in his club. Rumours that Ruby and Oswald knew each other have been repeated over and over again since the time that Ruby shot Oswald. Many conspiracy advocates have stated flatly that Oswald recognized Ruby just before Ruby pulled the trigger in the Dallas Police basement.

The Warren Report investigated numerous specific allegations that Ruby knew Oswald but found none that merited credence. Although it would be impossible to investigate all of these 'sightings' – which are uncorroborated and unsubstantiated, a clue why they arose in the first place may be gleaned from the commission's investigation of one particular sighting.

The Warren Commission stated:

> The testimony of a few witnesses who claim to have seen Ruby with a person who they feel may have been Oswald warrants further comment. One such witness, Robert K. Patterson, a Dallas electronics salesman, has stated that on Nov. 1, 1963, Ruby, accompanied by a man who resembled Oswald, purchased some equipment at his business establishment. However, Patterson did not claim positively that the man he saw was Oswald, and two of his associates who were also present at the time could not state that the man was Oswald. Other evidence indicates that Ruby's companion was Larry Crafard.

The Warren Commission concluded that Crafard, sometime in late October or early November, accompanied Ruby to an electronics store in connection with the purchase of electronic equipment.[32]

Furthermore, Oswald's wife Marina never believed that Oswald and Ruby would have associated with each other, 'How could Lee have known Ruby? . . . He didn't drink, he didn't smoke, he didn't go to nightclubs and, besides, he was sitting home with me all the time.'[33]

Ruby's True Motives
On the evening of JFK's assassination, Ruby met one of his dancers, Kay Coleman, and her boyfriend, Harry Olsen, a Dallas policeman. They talked for an hour and Olsen told Ruby, 'They should cut this guy [Oswald] inch

by inch into ribbons'. Ruby agreed and cursed Oswald. This may have been the beginning of Ruby's plan to kill Oswald. Ruby never mentioned the conversation until after his trial knowing it would be evidence of premeditation.

According to Rabbi Silverman, Ruby had seen a television broadcast on the Saturday morning in which a rabbi had been speaking about President Kennedy and the assassination. The next morning, 24 November, Ruby read in the newspaper that Jacqueline Kennedy might have to come to Dallas to testify at Oswald's trial. Ruby's rabbi was convinced of the sincerity of Ruby's explanation that he had killed Oswald because he was emotionally distraught over JFK's murder.

Melvin Belli, who became Ruby's lawyer after he shot Oswald, wrote:

> There was one weird trait. Unfailingly, at the mention of a member of President Kennedy's family, tears would start to course down his cheeks. It could even be a casual mention – later we tested his reaction by saying things like, 'Too bad Jack Kennedy won't be able to see the Giant's play' – and the tears would just flow out of there. It was too spontaneous to be an act. I am convinced of the sincerity of this affection.[34]

Ruby's sister, Eva Grant, has testified to the emotional turmoil Ruby was experiencing the weekend of the assassination:

> He was sick to his stomach . . . and went into the bathroom . . . He looked terrible . . . He looked pretty bad . . . I can't explain it to you. He looked too broken, a broken man already. He did make the remark, 'I never felt so bad in all my life even when Ma and Pa died . . . someone tore my heart out'.[35]

Cecil Hamlin, a long-time friend of Ruby's, said Ruby was 'very emotional . . . very broken up'. Buddy Raymon, a comedian, remembered that when Ruby telephoned him, 'He was crying and carrying on, "What do you think of a character like that killing the president?"', Ruby had asked him. George Senator said it was the 'first time I ever saw tears in his eyes'.

After the assassination Ruby had visited his synagogue and cried. His brother Hyman said, 'They didn't believe a guy like Jack would ever cry. Jack never cried in his life. He was not that kind of guy to cry.'[36]

Ruby described his actions that fateful Sunday morning:

I don't know what bug got a hold of me. I don't know what it is, but I am going to tell the truth word for word. I am taking a pill called Preludin. It is a harmless pill. And it is very easy to get in the drugstore. It isn't a highly prescribed pill. I use it for dieting. I don't partake of that much food.

I think that was a stimulus to give me an emotional feeling that suddenly I felt, which was so stupid, that I wanted to show my love for our faith, being of the Jewish faith, and I never used the term and I don't want to go into that – suddenly the feeling, the emotional feeling came within me that someone owed this debt to our beloved President to save [Jackie Kennedy] the ordeal of coming back [for Oswald's trial]. I don't know why that came through my mind.

James Leavelle, the homicide detective who was handcuffed to Oswald when he was shot and who also transferred Ruby to the County Jail, said that he asked Ruby why he shot Oswald and his answer was, 'I wanted to be a hero. It looks like I f***** things up'. Leavelle also said, 'Ruby told me an interesting thing when I was a patrolman which didn't make any sense to me at the time, but it did after. He told me, "I'd like to see two police officers sometime in a death struggle about to lose their lives, and I could jump in there and save them and be a hero."'

Ruby told Assistant District Attorney Bill Alexander, 'Well, you guys couldn't do it. Someone had to do it. That son of a bitch killed my President.'

Leavelle's reasoning for Ruby's actions are confirmed by many of Ruby's friends who believed the nightclub owner shot Oswald to become a hero. And Ruby, in the days after the shooting, believed he would soon be out of jail and running his nightclubs as usual, according to Ruby's bartender, Andrew Armstrong, who visited Ruby regularly in jail to report on the club's affairs.

Joe Tonahill, Ruby's lawyer, said:

In the beginning Ruby considered himself a hero. He thought he had done a great service for the community. When the mayor, Earle Cabell, testified that the act brought great disgrace to Dallas, Jack started going downhill very fast. He got more nervous by the day. When they brought in the death penalty, he cracked. Ten days later he rammed his head into a cell wall. Then he tried to kill himself with an electric light socket. Then he tried to hang himself with sheets.

In interviews conducted by the authors Ovid Demaris and Gary Wills, Armstrong and many of Ruby's friends and acquaintances had little doubt as to what went through Ruby's mind at the time he decided to shoot Oswald. 'At the club, after the first shock,' said Carousel Club drummer Bill Willis, 'we all said, "Well, it figures. Jack thought while he was downtown he might as well kill Oswald too."' Max Rudberg, another friend of Ruby's, said, 'Well, everyone was saying [he] needs killing, and Jack was anxious to please . . . he was bound to poke his head in and see what was happening. Wherever there was a crowd, he couldn't possibly pass it by'. Milton Joseph, a local jeweller and friend of Ruby's, had no doubt that Ruby killed Oswald to be in the limelight.[37]

Contrary to the claims of conspiracy writers, Ruby died telling the truth. There is no credible evidence he was part of a conspiracy. Ruby murdered Oswald for personal reasons – he wanted to show that 'Jews had guts'. He felt emotionally distraught about the Kennedys, and he wanted to fulfil his life-long dream of becoming a real hero.

Ruby was a small-time wheeler-dealer who could never have been a participant in a complex conspiracy. No one, least of all the Mafia, would have trusted such an incompetent small-timer to play a leading role in an elaborate and secretive plot. Most people who knew Jack Ruby agreed.

* * *

Commentary 2022

The Warren Commission and HSCA investigators were suspicious of Mafia involvement in the assassination of President Kennedy. In 1979, the HSCA gave the Mafia theory a boost with its conclusion that Kennedy's death was 'probably' the result of a conspiracy and that Mafia leaders had the 'means, motive and opportunity to kill the President'. They based their conclusions on one piece of evidence – the tape recording of gunshots in Dealey Plaza – but those scientific results were debunked by the National Academy of Sciences three years after the HSCA released its report.

New Orleans Mafia boss Carlos Marcello and Florida boss Santo Trafficante were prime suspects. But in addition to the lack of credible and corroborative evidence, there are two big problems with these accusations. The two men lasted as dons for decades, in part by running their enterprises without attracting attention, not trying to kill the President of the United States. FBI agent William Roemer insists that if the Mafia planned to kill Kennedy, he would have heard about it as he listened to Chicago Boss Sam Giancana (who helped the CIA plot to kill Castro) and other members of the Mafia's national commission scheme and brag. Additionally, Roemer believed that the mafia would never go after high-ranking government leaders.

Central to the idea that the mafia killed JFK, a number of questions are crucial. Why would the Mafia decide to kill President Kennedy when, one would assume, they held incriminating knowledge linking the president with the mistress of a mob boss? In the 1970s, President Kennedy and Chicago Mafia boss Sam Giancana shared a mistress, Judith Campbell Exner.

There were also statements made by mob-linked figures that Kennedy was having an affair with Marilyn Monroe and the Mafia was aware of it. Secondly – why would the Mafia kill Kennedy if they could get rid of him in a much 'cleaner' way – blackmail?

The information about these scandalous activities would have doomed Kennedy's chances for re-election in 1964. Kennedy's close friend ex-*Washington Post* editor Ben Bradlee has said the revelations would have led to Kennedy's impeachment by Congress. For the first time in the history of the United States, Mafia mob bosses had a president who was in their 'hip pocket'. Why on earth would they risk organizing a vast conspiracy, knowing they would be putting their own positions at extreme risk?

Another problem is Lee Harvey Oswald. It is difficult to think of a more unreliable, unlikely professional hitman than a paranoid loser like Oswald. If he was working for the Mafia, why did he try to assassinate retired General Edwin A. Walker seven months before he killed Kennedy, thus risking the whole enterprise? His job at the Book Depository was very convenient. But he got the job before the motorcade route was selected. There is no trail of phone calls between Oswald and the Mafia in the days before the assassination, nor does any evidence suggest the Mafia placed Oswald in the building overlooking Dealey Plaza.

Conspiracy theorists might also explain how some of the world's most notorious criminals might allow an incredibly complicated plot to be centred on men like Ruby and Oswald, who were unstable and unreliable individuals. Why would conspirators choose Oswald to participate in their plot, when they could have hired much more experienced assassins? Conspiracy theorists may counter that Oswald was a 'patsy' who was unaware of the plot.

We must then look at the many incriminating movements of Oswald which disproves he was innocently led – why did he leave the scene of the crime? Why did he shoot Tippit? – and so on and so forth. Instead, we can realistically conclude that there is no credible evidence of Mafia involvement in the assassination of President Kennedy.

The numerous books linking the Mafia with the murder of JFK provide nothing but second-hand accounts, speculation and obscure connections between the various and nefarious characters who dot the landscape of assassination literature. At most, these books have established that the Mafia hated the Kennedys, talked about killing them and wanted them out of their lives, but the idea that they carried out their wishes simply lacks inherent logic.

Chapter 4

The Alleged CIA Conspiracy

'Mark Lane: The Original Shyster', first published in Max Holland's Washington Decoded, *2012*

Commentary 2022

Lawyer Mark Lane was at the centre of the controversial circumstances surrounding the assassination of President Kennedy almost immediately after the killing, and remained there for almost fifty years. His 1966 book *Rush to Judgment*, an indictment of the Warren Commission's finding that Lee Harvey Oswald was Kennedy's lone, crazed assassin, became the first bestselling book to suggest conspiracy. He was a relentless self-promoter, often accused of sensationalism and hyperbole.

In fact, the cycle of endless myth-making about the Kennedy assassination began with Mark Lane and his modus operandi has been imitated repeatedly by countless other conspiracy authors.

In the weeks following the assassination the New York lawyer was 'hired' by Oswald's mother, a neurotic and unstable woman who shame-facedly told the press her son was a 'patsy' and a 'hero'. He began to scavenge any paper trail for another piece of the puzzle – a puzzle that continued with his distortion of Warren Commission testimony.

Long before scientists, medical experts and ballistics experts had a chance to clear up the anomalous evidence the Warren Commission failed to address, Lane published *Rush to Judgment*. It was a book inundated with false stories about Oswald which, for the most part, originated with so-called 'witnesses' telling fanciful tales and clamouring to be part of the story. It was an instant hit with the US public because the strange truth behind Lane's credulity was not intellectual but emotional. The US public simply could not accept that a misfit like Oswald could change the course of history all by himself.

Many decades later, in a debate with Lane, former Los Angeles prosecutor Vincent Bugliosi read transcripts of a recording Lane had made during an interview with Helen Markham, who witnessed Oswald shooting Dallas Police officer J.D. Tippit following the assassination of the president. Bugliosi then informed the audience how Lane had deliberately misquoted her. 'When I started to read Lane's shameful questioning of Mrs Markham', Bugliosi wrote, 'the embarrassment the audience felt for Lane was so pronounced that many began to dip their heads'.[1]

James Reston Jr, in the *Saturday Review*, described another of Lane's books as 'disreputable', in that all the reports contained in the book were 'unverified and lean[t] toward the salacious . . . Lane makes no pretence of distinguishing between fact and . . . embellishment'.[2]

* * *

The idea that Lee Harvey Oswald was somehow connected to the CIA is a legitimate line of inquiry considering how many allegations have been made that posit the agency has not released all its files pertaining to the assassination.

The non-release of some CIA files, including those of agency officers William Harvey (sealed until 2063) and George Joannides, only helps fuel suspicion that a cabal of operatives, known to be involved in an enterprise designed to either kill or topple Fidel Castro, enlisted Lee Harvey Oswald or used Oswald as a 'patsy' in a conspiracy to kill President Kennedy.[3]

Conspiracy writers have named singularly, or as a group, such CIA officers as William Harvey, George Joannides, James Angleton, David Atlee Phillips, E. Howard Hunt and David Morales, among others. It is the considered opinion of this reviewer that any additional CIA files will not support the allegations of CIA involvement in the assassination and will likely develop into a farce along the lines of the false Morales/Joannides/Campbell connection to the RFK assassination. However, the central ethical tenet for journalists and historians is to illuminate the unknown therefore it is in the interests of everyone that these files be released.[4]

Outside of the wild and speculative books that attempt to tie in the CIA to the JFK assassination, there have been a number of respected authors (including Bayard Stockton, Vincent Bugliosi, Gus Russo, Evan Thomas, Tim Weiner, Jefferson Morley and Peter Grose) who have researched the allegation. Most discovered curious, but essentially ephemeral, Oswald connections to anti-Castro Cubans and their CIA handlers. Additionally, alleged CIA/Oswald connections were investigated by the Warren Commission,

Rockefeller Commission, Senate Select Committee on Intelligence, Senate Select Committee on Assassinations (Church Committee), as well as the HSCA. All these investigatory bodies found no credible evidence to support CIA involvement or culpability in the assassination.

Vincent Bugliosi, in *Reclaiming History*, concluded that conspiracy theorists have been unable to come up with 'any evidence connecting the CIA to Oswald'. Bugliosi meticulously researched the JFK/CIA allegations that had been circulating since the 60s and observed that:

> . . . the only books written that suggest the CIA was behind the assassination are those by conspiracy theorists . . . on the other hand, a considerable number of books have been written about the CIA and its history, warts and all, and not one of their authors, even though they had every ethical, professional (Pulitzer Prize, esteem of peers, etc.) and commercial reason to expose the CIA . . . as being behind the assassination, found the need to devote no more than a paragraph or two in their long books to Lee Harvey Oswald and the assassination.[5]

Bayard Stockton, an ex-CIA agent who later worked as a journalist for *Newsweek*, may be the exception as he devotes a chapter of his 2006 book to the allegations. He researched the possibility of CIA involvement in the JFK assassination for his biography of CIA officer William Harvey. Stockton interviewed many former officials and Harvey's wife, all of whom reacted with 'horror and disbelief' about the allegations. Stockton wrote that although a conclusive decision could not be made until the CIA releases all its documents, there was no credible evidence to blame the CIA. 'I find it very hard to believe,' Stockton wrote, 'that sworn officers of the CIA plotted the death of the president of the United States. I think the Agency's top echelon knew more than it has admitted and was embarrassed that it had not yielded its knowledge instantly.'[6]

Those who have an interest in learning more about the purported role the CIA played in the JFK assassination will be disappointed in what Mark Lane offered in his book *Last Word: My Indictment of the CIA in the Murder of JFK*. He presented absolutely nothing new to the 'CIA-did-it' literature. He will also likely upset many serious researchers who have been receptive to claims of CIA malfeasance because he has partly built his arguments around preposterous propositions, including the notion that the witness testimony and physical evidence 'proves' a second shooter was involved in the assassination. Those old canards were debunked years ago.[7]

Judging from website reports, Lane's supporters are unaware of his previous shenanigans which stretch back to December 1963; yes, Lane was present at the creation. In 1966, Lane's first book, *Rush to Judgment*, was persuasive with the mainstream media who were taken in by Lane's lawyerly tricks and silver tongue as he debated supporters of the Warren Commission around the world. As commission lawyer Wesley Liebeler observed, Lane's antics during these debates reminded him of 'an old legend about frogs jumping from the mouth of a perfidious man every time he speaks . . . If [Lane] talks for five minutes, it takes an hour to straighten out the record.'

Even the counter-culture *Rolling Stone* magazine characterized Lane as a 'huckster' and 'hearse chaser'. Bugliosi describes Lane as having 'infidelity to the truth', a person who commits 'outright fabrications', 'a fraud in his preachments about the known assassin' and that he had 'deliberately distorted the evidence' and repeatedly omitted 'evidence damaging to his side'.[8]

In *Rush to Judgment*, Lane abused the Warren Commission testimony of Jack Ruby, Oswald's killer, and others like Charles Brehm, an alleged 'grassy knoll witness', who said Lane took his statements out of context and added a different meaning to them. Lane also omitted the statements of key witnesses like Johnny C. Brewer, who observed a nervous Oswald avoid police patrols after shooting Dallas Police Officer J.D. Tippit.[9]

But Lane has a long history of playing fast and loose with the facts. In the early 1970s he used unreliable testimony to accuse US soldiers of multiple atrocities during the Vietnam War, according to *New York Times* correspondent Neil Sheehan, a prominent critic of US involvement in the Vietnam War. Sheehan investigated the accounts in Lane's book, *Conversations with Americans Testimony from 32 Vietnam Veterans*, and found most of them to be bogus.[10]

In the late 1970s, as a lawyer for Martin Luther King Jr's assassin, James Earl Ray, Lane appeared before the HSCA, a congressional probe into the circumstances surrounding the separate assassinations of the Civil Rights leader and President Kennedy. HSCA said of Lane in its report:

> Many of the allegations of conspiracy that the committee investigated were first raised by Mark Lane . . . As has been noted, the facts were often at variance with Lane's assertions . . . Lane was

willing to advocate conspiracy theories publicly without having checked the factual basis for them . . . Lane's conduct resulted in public misperception about the assassination of Dr. King and must be condemned.[11]

With the publication of his latest book, Lane's modus operandi has clearly not changed. In fact, his new tome depends on readers' ignorance, and no independent knowledge of the dramatis personae of the assassination literature or how the CIA behaved at the time of the assassination. For example, the author of the book's introduction resurrects the myth that FBI agents listened to a tape recording of a 'Lee Oswald' at the Soviet embassy during the assassin's trip to Mexico City weeks before the assassination. The allegation that such a tape existed was debunked many years ago by the HSCA. The story of the existence of tapes had originated with only one FBI agent out of many who handled the transcripts of the tapes because the tapes had been copied over as per the CIA's usual procedures.[12]

There are literally tens of thousands of documents and items of evidence in the JFK case. There are, therefore, endless opportunities for conspiracy writers to add a word here or a word there to give a different contextual meaning to either a witness statement or a government document. The vast majority of readers simply do not have the time to wade through the relevant documents. As Victor Navasky observed in a 2010 article, 'The Rosenberg Variations' in *The Nation*, 'We live in a state of opinion trusteeship. None of us have the time and few of us the ability to do our own research on all the complex, problematic issues of our day.' Consequently, many conspiracy supporters mistake crude manipulation for scholarship.

Lane demonstrates how he can contort language to give a different meaning when he writes, '[former CIA Director Allen] Dulles told the [Warren Commission] members that they need not worry about anyone doubting their false conclusions. Maybe, he suggested, at worst many years will have passed before some professor might study the evidence and by then it would not matter.' Was the word 'false' Lane's, or did Dulles actually characterize the Warren Commission conclusions as 'false'? Lane does not tell us, so it is left to the reader to figure it out.[13]

Lane also demonstrates his technique of sowing doubt where none exists when he carefully places suspicion in the mind of the reader by making reference to the alleged sinister circumstances of the Robert F. Kennedy assassination. Lane describes how Bobby Kennedy was led out of the Ambassador Hotel pantry by his bodyguard 'FBI agent . . . William Barry'. Barry, according to Lane, 'changed the route at the last minute'. Lane goes on to state that Barry told an onlooker, 'No, it's been changed. We're going this way.'

At the time of the RFK assassination Bill Barry was a *former* FBI agent and the decision to change the route out of the Embassy Room was made by Bill Barry and RFK aide Fred Dutton to accommodate the realities of running for president – RFK had promised to meet with the print press who were in the Colonial Room and the simplest route was through the pantry, the scene of the assassination.

Additionally, RFK had asked to go the 'back way' to the Colonial Room instead of through the crowds in the Embassy Room. Yet via Lane's transparent innuendo readers will inevitably be left to wonder if a federal agency was responsible for the assassination of JFK's brother Bobby. It is therefore ironic that Lane has the gall to criticize Vincent Bugliosi for getting an address wrong in his book *Reclaiming History*. Lane sarcastically wrote, 'Did the publisher never hear of the term shared by the entire [publishing] industry: fact checker?'[14]

Lane also uses wild accusations to silence his critics by denouncing them as 'old CIA hand(s)', 'CIA assets', 'CIA media assets', a 'voice for the CIA', 'close to the CIA' or they work 'on behalf of the CIA'. He also uses innuendo to accuse anti-conspiracy writers of working for the agency in some undefined but nonetheless sinister fashion. These phrases will no doubt incite some of his less-than-rational readers. It is essentially McCarthyite in nature. To paraphrase Attorney Joseph Welch at the 1954 Army v. McCarthy hearings, 'Mr. Lane, you've done enough. Have you no sense of decency, sir? At long last, have you left no sense of decency?'[15]

Lane's omission of important facts about the two government investigations into the assassination also leaves his readers with an unenlightened understanding of the inquiries. He tells his readers that the HSCA 'concluded that probably a conspiracy was responsible for the murder [of JFK]'. What he does *not* inform his readers about is how the committee toiled for three years to uncover a conspiracy and failed.

At the eleventh hour, however, HSCA members were presented with a report from an acoustics firm which examined a Dallas Police recording, purportedly of the shots fired in Dealey Plaza. The acoustics experts concluded more than three shots had been fired at the motorcade therefore there must have been a second shooter. A narrow majority of the HSCA members concurred. In 1982, however, three years after the committee dissolved, the National Academy of Sciences found their acoustics findings to be seriously flawed.[16]

Central to Lane's the-CIA-did-it thesis is his chapter entitled 'The Indictment – The People of the United States v. the Central Intelligence Agency'. It is a regurgitation of his endlessly voiced but unproven vociferations that the CIA was not only at the centre of a conspiracy to murder President Kennedy but that Watergate burglar and former CIA agent E. Howard Hunt, along with others, had been part of the plot.

Lane's publishers promote the book by proclaiming Lane had successfully persuaded a jury that the CIA killed Kennedy. On the inside flap of the book's cover, they loudly state: 'Mark Lane has tried the only case in the history of America . . . in which jurors concluded that the CIA killed President Kennedy'. In fact, the jury concluded nothing of the sort.

Lane's story about CIA involvement in the assassination begins with a 1976 article published in an anti-Semitic magazine, *Spotlight*, which alleged that CIA agent E. Howard Hunt, one of the Watergate burglars, was in Dallas on 22 November 1963. The article, written by Victor Marchetti, a former CIA official, alleged Hunt had a role in the Kennedy assassination. The allegation had its origins in a photograph taken at the time of the assassination which purported to show three mysterious tramps in the railroad yards behind the infamous Book Depository being taken into custody by the Dallas Police. One of the tramps bore a resemblance to Hunt. It was not until the 1980s and the release of Dallas Police files that the tramps were identified, and they had nothing to do with the assassination.[17]

Hunt won a libel judgment against the magazine in 1981, but it was thrown out on appeal, and the case was re-tried in 1985 in Miami in a civil, not criminal, trial. Hunt lost his case. The jury's decision, with the exception of one member, was, however, based not on their belief that Hunt was a participant in a CIA plot to kill the president, but on the fact there was no 'actual malice' in the magazine's publication of the article – not that the article was necessarily true. When a 'public figure' like E. Howard Hunt is attacked in the media, he cannot win a libel judgment merely by showing that the attack is 'untrue and unfair'.

Lane claims the jurors accepted his premise that the CIA was responsible for murdering the president. Lane wrote, 'The evidence was clear, she [jury forewoman Leslie Armstrong] said. The CIA had killed President Kennedy. Hunt had been part of it, and that evidence, so painstakingly presented should now be examined by the relevant institutions of the United States trial government so that those responsible for the assassination might be brought to justice.'[18]

However, two of the jurors told the *Miami Herald* they did not believe Lane had proven that Hunt was a co-conspirator. Suzanne Reach said that the jury's verdict was 'absolutely not' the reason for the verdict. 'We were very disgusted and felt [the article] was trash', she said. 'The paper published material that was sloppy – but it wasn't malicious.' While Lane avoids literally telling lies in his book, he uses the same convoluted expositions he used before the Miami jury to persuade his readers that Hunt was indeed guilty of conspiring to kill the president.[19]

Lane trades on the sound presumption that the vast majority of his readers have no way of knowing what he's doing. In the Lane tradition of carefully concealing from his readers any information that might undermine his thesis, he portrays Hunt as having only two alibi witnesses at the trial, and denigrates these because they were CIA employees. But in fact, there were three CIA employees who testified at the trial, and three witnesses (two of Hunt's children and a domestic) who swore to the 1974 Rockefeller Commission that Hunt was in the Washington area, and not in Dallas, on the day of the assassination.[20]

In support of his allegations against Hunt, Lane makes reference to 'an alleged confession'. The circumstances of St John Hunt's interview with his father are fraught with problems, not least the fact E. Howard Hunt was heavily medicated at the time he 'confessed', but Lane does not disclose this to his readers. Hunt's memoirs were published posthumously, and he vehemently denies any involvement in the JFK assassination. Hunt did 'not believe the CIA had anything to do with JFK's death'. He even discloses that Lane's irresponsible accusations caused his family great suffering. Additionally, Hunt's 'confession' is nothing more than his own guesswork and ruminations as to who killed JFK. He may even have used this opportunity to vent his spleen over those in government who did not give him any support after he was indicted in the Watergate affair.[21]

Another central weakness in *Last Word*, as with all Lane's books, is to accept without context or criticism the false and misleading statements of so-called 'JFK assassination witnesses', including Jean Hill, deputy sheriff Roger Craig and disgraced Secret Service agent Abraham Bolden.[22]

Abraham Bolden is important to Lane because the former Secret Service agent bolsters his view that the Secret Service assisted the CIA in carrying out the assassination. Bolden claimed there had been a plot to kill Kennedy during a planned presidential trip to Chicago. When Kennedy's Chicago trip was cancelled, Bolden alleges, the assassination plans were then adapted to Dallas and Oswald became the designated patsy. The HSCA, however, said it 'was unable to document the existence of the alleged assassination team. Specifically, no agent who had been assigned to Chicago confirmed any aspect of Bolden's version.'[23]

The HSCA also said that 'one agent did state there had been a threat in Chicago during that period . . . but he was unable to recall details'. The existence of a 'serious threat' was hardly surprising as Kennedy received numerous death threats during his presidency. The HSCA concluded that Bolden's story was of 'questionable authenticity'.[24]

Lane also accepts the veracity of Marita Lorenz even though numerous researchers have proven her stories were not credible or they were constructed on outright lies. Marita Lorenz was the one single witness at the Miami trial who placed Hunt in Dallas on the day of the assassination. She said he was a co-conspirator in the JFK assassination who went by the name of 'Eduardo'.

Lorenz, a supposed CIA operative and mistress of Fidel Castro, was characterized by Lane as 'credible'. However, he fails to inform his reader of Lorenz's other claims about the assassination, and Hunt in particular, over the years. In conversations with other writers and investigators for the HSCA, she made a number of allegations that were proven to be false. Lorenz said Oswald was among the conspirators in a 'caravan' that drove from Miami to Dallas arriving on 21 November 1963. Numerous witnesses, however, placed Oswald elsewhere. Lorenz also claimed to have seen Oswald participating in training for the Bay of Pigs invasion at a time when Oswald was in the Soviet Union.[25]

During 1977 and 1978, Lorenz's allegations were extensively investigated by the HSCA. One of HSCA's investigators, Ed Lopez, a conspiracy advocate, told author Gerald Posner:

Oh God, we spent a lot of time with Marita . . . It was hard to ignore her because she gave us so much crap, and we tried to verify it, but let me tell you – she is full of shit. Between her and Frank Sturgis, we must have spent over one hundred hours. They were dead ends . . . Marita is not credible.[26]

In the end the sumptuous appeal of Lane's book, the deliberate demonization of a federal agency without any real proof, doesn't need to make sense. His work nourishes the appetite of a ready-made audience eager for stories that will prop up a belief system they are not willing to abandon. So, the question remains – will Lane's recitation of decades-old lies and myths about the assassination and alleged CIA responsibility provide ready-made paranoiacs with a larger arsenal of imagery and rumour? The answer to that is assuredly yes.

But those readers who are new to the subject and are sceptical of JFK conspiracy theories should read John McAdams' *JFK Assassination Logic* and/or Vincent Bugliosi's *Reclaiming History*. McAdams' intent is not to persuade the reader that there is no credible evidence to prove that JFK was assassinated as the result of a conspiracy. Instead, he concentrates on advising the reader how to think about conspiracy theories, especially the JFK assassination. By addressing the logical weaknesses in conspiracy books, he has been able to demonstrate how not to be duped by unscrupulous authors. And Bugliosi's volume is notable for its erudition and common sense.

After reading McAdams and Bugliosi, any reader should be in an excellent position to choose which title for Lane's book is more apt – *Last Word* or *Latest Lies*.

Chapter 5
Did Castro Kill JFK?

'Do Any of the New Books and Documentaries Prove Who Killed JFK?', first published by History News Network, November 2006

Commentary 2022

In September 1963 Lee Harvey Oswald took a short trip to Mexico City to visit the Cuban and Russian embassies. He had with him a scrapbook of newspaper clippings and other documents to demonstrate his support for Castro's revolution in hopes of winning a visa to Cuba. All three major investigations of the plots against Castro in the 1970s – the Church Committee, the Rockefeller Commission and the HSCA – rejected the idea of any causal link between Castro and the Kennedy assassination. When news came that Oswald had been arrested for the assassination of President Kennedy, Castro believed many Americans would blame him for the assassination because of Oswald's Cuban connections. He denied his government had any contacts with Oswald and said he had never heard of him.

In the years that followed, the idea that Castro had been involved persisted. The Cuban leader certainly had a strong motive. Castro's Cuba was the target of numerous CIA-led sabotage operations, assassination plots, support for anti-Castro guerrillas and encouragement of military coup plotters. The Kennedy administration efforts to rid the island of a communist dictatorship began with the attempted invasion of Cuba by Cuban anti-Castro exiles in April 1961. Operations to destabilize the Castro regime continued after the missile crisis in October 1962 and lasted until the end of the Kennedy administration.

* * *

Three books, *A Farewell To Justice* (2005) by Joan Mellen, *JFK and Sam – The Connection Between the Giancana and Kennedy Assassinations* by Antoinette Giancana, John R. Hughes and Thomas H. Jobe (2005), *Ultimate Sacrifice* by Lamar Waldron and Thom Hartmann (2005) and a German television documentary, *Rendezvous with Death* (2006), produced by Wilfried Huismann, helped return the United States' greatest 'whodunnit' to the media spotlight.

Mellen's book, for its part, purports to prove the CIA was behind the assassination. Giancana's book claims Chicago mob boss Sam Giancana ordered the assassination. Waldron and Hartmann maintain that Mafia dons Santo Trafficante, John Rosselli and Carlos Marcello called the shots and wanted to kill the president in retaliation for JFK's crackdown on the mob. Huismann points the finger of guilt at Castro or Castro's agents.

Giancana's book resurrects the same old myths about the assassination, including 'grassy knoll witnesses', discredited photo analyst Robert Groden's purported photographic 'proof' of grassy knoll gunmen and the alleged physical evidence which 'proves' Oswald's innocence. A central weakness in Giancana's and Mellen's books is the heavy reliance on so-called conspiracy witnesses whose outrageous tall tales have been investigated by the JFK assassination research community and found to be bogus. Their reliance on Madeleine Brown alone, a purported mistress of Lyndon Johnson, renders their overall thesis untenable. Brown's story was investigated by Max Holland, Gary Mack and Dave Perry who exposed her outrageous lies.[1]

Another major weakness is the authors' belief in the confessions of alleged assassin James Files. Again, the authors simply have not bothered to fully research Files' background as a reputed conman or the inconsistencies in his story. Files' story was fully researched by acclaimed JFK assassination writers Martin Shackleford, Dave Perry, John Stockwell, Edward Bell and Edward J. Epstein and found to be bogus.[2]

Wilfried Huismann's television documentary, *Rendezvous with Death*, which includes research by author Gus Russo, claims that former Cuban G2 Secret Service agent Oscar Marino, who fell out with the Castro regime, said the Cubans were desperate to eliminate Kennedy. Marino claims that Castro got Kennedy before Kennedy could assassinate the Cuban leader. He claims Oswald was pointed out to Cuban Intelligence by the Soviet KGB. 'There wasn't anyone else,' Marino told Huismann, 'You take what you can get . . . Oswald volunteered to kill Kennedy'. Newspaper reports about Huismann's documentary claim the Cuban agents paid Oswald $6,500 for the job.[3]

What emerges from Huismann's thesis are a number of truths. Oswald's wife, Marina, testified to Oswald's hero worship of Castro. She even said

Oswald had wanted to call their second child Fidel if it had been a boy. A friend, Michael Paine, said that Oswald 'wanted to be an active guerrilla in the effort to bring about the new world order'.[4]

Nelson Delgado, Oswald's friend in the Marine Corps, said that one of Oswald's heroes was William Morgan, a former sergeant in the US Army who became a major in Castro's army. In August 1959 Morgan received considerable press coverage when he lured some anti-Castro rebels into a trap by pretending to be a counter-revolutionary. Oswald emulated Morgan by acting as a counter-revolutionary in New Orleans when he visited Carlos Bringuier, an anti-Castroite, offering his services as a trained ex-Marine.

To Oswald, Cuba was indeed his last chance to fulfil his political fantasies. As Marina testified to the Warren Commission, 'I only know that his basic desire was to get to Cuba by any means and all the rest of it was window dressing for that purpose'.

However, while intriguing, there are a number of flaws in Huismann's thesis. Following the assassination, the US government became convinced that Castro's agents did not participate in the assassination of JFK. The National Security Agency, which intercepts communications, went all out to decipher intercepts of conversations, cable traffic, radio and telephone communications at the highest levels of the Soviet and Cuban governments. Together with information from human sources, the intercepts show clearly that both the Soviet and Cuban leaders were ignorant of the assassination and were frightened of receiving the blame.

Many years later it was revealed that Chief Justice Earl Warren had dispatched Warren Commission staff counsel William Coleman on a secret mission to Havana to investigate Cuban complicity in the assassination. Coleman has declined to speak about the trip except to say that it helped to convince him that Castro had nothing to do with the president's assassination. There are, however, problems with Coleman's story.

According to Anthony Summers he recently received a letter from Coleman denying the meeting with Castro took place. Summers wrote that, '[T]his is hard to explain, unless perhaps one notes that Mr. Coleman – himself a former Cabinet member – is close to senior officials in the Bush Administration. Perhaps the Bush people, who take a hard line on Cuba, prefer that dark rumours about Señor Castro remain unrefuted.'[5]

Fidel Castro told the 1976–9 HSCA the following:

That [the Cuban Government might have been involved in the president's death] was insane. From the ideological point of view, it was insane. And from the political point of view, it was a tremendous insanity. I am going to tell you here that nobody, nobody ever had the idea of such things. What would it do? We just tried to defend our folks here, within our territory.

Anyone who subscribed to that idea would have been judged insane, absolutely sick. Never, in 20 years of revolution. I never heard anyone suggest nor even speculate about a measure of that sort, because who could think of the idea of organizing the death of the President of the United States. That would have been the most perfect pretext for the United States to invade our country which is what I have tried to prevent for all these years, in every possible sense. Since the United States is much more powerful than we are, what would we gain from a war with the United States? The United States would lose nothing. The destruction would have been here.

He noted that murdering Kennedy brought to office a man – President Johnson – who would have been expected to be tougher toward Cuba. Richard Helms, deputy CIA director, commented, 'We would have bombed Cuba back into the middle ages'.[6]

There is, however, the possibility that Castro had known of Oswald's intent to kill Kennedy after Oswald visited the Cuban embassy in Mexico City in September 1963. Castro may have been told it was the rantings of a lunatic and because of the adversarial relationship between the United States and Cuba, the Cuban leader did not pass on the information to the US government.

Castro had given a speech on 27 November 1963, and mentioned that Oswald had made a 'provocative statement' when the assassin had visited the Cuban embassy in Mexico City the previous September. Castro related his story to Jack Childs (FBI code name SOLO), who, according to ex-FBI agent James P. Hosty, was historically one of the most important and reliable sources the FBI ever had. Childs, who was employed as the US Communist Party's financial advisor, met with Castro and confirmed the Cuban leader had known that Oswald had threatened to kill Kennedy.[7]

The FBI 'Airtel' memo which related Child's information was dated 12 June 1964. In part it stated the following:

Fidel Castro was not under the influence of liquor at the time he made the statements. Castro does not drink nor did he partake of any stimulants whatsoever . . . he treated the question as a very serious matter . . .

It was the impression of [SOLO] that Castro received the information about Oswald's appearance at the Cuban Embassy in Mexico in an oral report from 'his people' in the Embassy, because he, Castro, was told about it immediately. [SOLO] does not know the identities of the individuals who told Castro. [SOLO] advised that Castro said, 'I was told this by my people in the Embassy – exactly how he [Oswald] stalked in and walked in and ran out . . . he acted like a real madman and started yelling and shouting and yelled on his way out, "I'm going to kill that bastard, I'm going to kill Kennedy"' . . .

Castro was neither engaging in dramatics nor oratory but was speaking on the basis of facts given to him by his embassy personnel who dealt with Oswald . . . [SOLO] is of the opinion that Castro had nothing to do with the assassination.[8]

Another related scenario has suggested Castro's agents may have given tacit encouragement to Oswald during his trip to Mexico City. Such a sequence of events would have Kennedy shot in Dallas and Oswald fleeing to Mexico where he would have received safe haven by the Cubans and immediate departure for Cuba. Credible witnesses have said that Oswald met with not only KGB agents but with Castro agents as well – specifically Cuban Intelligence agents Luisa Calderon, the only person Castro would not let the HSCA speak with, Manuel Vega Perez and Rogelio Rodriguez Lopez – but they may not have taken him seriously.

The authors Gus Russo (*Live by the Sword* (1998)), ex-FBI agent James P. Hosty (*Assignment: Oswald* (1996)) and former counsel to the Warren Commission David Belin (*Final Disclosure* (1988)) believed in the possibility that Oswald had been encouraged by these Cuban Intelligence agents in Mexico City.

Russo, for example, wrote:

Certainly to the Soviets, and to the Americans, Oswald seemed an inconsequential figure before the assassination. Neither of these sophisticated countries had much use for him, and repeatedly marginalized him. Cuban diplomats, likewise fearing accusations of involvement, may have steered clear of Oswald as well . . .

Given what has been reported about his contacts and surroundings though, Cuban intelligence agents may have challenged Oswald to be the man of action he apparently vowed to be . . . Logic dictates that, with Castro's regime and very life being threatened by the Kennedys, a quick fix in the form of a bullet would not have been unwelcome in certain Cuban circles.[9]

Warren Commission lawyer David Belin wrote, 'Were it not for Oswald's lies about his trip to Mexico, I would state unequivocally that there was no conspiratorial complicity between Oswald and anyone else. I would suggest that the actions of Oswald were those of a loner and that he was not conspiratorially involved with any pro-Castro agents in Mexico.'[10]

James Hosty wrote, 'There is the dramatic, but insufficient, evidence that would directly implicate the Soviets or Cubans in the president's death . . . it is abundantly clear [however] why Oswald killed the president. Whether or not he was a KGB sleeper agent, Oswald was without question a Communist and Castro loyalist.'[11]

The paid-agent theory has a fundamental weakness. The claim that Oswald was paid $6,500 by the Cuban agents raises a number of questions. If Oswald had been paid this money, we would not have seen a virtually penniless Oswald trying to make ends meet in the two months prior to the assassination. Warren Commission investigators researched all of Oswald's financial transactions in the years prior to the assassination and discovered no large sums of money. His wife Marina confirms these facts.

Furthermore, a scenario that had Oswald leave the Texas School Book Depository with a handful of dollars then catching a bus makes some kind of assistance in the assassination unlikely. And of course, Cuban Intelligence agents would have had no way of knowing about the president's trip to Dallas, nor would they have known about the lucky chance of Oswald being given a job in a building on the motorcade route, a job which had been arranged by Marina's friend, Ruth Paine.

The figure of $6,500 cropped up in another tale of Cuban intrigue which was investigated by JFK researcher Anthony Marsh. Marsh wrote of how, on

25 November 1963, a Nicaraguan Intelligence officer who was sympathetic to the Cuban exiles, Alvarado Ugarte Gilberto, claimed that on 18 September 1963 he saw a Cuban consulate employee give $6,500 in cash to Oswald to assassinate the president.

Marsh wrote:

> . . . because Gilberto's story was so elaborate and because it fitted in with the prevailing suspicions in the intelligence community it was widely believed to be true. But under intense questioning by the CIA, Alvarado's story began to unravel. Oswald could not have been at the Cuban Consulate in Mexico on the day that he allegedly received the cash, because he was known to have been in New Orleans applying for unemployment insurance.

Marsh stated that Alvarado admitted that he had made up the story in hopes that the United States would be prompted to invade Cuba in retaliation.[12] According to Anthony Summers, Alvarado later reverted to his story after the retraction. Huismann and Summers tried to interview this witness but were unsuccessful. Summers believes he is now dead.[13]

While this evidence does not necessarily prove or disprove Oswald was hired by Russia or Cuba, it is tantalizing in that it suggests that Oswald may have offered to kill Kennedy as a way of proving his worth to them, but the Soviets and Cubans adopted a wait-and-see attitude. Anthony Summers concurs. Summers believes:

> . . . the Cubans had no real expectation that Oswald could or would do what he bragged he could do, that whatever mild encourage- ment they'd given him was more in the form of 'Go for it, if you want' and that their sin, maybe, was not to have said 'No, please don't do that' and to have warned the Americans what he might get up to. Which would have been a bit much to ask, given that they knew the US was trying repeatedly to kill *their* guy?[14]

Another flaw with Huismann's theory is that it does not factor in the actions of Jack Ruby. Had Ruby not killed Oswald the Cuban 'conspiracy' would have been put at risk by Oswald's arrest. And Ruby's appearance in the basement of the Dallas Police Station was pure coincidence.

Oswald was scheduled to be transferred from the Dallas Police Jail to the County Jail at 10 a.m. on Sunday, 24 November. Before his transfer to the County Jail, the alleged assassin was due a further interrogation by Captain Will Fritz and representatives of the Secret Service and FBI. Oswald's interrogation on Sunday morning lasted longer than originally planned because Postal Inspector Harry D. Holmes arrived. The arrival of Holmes delayed the transfer of Oswald because, unexpectedly, Fritz then turned to Holmes and asked whether he wanted to interrogate Oswald. Holmes accepted. It was for this reason the interrogation continued for another half hour or so. Ruby shot Oswald approximately 5 minutes after Ruby left the Western Union office. If Inspector Holmes had continued on to church with his wife that morning, as he had intended, the length of interrogation would have been shortened and Jack Ruby would never have had the opportunity to kill Oswald.

The Ruby factor is therefore a weakness in Huismann's thesis. Had Ruby not shot Oswald the assassin would have been in a position to reveal the details of the 'Cuban conspiracy' at his trial. Would Castro have taken that chance? It is unlikely. Had there been any evidence that Castro's agents had plotted to kill the US president an invasion of Cuba would have been inevitable.

A more compelling scenario is that Oswald read about Castro's threat to retaliate against CIA attempts to kill the Cuban leader or Cuban agents in Mexico City and this provoked Oswald by telling him about US efforts to murder his hero. Oswald saw this as an opportune moment to fulfil his revolutionary fantasies by taking unilateral action. The *New Orleans Times–Picayune* article with Castro's statement was prominently displayed on a day when Oswald was in the city and Oswald was an avid reader of newspapers. It was also common knowledge in New Orleans, certainly among anti-Castro groups, that Castro was a target for elimination. In his deluded state, Oswald may have thought that killing Kennedy was one way to win Castro's appreciation. It is unlikely that Oswald's purported meeting with Castro's Mexico City agents could have been an arrangement to plan Kennedy's assassination. They had no idea where Kennedy would be in the foreseeable future. But the Cuban agents may have implanted in Oswald's mind the idea that his impulsive outburst ('I'm going to kill that bastard Kennedy') was admirable sentiment spoken by a 'hero of the revolution'.

In *Ultimate Sacrifice: John and Robert Kennedy: The Plan for a Coup in Cuba and the Murder of JFK*, Lamar Waldron and Thom Hartmann argue that it wasn't Castro who murdered JFK, but the Mafia. Their 904-page book, complete with 2,700 footnotes, was the product of 17 years of research and interviews. It could not have been written, the authors say, without access to thousands of documents made available by the 1992 JFK Assassination Records Collection Act, which was passed into law after the public outcry surrounding Oliver Stone's 1991 pro-conspiracy movie, *JFK*.

The book's central thesis is that three Mafia chieftains – Santo Trafficante of Tampa, Carlos Marcello of New Orleans and John Roselli of Chicago – conspired to kill the president in retaliation for JFK's crackdown on the mob. This was not new.

What is new is the book's main disclosure that the Mafia believed it could get away with the president's assassination because it had inside CIA knowledge of a purported 'Kennedy secret' – the alleged 1 December 1963 plan to overthrow Fidel Castro in a violent coup (C-Day, they call it) then replace him with a pro-US puppet regime.

The authors argue that killing JFK would leave the Mafia protected because the government could not implicate the mob without revealing the invasion plans. If the plans had been revealed the United States would have risked another Cuban Missile Crisis.

However, the authors are far from proving their thesis. They rely for much of their conclusions on interviews with former Secretary of State Dean Rusk, no friend of Bobby Kennedy's, and Enrique 'Harry' Ruiz-Williams, a veteran of the 1961 Bay of Pigs debacle. Mr Ruiz-Williams was believed to be Robert F. Kennedy's closest friend and ally in the Cuban exile community.

Despite the collaboration of these distinguished 'witnesses', the authors fail to convince. Ruiz's statements to the authors can be characterized as wishful thinking and Rusk has provided no concrete proof that an invasion was pending. All the authors have succeeded in doing is presenting the reader with evidence that a contingency plan, not an actual plan, had been presented for JFK's perusal.

JFK's Defense Secretary, Robert S. McNamara, has given recent interviews claiming not to know of any such plot and rejecting the idea that such plans were in the works. Anyone who has viewed McNamara's honest and forthright (and apologetic) statements in the documentary *Fog of War* will soon realize that he is capable of telling the whole truth. Furthermore, there is a great deal of evidence to show that JFK was moving towards an accommodation with Castro at the time of his visit to Dallas and that plans for an invasion and/or assassination of Castro had been abandoned.

Another weakness with this book is the contention that the Mafia wanted to return to their lucrative Cuban casinos following Castro's elimination. The coup would have let the purported conspirators, Carlos Marcello, Santo Trafficante and Johnny Roselli, in on the start to regain control of organized crime in Cuba. But killing Kennedy would guarantee that the purported plans would be dropped.

The book's attempts to resurrect old myths about gunmen on the grassy knoll and magic bullets are an exercise in repeating every controversy connected to the Dealey Plaza shooting. The authors rely mostly on previously debunked theories about second shooters and purported photographs of gunmen which have been thoroughly debunked by the HSCA, ballistics experts and leading researchers in the scientific community.

For example, the authors quote former Kennedy aide Kenneth O'Donnell, who was in the motorcade and who told Tip O'Neill, former Speaker of the House, in 1968 that 'he had heard two shots' from the grassy knoll. They also quote former Kennedy aide Dave Powers, who was in the motorcade and who spoke to the authors before his death in 1998, that he felt they were 'riding into an ambush' because of shots from the grassy knoll. But, again, this is nothing new – many witnesses were confused as to the direction of the shots but this does not prove that more than one shooter was present in Dealey Plaza.

The reader should be directed, instead, to the work of real experts like Larry Sturdivan who decisively relegates the conspiracy buffs' criticisms of the scientific examinations of the JFK assassination to the dustbin of history.[15]

The true facts about JFK's assassination cannot now be established with absolute precision. Too many false leads have been sown, too many witnesses have died, the evidence can be misinterpreted by anyone who wishes to construct a false story – and time has a way of eroding the truth. Furthermore, the volume of material pertaining to the case can overwhelm the most erudite and conscientious researcher. However, despite attempts by JFK conspiracy advocates to present what they believe is compelling evidence of a conspiracy to kill JFK the simple truths remain – there is no smoking gun which would alter the fundamental conclusions of the Warren Commission Report that Lee Harvey Oswald alone fired the shots that killed President Kennedy.

* * *

Commentary 2022
Author Philip Shenon said he was:

> . . . intrigued by evidence – denied to the [Warren] commission's
> staff – suggesting that Oswald had talked openly about his plans
> to kill the president and that he may have been promised help if he
> were ever able to succeed. Much of that evidence involves his mys-
> terious visit to Mexico City several weeks before the assassination,
> when Oswald, a self-proclaimed Marxist, was apparently trying to
> get a visa to defect to Cuba.[16]

In 2008, two years after the above article was published, Gus Russo and
Stephen Molton claimed in their book *Brothers In Arms* that Fidel Castro knew
in advance that Lee Oswald planned to assassinate Kennedy during the president's trip to Dallas. A similar thesis was presented by Brian Latell in 2012 in
his book *Castro's Secrets*. Latell, who studied Cuban affairs as a CIA analyst in
the 1960s and became the agency's chief intelligence officer for Latin America,
said he was certain Castro knew of the impending hit on the president.

Brothers in Arms provides details of how the Soviets passed information
about Oswald on to the Cuban Intelligence agencies, who in turn decided
Oswald may be of some use in their attempts to hit back at the United States
for its efforts in trying to topple the Castro regime. Their investigation into
the movements of Cuban Intelligence agent Fabian Escalante Font – before
and after the assassination – is also central to their thesis that the assassination can be placed firmly at Castro's door. The authors utilized hundreds of
documents from KGB, Cuban, Mexican Secret Police and recently unre-
dacted US government files, and combined them with their own interviews
of the players in the JFK/Castro conflict to support their thesis.

Russo and Molton provided evidence that this self-styled revolutionary and
Castro worshipper may have had contact with Cuban agents when Oswald
visited the Soviet and Cuban Mexico City embassies a short time before the
assassination. They claimed that Castro had been aware of Oswald's desire
to murder the US president, and Cuban agents, either acting on their own or
with Castro's blessing, spurred him on.

This may have been true. The evidence the authors provide includes a
Cuban Intelligence agent's intercepted telephone conversation in which she
gleefully reports JFK's assassination, and hints she had prior knowledge of

Oswald's intentions to kill Kennedy, and multiple reports of Cuban agents stationed at the Cuban embassy in Mexico City quickly leaving and returning to Cuba after the Kennedy assassination. The inference is that Cuban agents directed Oswald each step of the way. However, there is also a compelling case to be made that Oswald simply presented proof of his authentic 'revolutionary' activities in New Orleans to the Cuban agents who then encouraged him to assassinate Kennedy but had no hand in the mechanics of the act.

Russo and Molton introduced the possibility that Oswald may also have had assistance from Cuban agents in Dallas or, at the very least, an observer to make sure the assassin carried out the crime which they encouraged. However, this remains, at best, speculative. Questions still remain about how Cuban Intelligence could have placed Oswald in the Texas School Book Depository and why they allowed Oswald to use his own less-than-reliable rifle to commit the assassination. The Oswalds' friend, Ruth Paine, and a neighbour, Linnie May Randle, were the two people responsible for securing the book-depository job for Oswald and it beggars belief that Cuban agents would want Oswald to use a cheap rifle which could have misfired at any time during the assassination attempt.

Additionally, Cuban agents would have had no way of knowing JFK's travel plans or the route the motorcade took in Dallas which placed the president in sight of his assassin – unless they formulated the purported plot only days before the campaign trip. However, would Cuban agents have allowed Oswald to threaten an FBI agent in a note he delivered to the Dallas FBI offices, complaining of how agents had harassed the ex-Soviet defector's wife? Would Oswald's co-conspirators have allowed the assassin to carry only a few dollars with him when he escaped from the Texas School Book Depository? Russo and Molton also cannot explain why Cuban agents would risk the possibility of Oswald giving up his co-conspirators in the 48 hours or so between the time he was arrested and his murder by Jack Ruby.

If Russo and Molton fall short of providing concrete proof that Castro organized the assassination of JFK, they have, nevertheless, come closer than anyone else to explaining Oswald's mysterious trip to Mexico City. With the eventual fall of the communist regime in Cuba, Russo and Molton may in time be proven to be correct and the truth of Castro's role in the assassination established. In the meantime, their thesis cannot either be ignored or rejected. This impressive work comes closer than any other author's efforts, with the exception of Vincent Buglisosi, in establishing the truth of the JFK assassination.

Brian Latell also argued that Oswald warned Cuban Intelligence officers in advance of his plans to kill the president. Latell wrote that Oswald, a belligerent Castro supporter, grew frustrated when officials at the Cuban embassy in Mexico City refused to give him a visa to travel to the island, and promised to shoot Kennedy to prove his revolutionary credentials. However, Latell does not say Fidel Castro ordered the assassination. 'I don't say Oswald was under his control,' Latell said, 'He might have been, but I don't argue that, because I was unable to find any evidence for that'.[17]

However, Latell's thesis is challenged by Vincent Bugliosi, author of the best-selling book *Reclaiming History*, and Peter Kornbluh, director of the Cuba Documentation Project at the National Security Archive and author of several books about US-Cuba relations in the Kennedy era. 'The notion of Castro being in any way connected to the assassination is preposterous on its face,' Vincent Bugliosi said.[18]

Both critics believe that if Castro had been responsible or had known his agents encouraged the assassin the CIA, FBI and the US State Department would have produced the evidence with alacrity.

Kornbluh said that any scenario involving Castro even indirectly in the assassination is unlikely. He noted:

> In the last several months of his life Kennedy sent several peace feelers to Castro. Kennedy even had a guy in Cuba [French journalist Jean Daniel] talking to Castro about rapprochement at the moment of the assassination. Why would Castro want to do anything that encouraged the murder of the first American president willing to talk about coexistence with the Cuban revolution?[19]

A month after Fidel Castro's death, on 19 December 2016, the tabloid *National Enquirer* published an article tinglingly titled 'Dying Castro Admitted Killing JFK!' The article's sensationalistic subtitle proclaimed 'Chilling New Evidence Blows Assassination Wide Open After 53 Years'. The *Enquirer* article is not only uncorroborated but false. The story consisted almost entirely of unverifiable and often highly unlikely allegations made by untrustworthy government informers or by anti-Castro zealots with an axe to grind and suspicious, misleading or altered or forged documents.

Both principal government investigations of the JFK assassination reached the conclusion that Castro's Cuba was not responsible. In its report, the Warren Commission concluded that it had 'found no evidence that Oswald was employed, persuaded or encouraged by any foreign government to assassinate President Kennedy, or that he was an agent of any foreign government'.[20]

In 1979 the US House of Representatives Committee on Assassinations agreed: 'The committee believes, on the basis of the evidence available to it, that the Cuban Government was not involved in the assassination of President Kennedy.'[21]

In short, the panels of leading experts which investigated the circumstances surrounding the death of the president knew that if there was any evidence of Cuban involvement, the US government would have exploited it for diplomatic advantage.

Another conspiracy story connected to the 'Castro-did-it' school of thought involved Oswald meeting with left-wing students and hinting they had given him some kind of help – which may have included putting him in contact with Castro agents. Journalist Óscar Contreras Lartigue said he'd been in a pro-Castro campus group and that Oswald had begged this group for help getting a Cuban visa. According to Contreras, Oswald spent two days with these National Autonomous University students, then met up with them again a few days later at the Cuban embassy.

According to witnesses from the Cuban and Soviet diplomatic missions, Oswald visited their embassies repeatedly during a visit he made to Mexico City a few months before the assassination. Disillusioned with the United States after his return in 1962 from the Soviet Union he was desperately seeking visas to those countries, which Americans were prohibited from visiting. Oswald was told his entry documents would take months to process which led him into an argument with the Cuban consul, Emilio Azcué, and when he visited the Soviet consulate he pulled out his pistol and burst into tears.

This story originated in March 1967, when Óscar Contreras Lartigue gave his account of meeting Oswald. However, it was debunked in 2020 by Gonzalo Soltero, who discovered numerous incidences of Contreras lying to the CIA and government investigators.[22]

The weakness of the theory that Castro ordered his agents to hire Oswald remains speculative at best. However, the notion that Fidel Castro had prior knowledge of Oswald's intentions remains compelling – Oswald read about Castro's threat to retaliate against CIA attempts to kill the Cuban leader and Cuban agents in Mexico City provoked Oswald by telling him about CIA efforts to murder his hero. Agents could also have told Oswald his assassination plans were 'heroic'.

The wannabe Castro revolutionary in turn saw this as an opportune moment to fulfil his fantasies by taking unilateral action. A clue to Oswald's thinking can be found in a statement he made to Michael Paine: 'You can read between the lines [in the newspapers] and see what they want you to do.'[23]

Part II
RFK

Chapter 6

Sirhan's Motives

'The Unaffiliated Terrorist – The True Motives of RFK's Assassin', first published by Frontline Magazine, *2005*

Commentary 2022

Just after midnight on 5 June 1968, presidential candidate Robert F. Kenndedy was shot and mortally wounded shortly after speaking at the Ambassador Hotel in Los Angeles. He died soon after in hospital. In the decades since RFK was killed, his assassin Sirhan Bishara Sirhan has repeatedly spoken about his motive for the crime and his animus towards the senator. Despite this simple fact conspiracy authors continue in their attempts to deny Sirhan had any motive for the crime. It is their way of persuading the public that a motiveless assassin was unlikely to have committed the crime.

The conspiracists' claims of Sirhan's innocence, which involve bizarre tales of the assassin's mumbo-jumbo speech, mirror-gazing, trance-like states and amnesiac episodes have succeeded over the years in obscuring just how explicit his motive was – as the reader will see in the following pages.

The conspiracy authors have also been given succour in recent years by the intervention of Hollywood celebrities including Oliver Stone, Alec Baldwin, Martin Sheen, Rob Reiner, David Crosby, Mort Sahl and two Kennedy family members – Robert F. Kennedy Jr and Kathleen Kennedy Townsend. In 2018 they called for a new investigation of the assassination. (The group also alleged that other political assassinations of the 1960s – JFK, MLK and Malcolm X – involved government malfeasance and cover-up and wanted the government to also re-investigate those crimes.)

It is no mystery why some Hollywood celebrities support the notion of an innocent Palestinian refugee railroaded into a notorious murder case. Many in Hollywood have endorsed and embraced the Palestinian cause mimicking the US left's decades-old support. Unable to gauge Sirhan's true character by reading the conspiracy books which ignore the assassin's political fanaticism, they would naturally assume Sirhan mysteriously acted at the behest of others who had an interest in eliminating the senator.

* * *

For nearly forty years conspiracy advocates have built their arguments not only around the controversies surrounding the ballistics evidence and the scene of the crime but the oft-repeated cry that the assassin had no real motive for his act. Yet there is a mountain of evidence to prove the contrary.

From the time he was a child, Sirhan had been indoctrinated in ideologies that are at the centre of his murderous act. Sirhan's hatred had its roots in the milieu in which he was raised and the education he received. Later, as a young adult, Sirhan sought meaning for his increasingly hopeless life by embracing anti-Semitism, anti-Americanism and Palestinian nationalism.

As a child Sirhan had been taught by Arab teachers who instilled in him the principles of the Palestinian cause. They promoted the cause of Palestinian nationalism and made constant references to the great Arab warrior, Saladin, who had expelled the foreign crusaders from Jerusalem. Teachers would attempt to inspire the children in their care to fight for Palestinian rights.

During Sirhan's trial his mother related how the intense feelings of the Palestinians remained with the family even though they had been far removed from the conflict when they emigrated to the United States. She told of how her family had lived in Jerusalem for 'thousands of years' and she spoke of the bitterness and hatred of the Israelis who had 'taken their land'. Mary Sirhan believed her son had killed Robert F. Kennedy because of his Arab nationalism. She said, 'What he did, he did for his country.'[1] A friend of Sirhan's, John Strathman, believed the young Arab was heavily influenced by his mother's views.

But Sirhan was doubtlessly influenced by the opinions of both his parents. Child psychologists have long known that the nature of early childhood suggestions by parents can lead to a lifelong influence on the individual's self-concept. In Sirhan's case his parents taught him the Jews were 'evil' and 'stole their home'.

Sirhan's father, Bishara, regretted Kennedy's death but his hatred and contempt shone through in a statement he made to reporters in the days following his son's arrest. Bishara, himself a victim of Palestinian propaganda, said:

> I can say that I do not regret his death as Kennedy the American politician who attempted to gain the presidential election by his

aggressive propaganda against the Arab people of Palestine . . .
Kennedy was promising the Zionists to supply them with arms
and aircraft . . . and thus provoked the sensitive feelings of Sirhan
who had suffered so much from the Jews . . . It is not fair to accuse
my son without a full examination of Zionist atrocities against the
Arabs – those atrocities which received the support and blessings
of Robert Kennedy.[2]

What was never considered by writers and journalists, in their quest to
find a motive for Sirhan's act of murder, was the effect that teachers and influ-
ential adults in Jerusalem's Arab community had on the young Palestinian.
The way a nation educates its children on the characterization of other races
and religions will often determine the relations between them. Populations
are not culturally prone to hatred – they are educated toward it, as studies
of Nazi Germany show. The anti-Semitism inculcated in German children
in the 1930s and 1940s remained with them into their old age and the West
German government's post-war attempts to promote anti-fascism had no
effect on those who grew up during the Third Reich.

The propaganda used by Palestinians had no less an effect on the younger
generations of children from the 1940s to the present day. From an early
age Sirhan had been taught by educators, family members and friends that
the Jews were 'treacherous', 'an evil enemy' and that it was his 'duty' to rid
Palestine of Jews. Sirhan's generation was taught to hate, despise and fear
Jews, to believe that it was not only right for every self-respecting Arab to fight
the Jewish state and that it was just and desirable to destroy it. Undoubtedly,
this milieu of hatred had an intense effect on Sirhan as he grew up.

Sirhan's irrational enmity and anger towards the Jews did not originate
with any mental illness he may have suffered. In fact, his attitude was
no different from that of the majority of Palestinians and the rest of the
Arab peoples. His ideas were entirely rational within the norms of the
Arab world. As Glubb Pasha, an Arab military leader and British officer
(and no lover of Jews), reported in 1945, 'They [the Arabs] were painfully
conscious of their immaturity, their weakness and their backwardness.
They show all the instability and emotionalism of the adolescent [charac-
terized by] their touchiness and . . . readiness to take offence at any sign
of condescension by their "elders". Slights gave rise to outbursts of temper
and violent defiance.'[3]

There is little doubt the conflict and the situation Palestinians found themselves in, following the 1948 diaspora, had its effect on all Palestinian children. Their dark rage and despair originated from poor leadership within the Palestinian communities and the feeling they had gone unnoticed by the rest of the world. Theirs were memories of a 'lost homeland', the yearning for return passed down from generation to generation and above all outrage, shame, anger and humiliation. As writer Sana Hassan eloquently testified:

> Living in Beirut as a stateless person for most of my growing up years, many of them in a refugee camp, I did not feel I was living among my 'Arab brothers' . . . I was a Palestinian. And that meant I was an outsider, an alien, a refugee and a burden . . . It defeated some of us. It reduced and distorted and alienated others. The defeated, like myself, took off to go away from the intolerable pressures of the Arab world . . . The reduced, like my parents, waited helplessly in a refugee camp for the world, for a miracle, or for some deity to come to their aid. The distorted, like Sirhan Sirhan, turned into assassins. The alienated, like Leila Khaled, hijacked civilian aircraft.[4]

Before Sirhan emigrated to the United States at the age of 12 he had been schooled in East Jerusalem which had been annexed by Jordan during the 1948 conflict. After 1948, East Jerusalem and West Bank schools followed the Jordanian curriculum. In the Arab world, including Jordan, educational systems were riven with notions antithetical to the values of tolerance and understanding that are so intently promoted in the West. Hundreds of books published from 1948 in Egypt, Syria, Lebanon, Jordan and Iraq promoted the theme that the liquidation of Israel was not only a political necessity, but also a moral imperative. Israel and its people were an evil entity and that it was permissible to destroy them. The textbooks contained material that went beyond the worst excesses of Nazi Germany.[5]

Arab leaders compiled a curriculum of hatred for use by their children and the anti-Israeli and anti-Jewish teachings became a basic element in the study of history in the schools. Arab children were taught that Jews were the ultimate embodiment of evil and should be 'destroyed'. Although Sirhan's school was nominally Christian, teachers were mainly drawn from the Arab community, which was predominantly Muslim, with some input from foreign missionary workers. Christian Arabic children used Jordanian textbooks.

From 1948 to 1967, Christian schools in East Jerusalem were required to teach the Koran. Following his arrest for the murder of Robert F. Kennedy, Sirhan told of how he had been influenced by one particular teacher in his school, 'Mr Suheil', who angrily denounced present-day Arabs and compared them to the Arab warrior Saladin. Suheil tried to indoctrinate his pupils in Arab nationalism and urged them to be like Saladin and fight for the Arab cause.[6]

As the Arab world ignored the United Nations' call to legitimize the State of Israel Arab Jordanian school textbooks continued to refer to Israel as 'foreign occupied Palestine'. The texts called for Israel's destruction and made reference to the obligation Palestinians had to defend Islamic land. In the textbooks Jews were portrayed as thieves, occupiers and 'enemies of the prophets', 'cunning', 'deceitful', 'wild animals', 'locusts' and 'treacherous'. The curriculum also exhorted children to violence and described the Jewish state in Nazi-like terms. They always described Arabs as 'victims'. In fact, the purpose of Arab schooling in Jordan and Egypt was to mobilize the population for future conflict with Israel.

The Israeli educational textbooks during this period were not without their own bias and many used less than flattering descriptions of Arabs and were essentially racist towards 'goyin' (non-Jews). History textbooks also contained many biases, distortions and omissions concerning the depiction of Arabs and the history of the Arab-Israeli conflict. However, the books omitted the incitement to hatred and violence that was present in the textbooks used by Palestinian refugees in Jordan and Egypt. In fact, beginning in the 1950s, Israel did much to promote the concept of peaceful co-existence. Study of Arabic culture and language was introduced in elementary schools and the works of Arab authors and poets, even those writers hostile to Israel, have been included in the curriculum.[7]

In December 1956, when Sirhan was 12 years old, the Sirhan family moved to the United States. At first Sirhan was not impressed with his new life, but he was hopeful that his position as one of an 'oppressed' minority would improve. The 12-year-old asked his mother if, by becoming a US citizen, he would get blonde hair and blue eyes. From an early age he would always refer to himself as a 'Palestinian Arab', even though he was, technically, a Jordanian citizen.

The effect of seeing US students from wealthy backgrounds socializing among themselves had an impact on Sirhan; an impact long recognized by educators who have understood how school populations, differentiated by social class, material possessions and social groupings, can experience resentment and bitterness. Sirhan began to recognize that, for him at least, the United States was a society of the 'haves' and 'have-nots'. He identified with the 'have-nots' and characterized the 'haves' as students who had 'blonde hair and blue eyes'. Sirhan was beginning to identify himself along racial lines. At this time, he was described by friends and fellow students as 'taciturn', 'surly', 'hard to get to know', 'withdrawn and alone' but also 'pleasant and well-mannered'.

Sirhan's hatred and anger towards the Jews remained with him as he settled in his new country. He continued to believe Jews ran 'the whole country', headed major organizations of the media and were responsible for the slanted view the media gave of Arabs. According to Mohan Goel, an acquaintance of Sirhan's, '[Sirhan] couldn't understand the Americans, that they let the Jews suck the blood of the nation, and keep putting money in the banks'. Sirhan confessed he still felt 'towards the Jews as they (the Jews) felt towards Hitler. Hitler persecuted them and now they're persecuting me in the same style'.[8]

At Pasadena's John Muir High School, Sirhan became interested in politics and began to express his political views. Once he gave a talk to the school's Foreign Relations Club. Arriving at the venue, Sirhan became disgusted at the audience which he believed was made up mostly of Jews. Asked if Arabs should accept the status quo and also accept peace, Sirhan became inflamed. He berated his questioner and asked, rhetorically, 'Give up our own houses? You want us to give up our own houses?'[9]

The Sirhan family continued to resist acculturation. Conversation at home was always Arabic and they listened to taped Arab music all day long, especially the music of Umm Kulthum. They read Arab newspapers and observed Arab customs, read Arab literature and their way of thinking was always the 'Arab way'. Arab pride was also important to them, which is the reason why Sirhan became angry when his lawyers argued that he had been 'mentally ill' when he shot Robert F. Kennedy. Sirhan reacted this way because in Arab culture there is a great stigma attached to mental illness. In most Arab countries it is better to be a criminal than to admit insanity.[10]

Despite his all-English education, Sirhan's mother tongue remained Arabic, although Sirhan claimed to think in English. The family spoke Arabic among themselves and all the brothers described themselves not as 'Christian Arabs' but as 'Palestinian Arabs'. The brothers also strongly disapproved of their sister Aida not marrying an Arab.[11]

During a period of unemployment in 1966–7 Sirhan frequently visited the Pasadena public library, especially during summer 1967 when he read everything he could get his hands on about the Six-Day War. He avidly read *B'nai B'rith Messenger* (which had chronicled Jewish life in Los Angeles since 1897), keeping track of what he described as 'Zionist intentions'. Angry and bitter at the Arab defeat, Sirhan frequently railed against the purported pro-Israeli US television news and the 'bias' of the likes of *Time, Newsweek, US News* and *World Report*.

The war had an intense effect on him. He had seen photographs of Israeli soldiers triumphantly taking control of the Suez Canal and later he would remark, 'If I had seen those guys personally, I would have blasted them . . . I would have killed them'. His anger against Israel provoked him to write the following in his notebooks, '2 June 1967, 12.30pm – A Declaration of War Against American Humanity, when in the course of human events it has become necessary for me to equalise and seek revenge for all the inhuman treatments committed against me by the American people'. Another entry declared, 'Long Live Nasser . . . Long live the Arab Dream'.

Between September 1967 and March 1968 Sirhan had been employed by health-food store owner John Weidner and the two discussed politics, religion and philosophy. One of Weidner's assistants recalled that Sirhan was 'a fanatic when it comes to a discussion of religion or politics'. According to Weidner, Sirhan believed he was 'an Arab . . . till the end'.

Weidner also quoted Sirhan as saying, 'They [the Jews] have stolen my country. They have no right to be there. It belongs to Jordan and they have taken it.' Weidner said Sirhan believed:

> The Jewish people were dominating, they had a lot of wealth, a lot of power, and he say [*sic*] there is no freedom in America . . . he always had the attitude of resenting authority . . . he could be very nervous and arrogant . . . he was thinking alone . . . knowing his hate of the Jews . . . and knowing his complex of inferiority, seeing in Kennedy a man who has a big name, rich, successful life, happy – now Sirhan, you have got to do something big.[12]

It was because of Sirhan's 'touchiness', arrogance and his feelings of inadequacy and inferiority that friction between employer and employee developed. Weidner said he sometimes:

. . . felt that [Sirhan] had turned against the whole American way of life, and that he was an anarchist in revolt against our society. And yet he had beliefs and principles. Personal honour and his self-respect were important to him. And second only to that he esteemed patriotism. He had strong patriotic feelings for his country [Palestine]. Yes, I would say he loved his country.[13]

Weidner also engaged Sirhan in many discussions about the problems of the Middle East. According to Weidner, 'he hated the Jews because of their power and their material wealth, they had taken his country from his people who were now refugees. Because of Israel, he said, his family had become refugees, and he described to my wife how he himself had seen a Jewish soldier cutting the breast off an Arab woman in Jerusalem.' He told Weidner, 'There is no God. Look at what God has done for the Arabs! And for the Palestinians! How can we believe in God?'[14]

During the Easter vacation of 1968, Arab-American Lou Shelby, who hired Sirhan's brother Adel as a musician for his club the Fez, visited the Sirhans. Shelby thought the family was 'strange'. He had previously visited them in Pasadena on a number of occasions for musical rehearsals and was able to see them in a social setting. According to Shelby:

The Sirhans always struck me as being a weird family. By that I mean something quite strange and unusual. Perhaps the best way to explain it is by saying that though they were Christians, the general quality, the atmosphere, of their family was that of a Muslim family. It was serious and heavy and lacking in the adaptability and quickness which most Arab Christian families here have. And there were their relations with their mother; the sons were fond of her, of course, but she had little influence on them, and they didn't take her wishes or feelings into account.[15]

Shelby had known Adel for seven years, but it was the first opportunity to talk to his younger brother. According to Shelby:

We had a really big argument on Middle East politics . . . we switched back and forth between Arabic and English. Sirhan's outlook was completely Arab nationalist – the Arabs were in the right and had made no mistakes. I tried to reason with him and to point out that one could be in the right but still make mistakes. But he was adamant. According to him, America was to blame for the Arabs' misfortunes – because of the power of Zionism in this country. The only Arab leader he really admired was Nasser and he thought Nasser's policies were right. The Arabs had to build themselves up and fight Israel, that was the only way. The only outside friend the Arabs had was Russia, but, according to Sirhan, Russia had not proved a good enough friend during last June's fighting [the Six-Day War].[16]

Following his arrest, Sirhan told one of the court-appointed psychiatrists, George Y. Abe, about his political philosophy. Sirhan told him he was solidly anti-Zionist and disgusted at the way Jews in the United States had such a strong influence within the US political system. Sirhan said he believed Robert F. Kennedy listened to the Jews and he saw the Senator as having sold out to them.[17]

As the years went by Sirhan's hatred of the Jews did not dissipate. He once denounced one of his brothers for dating a Jewish girl and he rejected another girl he dated because she was Jewish. He became incensed when he saw the movie *Exodus*. 'Every time I hear that song,' he later told author Robert Kaiser, 'I shut it off. It bugs me. The memories. Those Jews . . . "The f****** Arabs" is what they're trying to say every time they play that song.'[18]

Sirhan refused to see the movie *Lawrence of Arabia* as he believed it to be anti-Arab. He also disliked the movie because it had a Jewish director, Sam Spiegal. In fact, Sirhan became paranoid about Jews in the United States: 'The Jews are behind the scenes wherever you go. You tell them your name and they freeze; "SUR-HAN".' He felt slighted every time someone mentioned his double-barrelled name. He said, 'My name! My name! As soon as anyone heard it, everything else stopped.' He confessed that he was not 'psychotic . . . except when it comes to the Jews'.[19]

Childhood friend and fellow radical Walter Crowe said Sirhan was virulently anti-Semitic and professed hatred for the Jews and the State of Israel. Crowe believed Mary Sirhan propagated these views to Sirhan. Crowe, who studied Arabic, attended a meeting of the Organization of Arab Students with Sirhan in 1964. In 1965 Sirhan told Crowe of his admiration for President Nasser and expressed the wish that the Arabs would someday rid Palestine of the Jews.[20]

At Pasadena College, Sirhan said he realized:

> . . . being an Arab is worse than being a Negro. Oh, I worked hard
> . . . but I stood out in class . . . just my name gave me away. I stood
> out for that teacher as an example to prove the points he wanted to
> make to the class about 'acculturation'. Once, during a discussion
> of adaptation, the problem, the issue of Palestine came up. This
> was my chance to speak. I really wanted to clobber this fellow, this
> blond son of a bitch and I did. I put him where he really belonged.
> I talked for one solid hour. There were two or three coloured peo-
> ple in the class. They had to applaud. I was on their side when they
> got up to tell about their grievances. My argument? Well, I said
> that if the US was really as benevolent as it claimed to be, why did
> it send Hitler's Jews to Palestine? Why not to the Mojave Desert?
> Then see how much milk and honey they could produce![21]

For a brief period, a few years before the assassination, Sirhan had secured
employment as a part-time gardener, and he came to hate the Jews whose
gardens he tended. He referred to them as those 'f****** Jews', 'the goddamn Zionists' and the 'f****** Zionists'.

A number of people who knew Sirhan, including friend John Strathman,
said Sirhan had been impressed by Hitler's *Mein Kampf* and also of the
German leader's solution to the 'Jewish Problem'.[22] Sirhan believed Hitler
had had 'hypnotic powers' over the German people. John Weidner, said,
'I soon discovered he had a dislike for the Jewish people as a nation . . . he
said that in America, the Jewish people were on the top and directed things
. . . He said they had taken his home.'[23]

However, it was the Arab-Israeli War of 1967 that provoked the worst of
Sirhan's anti-Semitic rages. Kanan Hamzeh, president of the Organization of
Arab Students (OAS) in Pasadena, said Sirhan had 'intense feelings about the
Israelis'. According to John Strathman, Sirhan was 'intense' and 'mad' about
the Six-Day War. Strathman's wife, Patricia, said Sirhan became 'burning
mad . . . furious' about the war.[24]

The Sirhan family watched television news reports about the war and
they read the Los Angeles newspapers. The *Los Angeles Times* editorial of
6 June 1967 said that the United States had an obligation to maintain the
territorial integrity of Israel and from the week beginning 5 June 1967, the
newspaper devoted many pages depicting Arabs as figures of ridicule.

Television comedy shows made reference to anti-Arab jokes and the general atmosphere throughout the United States was joy at the Israeli victory. Arabs living in the United States found it difficult to understand why the United States sided with Israel, despite the oft-stated view of US leaders that Israel was viewed as an island of democracy in a sea of dictatorships. Arab communities in the United States also failed to understand how the US people supported Israel because it was seen as the underdog, a small nation standing up to the aggression from large Arab states. Furthermore, support for Israel had been linked to the Cold War realities of a superpower's response to the growing friendliness between Arab states, especially that of Nasser's Egypt, with the Soviet Union.

One year later, on the anniversary of the Arab defeat, Sirhan saw, on his way to the Ambassador Hotel on the night of 4 June 1968, an advertisement announcing a march down Wilshire Boulevard to commemorate the first anniversary of Israel's victory in the Six-Day War. It was a 'big sign, for some kind of fund, or something . . . a fire started burning in me . . . I thought the Zionists or Jews or whoever it was were trying to rub it in that they had beat hell out of the Arabs.'[25]

At his trial Sirhan stated:

> That brought me back to the six days in June of the previous year
> . . . I was completely pissed off at American justice at the time . . .
> I had the same emotionalism, the same feelings, the fire started
> burning inside me . . . at seeing how these Zionists, these Jews,
> these Israelis, . . . were trying to rub in the fact that they had beaten
> the hell out of the Arabs the year before . . . when I saw that ad, I
> was off to go down and see what these sons-of-bitches were up to.[26]

Sirhan was not alone in his anger. An unnamed girlfriend of Adel's told reporters it was no secret that the Arab community in Los Angeles was upset at the US government's overt support of Israel. In 1967 and 1968 she and others joined in a demonstration with marches on Hollywood Boulevard and the Hollywood Bowl.

Sirhan had developed the idea of 'striking out' in the year following the Arab defeat and his feelings climaxed during the 1968 primary elections. Furthermore, in the years leading up to the shooting, his Arab nationalism was fuelled by the Arab newspaper *Al Bayan*, published in Brooklyn, which promoted anti-Israeli rhetoric. Some of its articles were overtly anti-Semitic.[27]

As an avid reader of US political periodicals, Sirhan became angry at the way the US press was treating the Arabs. He told one of the doctors involved in the case, 'I read this magazine article on the 20th anniversary of the state of Israel . . . I hate the Jews. There was jubilation. I felt they were saying in the article, "We beat the Arabs". It burns the shit out of me. There was happiness and jubilation.'[28]

There is some evidence that Sirhan was not incorrect in his assumptions that the US media had a bias against Arab states. In a July 1967 *Time* magazine article entitled 'The Least Unreasonable Arab', Jordan's King Hussein was described as the only moderate leader in the Middle East. The magazine stated, 'Instead of trying to salvage what they can, the Arabs are busy blaming just about everybody but themselves for the fact that great [amounts] of territory lie in Israeli hands.' In its article, *Time* continued: 'Desperately in need of survival training for the 20th century . . . a case of arrested development . . . emotional and political instability . . . suffering from one of history's worst inferiority complexes'.[29]

The idea that Sirhan's self-confessed political motivation was spurious did not originate with conspiracy advocates. From the beginning both Sirhan's lawyers and the US media sought to portray the assassination of Robert F. Kennedy as the act of a deranged individual bent on seeking fame and notoriety.

The New York lawyer Emile Zola Berman, a Jew, became one of Sirhan's lawyers and was praised for defending a Palestinian. However, he may well have been used by the defence team to prevent the political aspects of the crime from being addressed. It was Berman who advocated Sirhan's defence be built around the plea of 'diminished capacity', to prove that Sirhan had been 'mentally ill'. Sirhan protested and told his lawyers, 'Have you ever heard the Arab side of the story? . . . I mean on the TV, the radio, in the mass media? . . . That's what bugs me! There's no Arab voice in America, and goddamn it, I'm gonna show 'em in that courtroom. I'm gonna really give 'em hell about it.' During the trial, Sirhan repeatedly voiced his political motives but his lawyers went ahead with their trial strategy.[30]

The act of killing Kennedy can only be seen as an 'absurd' one if there was no obvious rational motive to consider. Yet Sirhan's crime was indeed explicable and rational both in personal and political terms, as the Arab communities in the United States recognized as soon as the facts of the case were publicized. Henry Awad, the editor and publisher of the *Star News and*

Pictorial, the largest Arab newspaper in the United States at the time, said, 'The Arab community wants this trial. We think it's the only way the US will hear about the Arab cause . . . Every single Arab in America regrets the killing, but the trial will bring us a chance for publicity.'[31]

The *New York Times* interviewed a celebrated spokesman for the Arab-American community in the United States, John Jabara, who believed the trial of Sirhan would bring an 'understanding of the Arab cause'.[32] *Al Anwar*, an Arab newspaper in Beirut, commented on 10 June 1968, that 'regardless of everything, Sirhan's blood-stained bullets have carried Palestine into every American home. The act may be illegal, the price high and the assassination unethical. But American deafness to the cause of the Palestine people is also illegal, unethical and carries a high price.'[33]

There were a few media outlets in the United States that recognized the true nature of Sirhan's act, but their voices largely went unheard. The *Jewish Observer* acknowledged that Robert F. Kennedy's assassination would leave a 'deep scar on America's relations with the Arab world', and it noted how the State Department played down Sirhan's Arab origins in order not to offend Arab states. They also observed that members of Congress were avoiding all reference to the Arab-Israeli conflict.

Psychiatrist Dr George Y. Abe, who interviewed Sirhan in the pre-trial period, implied that Sirhan's political ideas were irrational. Sirhan, he said, had 'paranoid-inclined ideations, particularly in the political sphere, but there is no evidence of outright delusions or hallucinations'.[34]

Yet the assassin's motives were anything but 'paranoid' and reflected the thinking of millions of Arabs both in the Middle East and the United States. Dr Philip S. Hicks, a psychiatrist who interviewed the assassin in 1986, said that the assassination stemmed from 'political fanaticism rather than psychotic violence'.[35]

When the United States voiced its support for Israel in the United Nations Assembly it enraged Sirhan. He later confessed, 'At the time I would have killed [US Ambassador to the United Nations, Arthur Goldberg] if I had a gun'.[36] Sirhan also developed an intense hatred for other leading US politicians, although at his trial he expressed admiration for President Kennedy. He said he had 'loved' the president because JFK had been working with Arab leaders to try to bring about a peace settlement in the Middle East. Sirhan believed President Kennedy 'was going to put pressure on Israel . . . to help the refugees . . . he was killed and it never happened'.[37]

But Sirhan reserved his burning contempt for Robert F. Kennedy, who he believed had made statements in support of Israel that went beyond any expressed by the other presidential candidates. He imagined Kennedy had 'betrayed' him when he discovered that Kennedy, the candidate who expressed allegiance to the 'underdog', had now become his bitter enemy. He also targeted Kennedy because of the Senator's greater potential in becoming the next president. Sirhan knew RFK's assassination would engender greater publicity for the Arab cause.[38]

At his trial Sirhan said he had wanted Robert F. Kennedy to be president, but that love turned to hate when he saw television reports of RFK participating in an Israeli Independence Day celebration. Asked by his lawyer, Grant Cooper, if anyone had put it in his mind that Robert F. Kennedy was a 'bad person', Sirhan replied: 'No, no, this is all mine . . . I couldn't believe [RFK's support for Israel]. I would rather die . . . rather than live with it . . . I have the shock of it . . . the humility and all this talk about the Jews being victorious'.[39] Sirhan said he heard a radio broadcast when the 'hot news was when the announcer said Robert Kennedy was at some Jewish Club or Zionist Club in Beverly Hills'. Speaking at the Neveh Shalom Synagogue, Kennedy said, 'In Israel – unlike so many other places in the world – our commitment is clear and compelling. We are committed to Israel's survival. We are committed to defying any attempt to destroy Israel, whatever the source. And we cannot and must not let that commitment waver.' Sharif Sirhan told Egyptian journalist Mahmoud Abel Hadi that, following the broadcast of the speech on television, '. . . he (Sirhan) left the room putting his hands on his ears and almost weeping'.[40]

Sirhan had been aware that Palestinian organizations were beginning to carry out terrorist acts in the 1960s. In conversations Sirhan held with his friend, Walter Crowe, the two politically aware and leftist young men discussed Arab nationalism. Crowe told Sirhan that the Arab cause was a fight for national liberation. Echoing sentiments held by many left-wing radicals of the time, Crowe said the conflict in Palestine was an internal struggle by Palestinians who were oppressed by the Israelis. Crowe believed Al Fatah's terrorist acts were justified and that Palestinian terrorists had gained the respect of the Arab world. Sirhan agreed and spoke of 'total commitment' to the cause. Sirhan was for 'violence whenever, as long as it's needed'. Crowe recalled that Sirhan 'could have seen himself as a fighter', and he believed that Sirhan saw himself as a committed revolutionary willing to undertake revolutionary action. Later Crowe would come to feel guilty about the part he may have played in putting ideas of terrorist acts into Sirhan's head and reinforcing Sirhan's resolve.[41]

Since June 1967 Al Fatah had been promoting their interests in the United States. From 1965 to 1967, Fatah pursued a policy of terrorist attacks on Israeli settlements. Only a few incursions into Israel were aimed at military targets. In March 1968, a group of terrorists used a land mine to destroy a school bus in Israel's Negev Desert. Two adults were killed, and twenty-eight children wounded. In April 1968, a passenger bus was stopped by Israeli police a few miles east of the Sirhan's former West Bank village of Taybeh. Three young Palestinian terrorists were shot and two of the victims died. The stories were widely circulated within the United States.

As a keen student of politics and Middle-Eastern affairs, Sirhan could not have failed to read about Fatah's exploits. On the US West Coast, Arab students had been receiving political literature from a number of Arab groups, including Al Fatah. Students received copies of Al Fatah statements and communiqués, according to the *Christian Science Monitor*'s Beirut correspondent. The statements exhorted Palestinian Arabs to pursue a more violent agenda to rid the Jews from Palestinian soil.[42] There is no evidence, however, that Sirhan had met with any representatives of terrorist groups. However, the Arab community in Los Angeles gave their wholehearted support for the actions of Palestinian terror groups and this no doubt influenced and inspired Sirhan.

Sirhan was a student at Pasadena City College from September 1963 until 18 May 1965. During this period two Arab groups were active on campus – The International Club and the OAS in the United States and Canada. Neither was recognized by the college. According to writer James H. Sheldon, in an article entitled 'Anti-Israeli Forces on Campus', the OAS was dangerously active in spreading extremist and violent ideas during this period.

Sirhan was involved with OAS and met the president of the organization, Kanan Abdul Latif Hamzeh, through his brother, Sharif, who was an active member. Sirhan became a de facto member of the organization which, purportedly, had been set up to assist Arab students in adjusting to academic life away from home but, in reality, was more politically active than its mission statement professed. According to Hamzeh, Sirhan volunteered to assist in organizing meetings, setting out chairs and procuring refreshments. Hamzeh also said Sirhan had intense feelings against the Israelis.

Sirhan believed his crime of assassinating Robert F. Kennedy was legitimate and he was intensely proud of his act. Robert Kaiser tried to fathom Sirhan's true motives and in December 1968 he told him he did not believe his expressed pro-Palestinian motives. Sirhan had been 'putting him on', he thought. Sirhan replied: 'I could be sometimes. But it's in me . . . You know, women, money and horses were my thing, but I still maintain this thing (the assassination) had a political motivation. There was no other . . . involving factor.' [43]

John Weidner said, 'I think he did it because he thought he was doing something for his country . . . [Sirhan] told me that when he was a child, he saw members of his family killed by Jews and he had to flee Jordan when he was a child. He was not a citizen and didn't like the United States.' [44]

By killing Kennedy, Sirhan had been advancing the cause of the Palestinians, a cause that promoted the return of Arab land from the state of Israel. 'They [the Palestinians] want action. They want results. Hey! I produced action for them. I'm a big hero over there.' [45]

Sirhan knew that his crime 'propagandized' a political or ideological point of view – 'a propaganda of the deed' as the 1969 National Commission on the Causes and Prevention of Violence described it. Sirhan attempted to advance his cause through publicity and there was a 'cause and effect' relationship to his crime. Sirhan, therefore, was an 'unaffiliated terrorist' and the motive for his act was established on the night he murdered Robert F. Kennedy when he cried out, 'I did it for my country'.

* * *

Commentary 2022

Every conspiracist who wrote about the Robert F. Kennedy assassination has attempted to show that Sirhan was not interested in politics, had no animus towards Senator Kennedy and was non-violent. Authors Philip Melanson and William Klaber, for example, wrote: 'A review of Sirhan's interviews with his doctors and lawyers reveals that he is noteworthy for his lack of hatred for his victim. His notebooks hardly constitute a shrewd posture for his legal defence, and other than that he has Arab origins and has voiced anti-Israeli sentiments, he has remarkably little in common with Black September.' [46]

In 2008, the conspiracy author Shane O'Sullivan attempted to remove the political motive for the crime when he interviewed Sirhan's brother

Munir for his video documentary *RFK Must Die*. It was yet another exercise by conspiracy promoters in whitewashing vital facts about Sirhan's character and political motives.

Munir's characterization of the Sirhans was of 'a, normal, happy, God-fearing family' and that his brother Sirhan had no real interest in politics. 'It was horrifying to go through this. It was unbelievable. He had never said anything about Kennedy either way,' Munir said, 'From the start, I doubted the charges because Sirhan couldn't hurt a fly . . . He wasn't capable of it, running at someone and shooting them . . . [He's] always been a Christian, a devout Christian.'[47]

This is, as I found out while researching Sirhan's life, arid nonsense. O'Sullivan used Munir Sirhan to create the myth the assassin was a non-violent devout Christian. His book left his readers unaware that Sirhan had abandoned his Christian faith and embraced atheism and the occult many years before the assassination. An associate pastor at the Baptist church in Pasadena, which was attended by Sirhan's mother Mary, had several conversations with him and described Sirhan as 'a very intense atheist'.[48] Sirhan told his boss, John Weidner, he did not believe in God.[49] O'Sullivan's readers were also left unaware of Sirhan's frequent and angry anti-Semitic and anti-American outbursts, his pathological hatred of Jews and his stated desire to eliminate US leaders who had given their support to Israel.

According to the star witness at Sirhan's trial, Alvin Clark, the assassin was, 'very prejudiced towards white people'.[50] Sirhan said, 'Robert Kennedy was a fascist pig. [Black Panther leader] Eldridge Cleaver said so.'[51] In fact, during his trial, Sirhan emulated the Black Panther clenched fist salute. According to his brother Munir, he also became enamoured with the Black Muslims who were more like him culturally. After attending the Black Muslim Temple in Central Los Angeles, Sirhan was told he could not join the organization because he was not black. He did, however, purchase some Black Muslim literature.[52]

In August 1968, when he was awaiting trial, Sirhan told his lawyers that Hubert Humphrey was a 'chicken-faced son-of-a-bitch . . . Humphrey, you better have a million guards around you, because you're gonna get it, you goddamn bastard!' He also railed against Richard Nixon and Ted Kennedy. He told his lawyers, 'Nixon! He's worse than Kennedy. To get the Jewish vote, he said he'd help the Israelis. But what good did it do him? Hell, he only got four percent of the Jewish vote. Humphrey got most of it, the son-of-a-bitch. Nixon! Hell, I gave him the election! Hell, I gave it to him!'[53]

Sirhan even believed that, since he had given the election to Nixon, the new president should free him and give him a Jordanian passport and a million dollars. During his pre-trial incarceration at the Los Angeles County Jail, he also made numerous statements which revealed his contempt for the Kennedy family. During one conversation he had with his lawyers he said that if Ted Kennedy ran for president, it would be like 'putting the exercise boy on [a winning racehorse]'.[54] He wanted to kill Arthur Goldberg, US representative to the UN. He wrote in his diary, 'Ambassador Goldberg must die – Goldberg must be eliminated.'[55]

Contrary to O'Sullivan's somewhat distorted description of the Sirhan family, they can best be described as dysfunctional. The father, Bishara Sirhan, had deserted his family shortly after they arrived in the United States, disappointed at having lost control over his sons who he feared were becoming westernized. All the brothers, with the exception of the oldest, Adel, had been in trouble with the police.

At the time of Bobby Kennedy's assassination, Sharif was 38, Saidallah 36, Adel 33, Sirhan 24 and Munir, the youngest, 19. Sharif was arrested for attempting to murder his girlfriend and, like Sirhan, hated Jews. Mary Sirhan, who had indoctrinated her sons to hate Jews, had no control over her sons and often asked Arab friends to intervene in their disputes among themselves and with her. Saidallah was arrested for drunk driving and drunken disturbances. And Munir was a disciplinary problem in school, was involved in a high-speed pursuit by the California Highway Patrol and had been arrested for selling marijuana. Munir also lied to police about the provenance of the RFK murder weapon. In recent years Munir has stated his brother Sirhan is 'not a Muslim; [he's] always been a Christian, a devout Christian'.[56]

The *New York Times* reviewed O'Sullivan's book and video and concluded, 'Like a dog unleashed in a field full of rabbits, [O'Sullivan] chases one shard of "evidence" after another – a second gunman, a girl in a polka-dot dress – without bothering to arrange them in any coherent pattern'.[57]

Chapter 7

Did the CIA Assassinate Robert F. Kennedy?

'Still Guilty After All These Years: Sirhan B. Sirhan', first published in Max Holland's e-zine Washington Decoded, *in 2008*

It has often been said that lurid theories about the Lincoln and JFK assassinations have thrived because neither John Wilkes Booth nor Lee Harvey Oswald received their day in court. The concept of due process is so embedded in the US psyche, in other words, that its denial inexorably gives rise to conspiratorial explanations.

The aftermath of Robert F. Kennedy's June 1968 assassination, however, challenges this somewhat comforting observation. In this instance, the assassin was literally caught red-handed – tackled by Kennedy's bodyguards, moments after the shots were fired, a .22 calibre revolver still in hand. When the trial of Sirhan Bishara Sirhan opened seven months later, his defence counsel explained, 'There will be no denial of the fact that our client . . . fired the shot that killed Senator Kennedy'.[1] Instead, Sirhan's lawyers mounted a defence of not guilty because of 'diminished capacity', the only way to spare their client from what seemed to be his likely fate, the gas chamber at San Quentin.

Sirhan's counsel had no other choice because the presiding judge, Herbert Van Walker, exercising his discretion, had summarily rejected a plea bargain that would have exchanged life imprisonment for a guilty plea. 'We don't want another Dallas,' Walker reportedly observed, repeating the mantra uttered moments after Sirhan's apprehension.[2]

Walker believed, presumably, that prosecuting Sirhan to the full extent of the law would avert the uncertainty that was already rampant with respect to the first Kennedy assassination. The Sirhan case was being tried at virtually the same time the awful miscarriage of justice in New Orleans – the circus-like persecution of Clay Shaw by District Attorney Jim Garrison –

was coming to a head. And that debacle was the direct outgrowth of the doubt and disbelief which existed because of Jack Ruby's vigilantism, and the denial of due process for Oswald.

Sirhan Sirhan had his day in court, indeed, several months. Because of the extraordinary security precautions employed, Sirhan's prosecution was judged the most expensive US trial ever held, costing the county of Los Angeles $900,000 ($5.3 million in 2007 dollars).[3] And despite the best efforts of his lawyers, Sirhan received the ultimate sanction. The only factor which saved him from being executed decades ago was that three years after the penalty was handed down in May 1969, the state Supreme Court declared California's death penalty unconstitutional. Sirhan's sentence was commuted to life imprisonment, and Corcoran State Prison near Fresno, an infamous maximum-security facility, is where he remains to this day – along with other notorious inmates such as Charles Manson.

Judge Walker was not a naïve man, but even a cynic might have been hard-pressed in 1969 to foresee how conspiracy theorists would succeed in twisting the facts in a ceaseless effort to raise doubts about what amounted to an open and shut case. Today it comes as little surprise, given the absence of any editorial vetting on the Internet, to find many websites and blogs saturated with bogus revelations and mindless repetition of supposed 'facts' that were, in actuality, refuted or rationally explained years ago.[4]

The tide of nonsense is sufficiently high that on occasion, and as if by osmosis, palpable falsehoods are accepted and propagated by even the most venerable news organizations, as will be seen below. There were, to be sure, apparent anomalies in the evidence, including problems with the ballistic and forensic evidence. In addition, some eyewitness statements, if taken completely at face value, at least raised the possibility that Sirhan had not acted alone in the pantry of the Ambassador Hotel. But such incongruities are entirely normal in most murder investigations, which are far from being as neat and tidy as an episode of *CSI*. It is particularly true of major investigations, where the possibility of human error is compounded because of the vast amounts of paperwork and physical evidence that must be processed. Then, too, police forces forty years ago were simply not as careful about securing a murder scene as they are trained to be now.

What is immediately apparent when the historiographies of the JFK and RFK assassinations are placed side by side is their similarity, independent from the reality that Sirhan confessed, was tried and convicted. It would not be an exaggeration to say that the assassination mimicry serving as inspiration for Sirhan's crime in the first place has extended to the post-assassination arc of the RFK case. Though not in the same order, many of the same tactics used to put the official story of the JFK assassination in disrepute by 1968 have been employed in the RFK case – sometimes by the very same people.

Purported Involvement of the CIA

It took four years before allegations of CIA involvement in the JFK assassination achieved critical mass in the public mind, courtesy of Jim Garrison. In the RFK case, the allegation was levelled far more quickly, owing to the noxious political atmosphere generated by Garrison and comrades such as Mark Lane in the late 1960s.

Even as a special unit of LAPD detectives was investigating Sirhan's every movement and association prior to 5 June, some of the conspiracists who had attached themselves to Garrison's probe were contacting the LAPD to report a 'CIA conspiracy' in the Senator's assassination. These freelance researchers, or 'Dealey Plaza irregulars' as they were dubbed, claimed that RFK was killed because the CIA feared he would launch an investigation into agency 'involvement in his brother's death' if elected president in 1968.[5]

Garrison himself was uncharacteristically silent on the subject, perhaps because he had accused the former attorney general, prior to June 1968, of obstructing the DA's probe into the JFK assassination. The truth, Garrison alleged, threatened to 'interfere with [RFK's] political career'.[6] In fact, within the DA's bizarre world, according to Tom Bethell, who worked on the investigation, Robert F. Kennedy was considered a *suspect* in the JFK case until his own death.[7]

The theme of CIA involvement in the RFK case waned in subsequent decades, but was resuscitated with the success of Oliver Stone's 1992 film *JFK*. The most persistent purveyor of this meme was Lawrence Teeter, a criminal defence attorney who took up Sirhan's case in 1994 and immediately began petitioning state and federal courts for a new trial. Taking a leaf from two earlier, conspiratorially minded books about the case, Teeter never denied that Sirhan fired a handgun shortly after midnight, but claimed the assassin was a victim of hypnotic programming, à la Richard Condon's 1959 book *The Manchurian Candidate* (later a film by John Frankenheimer).[8] In Sirhan's case, however, he was not a tool of a foreign power and Stalinist mother, Teeter contended, but was controlled by the CIA, the 'military industrial complex' – or both.[9]

As inexorably happens, the latest incarnation of this fantasy is even more baroque and involved than its precursors. That did not, however, prevent it from being propagated by the BBC. On 6 November 2006, *Newsnight*, the BBC's flagship news programme, broadcast a 12-minute segment about a forthcoming 'documentary' on the assassination, written by Shane O'Sullivan, an Irish screenwriter. Though not previously known for his investigative prowess or non-fiction writing, O'Sullivan claimed to have uncovered new video and photographic evidence that proved 'three senior CIA operatives were behind the [RFK] killing'. In the BBC report, and a companion article published in *The Guardian* on the same day, O'Sullivan even named names: David Sanchez Morales, Gordon Campbell and George Joannides, all three of whom were involved in anti-Castro activities out of the CIA's station in Miami in the early 1960s.[10]

There was only one problem – well, actually there was more than one, but one will suffice – with O'Sullivan's allegation. Those CIA officers he claimed were the real sponsors of the assassination were not at the Ambassador Hotel on the night in question.[11]

Primarily because my own work on the RFK assassination, *The Forgotten Terrorist*, was coming out in a matter of months, I immediately undertook to investigate O'Sullivan claims. Through Don Bohning, the former Latin America editor for the *Miami Herald* (and author of *The Castro Obsession*), whose contacts regarding this subject are unrivalled, former colleagues who knew David Morales and/or Gordon Campbell very well were promptly located.[12] All three positively and without hesitation stated that the dubious witnesses O'Sullivan had relied upon – Wayne Smith, Bradley Ayers and David Rabern – were wrong in their identifications of Morales and Campbell.[13]

Following my article, two other journalists, David Talbot and Jefferson Morley, began investigating O'Sullivan's story, because they, too, were working on projects with equity in the allegation. Talbot was putting the finishing touches on *Brothers* (2007), his biography of Robert F. Kennedy post-1963. Talbot was going to argue that JFK had been killed as a result of a conspiracy involving CIA operatives, and he obviously needed to understand if a similar 'plot' extended to RFK. Morley had a keen interest because he had single-handedly transformed George Joannides from an all-but-forgotten officer into the crucial link that would supposedly unravel the CIA's alleged

President and Mrs Kennedy arrive at Love Field airport for their motorcade through the streets of Dallas, 22 November 1963. (*JFK Presidential Library*)

The Texas School Book Depository. When the JFK limousine reached the corner of Houston Street, seen above, it slowed down to make a sharp left turn on to Elm Street. (*Copyright Mel Ayton*)

Elm Street, Dealey Plaza, Dallas. The fatal shot came as the presidential limousine was in the approximate position of the first car in the centre of the photo. (*Copyright Mel Ayton*)

The Texas School Book Depository and the window, six floors up from ground level, where Oswald fired his three shots at JFK. (*Copyright Mel Ayton*)

When Robert Kennedy campaigned for the 1968 Democrat Party nomination his security was woefully lacking. During the June California Primary his bodyguard protection consisted of three friends, armed ex–FBI agent Bill Barry and unarmed celebrity sportsmen Rafer Johnson and Rosey Grier. (*Copyright JFK Library*)

Colonel Manny Chavez, seen here with his wife Bernice, was a former air force intelligence officer who served in Venezuela as a military attaché and later was assigned to the CIA Office in Miami from 1960 to 1964. Chavez and other former intelligence agents who the author contacted were instrumental in debunking the bogus BBC story, authored by conspiracist Shane O' Sullivan, that CIA agents were present at the Los Angeles Ambassador Hotel when Robert Kennedy was assassinated. (*http://news.fiu.edu*)

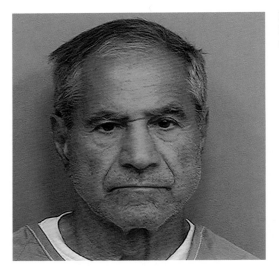

Prison photograph of Sirhan Sirhan, 2016. (*California Department of Corrections and Rehabilitation*)

The infamous 'Hey Punk' letter written by Sirhan after his arrest in which he threatens author Robert Blair Kaiser. The letter puts the lie to the claims of Sirhan's defenders that the assassin was a mild-mannered and non-violent individual. (*www.moldea.com*)

A page from Sirhan's notebooks in which he expresses his desire to kill Robert F. Kennedy. (*California State Archives*)

At least nine original testimonies can be found in the FBI's 'Kensalt' Files and the LAPD Files in which witnesses talk about having seen a 'mysterious polka-dot-dress girl' at the Ambassador Hotel the night of Robert F. Kennedy's shooting, purportedly accompanying Sirhan Sirhan. However, there are considerable differences in the descriptions, time periods and exact locations of the 'polka-dot girl' – she has black hair, other times blonde or brown hair. In fact, there was no mystery about the girl in the polka-dot dress – no credible evidence exists to show such a person ever accompanied the assassin on the night of the assassination. (*California State Archives*)

An image I captured from television news film footage showing a Sirhan look-alike standing next to a woman some witnesses described as 'pretty' and wearing a polka-dot dress in the Ambassador Hotel's Embassy Room during RFK's final speech. This may be the origin of why some witnesses stated they saw Sirhan with a 'girl in a polka-dot dress'. The man with the girl is unidentified. Sirhan is pictured on the right. (*California State Archives*)

Another Sirhan look-alike
in the crowd of the Embassy
Room who may have been
mistaken for the assassin.
(*California State Archives*)

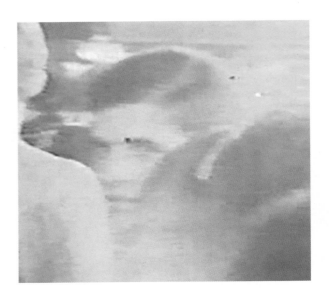

After speaking to the crowd of supporters in the Embassy Room, Robert F. Kennedy walked through the door at the rear of the stage, turned right and passed through the kitchen swing doors to the pantry where he was shot next to the steam tables. (*California State Archives*)

cover-up of its embarrassing involvement with Lee Harvey Oswald prior to the JFK assassination. If Joannides had been at the Ambassador Hotel, Morley also needed to know it immediately.

Despite their predisposition to believe in conspiracy theories when it came to one or both Kennedy assassinations, not even Talbot and Morley could countenance O'Sullivan's flimsy proof.[14] After six weeks of crisscrossing the country, their investigation not only confirmed the mistaken identifications of Morales and Campbell, but took the debunking of O'Sullivan's allegation two steps further. In an essay posted in spring 2007, they proved that Campbell could not possibly have been in Los Angeles in 1968 because he had died in September 1962. In addition, utilizing Morley's familiarity with Joannides, Talbot and Morley quoted five close friends/relatives who said the man who 'looked Greek' to Shane O'Sullivan was definitely not Joannides.[15]

In a brief rebuttal, O'Sullivan claimed to 'welcome this new evidence', although he found the tone of Morley and Talbot's article 'absurdly pompous', given that they, too, had initially been titillated and intrigued by the allegation (according to O'Sullivan). In any case, the Irish screenwriter promised to address the issue again in more detail when his feature-length documentary was released in a matter of months.

When *RFK Must Die* was finally released in 2007, a reasonable person might have predicted that a chastened O'Sullivan would back off from his claim of CIA involvement. Quite the contrary.

O'Sullivan devoted 45 minutes of his 138-minute 'investigative documentary' to the supposed controversy over CIA operatives allegedly at the Ambassador. To his credit, O'Sullivan showed Ruben Carbajal, one of David Morales' best friends, denouncing those who allege the CIA officer was present at the Ambassador Hotel in June 1968. But then O'Sullivan devoted even more footage to the supposed identifications of Morales and Joannides, made by the likes of Wayne Smith, Bradley Ayers, David Rabern and Edwin Lopez. Even more astounding was O'Sullivan's subsequent disclosure that upon further investigation, he had actually discovered the real identifies of the men he previously claimed were as 'Gordon Campbell' and 'George Joannides'.

From LAPD files, O'Sullivan had learned these men were two now-deceased executives from the Bulova Watch Company, who had been attending a company convention at the Ambassador at the time of the California primary. 'Campbell' was actually Michael Roman, Bulova's national sales manager in

1968, and 'Joannides' was, in reality, Frank Owens, a regional sales manager. But O'Sullivan then went on to insinuate, incredibly, and without citing a shred of evidence, that Bulova – a fabled New York company founded in 1875 by a Czech immigrant – was a well-known CIA 'asset', 'cover' or 'front'.[16]

In all the investigations ever conducted into the CIA, no information has ever surfaced to suggest that Bulova was utilized for cover purposes or acted as a CIA front – though, in all likelihood, some officers undoubtedly wore the company's popular 'Accutron' wristwatch in the mid-1960s. Perhaps O'Sullivan made the connection because Bulova used to advertise the 'Accutron' in 1966 on the popular TV spy show *The Man From U.N.C.L.E.* If so, that should have raised, by the reasoning and logic O'Sullivan consistently employs, some questions about the actor Robert Vaughn, who played Napoleon Solo in the TV series, and just coincidentally happened to be one of RFK's most prominent backers in Hollywood.

Was Vaughn actually playing a dual and sinister role? Perhaps using his access to Kennedy to telegraph the Senator's schedule and whereabouts? Where *was* Robert Vaughn shortly after midnight on 5 June 1968? And was he wearing a Bulova?

Insinuating CIA complicity, of course, is only one of the tactics shared by those who stoke conspiratorial explanations for the Kennedy assassinations. Another is to call into question the ballistics evidence. Championed by former Representative Allard K. Lowenstein (Democrat; New York) and former RFK aide Paul Schrade, this mode of criticism reached its first peak in December 1974 and took three years to wane.

On the fortieth anniversary of RFK's slaying there was another supposedly new challenge to the forensic evidence. In March 2008, ABC News reported that two 'forensic scientists', Robert Joling and Philip van Praag, had developed startling new evidence that undermined the notion Sirhan was the only one who fired a gun in the Ambassador's pantry. In their new, self-published book, *An Open and Shut Case* (2008), Joling and van Praag asserted that an audio recording of the assassination proved at least thirteen shots were fired, which exceeded by five the number of bullets that Sirhan's revolver could fire. According to ABC, the authors also claimed the bullet that killed Kennedy had entered the back of his head, and Sirhan was believed to be facing RFK at all times. 'It can be established conclusively that Sirhan did not shoot Senator Kennedy,' Joling told ABC. 'And, in fact, not only did he not do it, he could not have done it.'[17]

While ABC News' lack of judgment here was not as bad as the BBC's, it was only so by a very small margin. The ABC story included this sentence: 'But other forensic scientists dismiss these theories, saying the analysis is flat-out wrong.'[18] That was plain lazy 'on-the-one hand, on-the-other-hand' journalism. Given the seriousness of the allegation, it was incumbent upon the network to do its own rudimentary vetting of the story. If ABC had, it would have discovered the Joling/van Praag allegation is neither novel nor accurate, and thus not news.

The notion that Sirhan was never in position to shoot Senator Kennedy in the back of the head is very old, but oft-repeated, buncombe – not dissimilar from the canard that there was something 'magic' about the bullet that passed through President Kennedy before striking Governor Connally.[19] Vincent DiPierro, an Ambassador waiter in 1968, was standing 5ft behind the senator in the pantry and had an unobstructed view of the shooting. As he told the *Washington Post*'s Ronald Kessler in 1974, it was true that Sirhan was standing about 3ft in front, and slightly to the right, of Kennedy. But a moment before Sirhan whipped out his handgun, Kennedy turned to his left to greet some busboys. As Sirhan began firing, he lunged forward, bringing the muzzle of his Iver Johnson revolver to within inches of Kennedy's head.

'It would be impossible for there to be a second gun,' DiPierro told Kessler. 'I saw the first shot. Kennedy fell at my feet. His blood splattered on me. I had a clear view of Kennedy and Sirhan.'[20]

After Kennedy was shot, according to DiPierro, Sirhan continued to fire wildly and rapidly, while bystanders slammed his gun hand down on a nearby table in an effort to wrest it from him. There are at least three more eyewitness statements corroborating DiPierro's account that Sirhan, and no one else, shot Kennedy at point-blank range.

The allegation that more than eight shots were fired is also a concoction, although of a more recent vintage. It has the same odour as the HSCA's 1979 discovery of a fourth shot in the JFK case, because it, too, cannot withstand scientific scrutiny.

The story here begins in early 2006. While I was conducting archival research for my account of the RFK assassination, *The Forgotten Terrorist*, I learned from a source that the RFK-related holdings of the California State Archives contained a previously unreported tape recording of the gunshots in the pantry. The 35-minute recording had been made by Stanislaw Pruszynski, a freelance journalist at the time, and is the only extant recording of all the shots fired.

At my request, Philip Harrison of J.P. French Associates, the oldest independent forensic speech and acoustics laboratory in the United Kingdom, analysed a digital copy of the Pruszynski tape. During this process, Harrison would consult both his laboratory colleague, Professor Peter French, who is also a lecturer in forensic speech and audio analysis at the University of York, and Steve Barber, who is well-known for having exposed HSCA's bogus claim of a fourth shot in the JFK case. Harrison was able to identify seven impulse sounds (which are characterized by a sharp onset and rapid decay) that corresponded to Sirhan's gun being fired to the exclusion of another weapon (the seven impulses all exhibited very similar characteristics).

An eighth shot could not be clearly identified on the spectrogram made from the tape recording; this sound appeared to be masked by other noise, including screams. Harrison's report was printed as an appendix in *The Forgotten Terrorist*, first published in May 2007. A trio of Americans, led by Steve Barber, who had begun to analyse the Pruszynski recording even before Harrison became involved, also concurred with Harrison's finding. Their analysis was published online in March 2007 on History News Network.[21]

The following month, the Discovery Times Channel broadcast an episode of its *Conspiracy Test* series in which it was claimed that 'forensic audio experts' had detected not seven or even eight, but as many as thirteen shots on the Pruszynski tape. One of the experts, Philip van Praag, insisted there were thirteen identifiable sound signatures, while the other, Wes Dooley, found ten.[22]

It could be argued that Harrison's analysis simply ought to be given more weight than van Praag's or Dooley's on the basis of Harrison's superior expertise and experience. A trained acoustic engineer, Harrison has worked on more than 1,000 cases for one of the leading forensic firms of its kind in the world. Van Praag is actually an audio engineer by profession, which is quite a different thing, and his experience is simply not comparable to Harrison's; nor is Dooley's. It could also be argued that the vast majority of earwitness testimony comports with Harrison's analysis and contradicts van Praag's and Dooley's assertions.

But the most revealing aspect of all is that neither van Praag nor Dooley has been willing to discuss their respective findings in detail, despite several appeals. Indeed, Dooley disclosed to Harrison that he had had to destroy his files after the documentary was filmed, and that he did not consider his findings to be as conclusive as the documentary made them seem.[23]

This is not the method of science. It is pseudo-science. *(Author's note: As readers will learn later, in 2018 Philip Harrison's work was corroborated by a new scientific study of the gunshots by Ed Primeau, a forensic audio expert who used newly invented computer technology to examine the Pruszynski tape.)*

Facts Irrelevant

Whether they are relative neophytes, like Shane O'Sullivan, or grizzled veterans, like Robert Joling, who has cried conspiracy and cover-up in the RFK case for nearly forty years, the tactics and gambits employed by conspiracists are easily identifiable. If caught in a lie, they shamelessly manufacture a new one. Facts don't matter, because their conspiracy mongering is seldom, if ever, about the facts. As far back as 1971, Lynn D. Compton, the chief prosecutor in the Sirhan case, noted that conspiracy theories about the second Kennedy assassination were unlikely to cease because the allegations were not rooted in the facts of the case, but stemmed from the critics' political agenda.[24]

To be sure, conspiracy notions about RFK's political murder have never gripped Americans' collective psyche to quite the same degree as in the assassination of his brother. The pantry has no grassy knoll, and 'Ambassador Hotel' never connoted the same instant chill as the words 'Dealey Plaza'. The Los Angeles County District Attorney and LAPD chief never became household names overnight. The city of Los Angeles never bore the kind of burden visited upon Dallas.

Perhaps that is because Robert F. Kennedy was not president when he was assassinated, and the shock of the sequel was more like a numbing aftershock than a political earthquake. There is also the fatigue factor: just how many conspiracies must a citizen keep track of? Finally, one would like to think that the due process accorded Sirhan has something to do with the relative deficit of interest in conspiracy theories about RFK's assassination.

But this much is true: the public's lack of interest has not stemmed from conspiracy theorists' lack of effort.

* * *

Commentary 2022

I first broke the story about Shane O'Sullivan's bogus CIA tale in a History News Network article. Through my contacts with former *Miami Herald* Latin America editor Don Bohning and retired intelligence officer Colonel Manuel Chavez I placed five people on record as stating O'Sullivan misidentified the men he claimed were CIA agents present at the Ambassador Hotel the night of the RFK shooting. My sources stated that two of the men O'Sullivan mistakenly identified – David Morales and Gordon Campbell – were definitely not the men captured in the news-video footage.

My five sources were:

1. Manny Chavez – a former air force intelligence officer who served as a military attaché in Venezuela during 1957–9 while Dave Morales was assigned to the CIA office for a year during the period 1957–8. After examining the photo clips of the LAPD film footage used by O'Sullivan, Chavez stated: 'I was assigned to the CIA Office in Miami from 1960 to 1964. Dave Morales worked in my office (we shared desks) during a 4-month period (1961), until they moved to their own JM/Wave location in Southwest Miami. We often socialized . . . the tall dark man (in the LAPD film footage) does not look like Dave Morales . . . [He] looks like a young, late 30s early 40s, Afro-American . . . I worked on the photo to make it clearer and am more convinced that the person in the photos is not Dave Morales as I knew him up until 1963.'
2. Manny's wife Bernice who socialized with Morales identified the man as 'not Morales'.
3. CIA intelligence officer Grayston Lynch who worked with Morales said the man was 'not Morales'.
4. Lynch's wife, who knew Morales well, concurred.
5. Luis Rodriguez, a close friend of David Morales, said the man was 'not Morales'.

Following the publication of my article reporters Jefferson Morley and David Talbot followed up my research. Manuel Chavez, who was interviewed by the two journalists after my HNN article was published, wrote to me, expressing 'regret that David Talbot did not give you credit for having debunked the Morales involvement first, which you certainly did and deserving of at least an acknowledgement'. Chavez continued, '[Talbot and Morley's] interviews all took place two or three weeks after we had sent you our reports, so rest assured you were Numero Uno to debunk the story'.[25]

Chapter 8

Hypnotized Assassin?

*'The JFK and RFK Assassinations and the "Manchurian Candidate" Theory',
first published by John McAdams*, The Kennedy Assassination, *2009*

Commentary 2022

Many people have held a strong belief that Robert F. Kennedy's assassin had been hypnotized by the CIA and had been telling the truth when he announced he could not remember shooting Kennedy. Ipso facto – the conspirators also hypnotized Sirhan to forget his crime. This belief exists in spite of overwhelming evidence to the contrary.

Instructive in Sirhan's behaviour is the work of Theodore Dalrymple, the author of *The Knife Went In* (2017). Dalrymple worked as a psychiatrist in the UK prison system for decades. The criminals in his account are characterized by a pathological inability to take responsibility for their actions. One prisoner on remand for murder told Dalrymple, 'A fight broke out, a gun arrived, I accidentally took it and it went off.' As Dalrymple points out, 'The only human action that he admitted to was the accidental discharge of the gun, by happy chance killing an enemy.'

In this spirit, another of Dalrymple's patients, imprisoned for throwing acid in the face of his then girlfriend, tells the young doctor that he couldn't have done it – because he did not remember having done it. 'I asked him my usual question – "How, then, do you know that you didn't do it?" He replied, "Because I don't do them things."' In other words, he knew he didn't do it because it wasn't the type of thing he did, even if he could not say exactly what he was doing at the time in question. Sometime later the doctor asked the man if he had been in prison before. 'Yes,' he replied, 'I threw ammonia in a girl's face.'

Part of this must have been the as yet un-convicted killer preparing the grounds for his not guilty plea. But it is much more than that – criminals are frequently the best examples of Nietzsche's aphorism: 'Memory says "I did that." Pride replies, "I could not have done that." Eventually memory yields.'

* * *

To coincide with the fortieth anniversary of Senator Robert F. Kennedy's assassination, conspiracists again raised the possibility that RFK's assassin, Sirhan Sirhan, had been hypnotized to murder Senator Kennedy. And other writers used the RFK assassination anniversary as a vehicle to promote their Lee Harvey Oswald 'Mind Control' theories.

In a 2007 documentary, *RFK Must Die*, and a subsequent National Geographic channel documentary, *CIA – Secret Experiments* (2008), a number of conspiracy advocates alleged Sirhan was a Manchurian Candidate-type assassin – an unwitting tool of faceless conspirators in the CIA and the military industrial complex. As mentioned previously, the conspiracy writers say the same conspirators who were responsible for JFK's death had plotted RFK's murder to stop him from enquiring into the death of his brother when he became president.[1]

Some conspiracy writers have also alleged Lee Harvey Oswald had been manipulated by mind-control experts to carry out the assassination of JFK. Jerry Leonard, Lincoln Lawrence and Kenn Thomas believe that Oswald's bizarre behaviour was remarkably consistent with that of an unwitting 'hypno-programmed spy'. They also believe that Oswald's alleged links to the CIA and the further allegation that George Sergius de Mohrenschildt was Oswald's 'handler' or 'controller' were proof enough that Oswald had been brainwashed to kill President Kennedy.

Dick Russell also alleged Oswald had been a hypnotized assassin in his book *The Man Who Knew Too Much* (2003), an account of Russell's investigation into the subject of Richard Case Nagell. Nagell stated that during the summer of 1963 he had discovered that Oswald was 'undergoing hypnotherapy' from JFK conspirator David Ferrie. The story, however, had originated with a notorious fabricator, Jack Martin, who later admitted the story was false.[2]

The only plausible JFK 'Manchurian Candidate-type' theory comes from Ion Mahai Pacepa, head of Romania's secret security agency before defecting to the United States in 1978. In his book, Pacepa maintains that Khrushchev plotted the assassination, only to have a change of heart, but Soviet agents were unable to deprogramme Oswald. Pacepa also claims that Carousel Club owner Jack Ruby was working as an intelligence agent for the Cuban Dirección General de Intelligencia. However, there are fundamental flaws in Pacepa's story. KGB officers who had an interest in Oswald when he was in the Soviet Union have testified that the KGB found him to be unstable and untrustworthy. It is therefore extremely unlikely the Soviets would have wanted to employ someone of Oswald's calibre.

Additionally, Pacepa is on shaky ground when he alleges that Ruby acted at the behest of the Cuban regime, and was later poisoned in order to silence him. That allegation, of course, would have to take into account the implausible notion that Ruby's doctor was part of the conspiracy. Furthermore, Ruby died from a pulmonary embolism and cancer of the lungs and brain more than three years after he murdered Oswald, raising the question of why would an apparently all-powerful intelligence agency wait that long? If Ruby had wanted to spill the beans, he had plenty of opportunity. As it turned out the only conspiracy Ruby complained about was a conspiracy to 'kill the Jews', a product of his mental illness.

Pacepa offers no convincing Soviet motive for the assassination. Furthermore, as Vincent Bugliosi said in his examination of the allegations that the Soviet Union planned and carried out the assassination, 'Russia had absolutely nothing to gain but much to lose in killing Kennedy'. And, according to the State Department and counter-intelligence officers who debriefed Pacepa, changes to his defection story cast doubt on his veracity.[3]

There is nothing in Oswald's background that could remotely infer he was hypnotically controlled by the CIA despite the speculative accounts by some JFK assassination writers. But there were tantalizing hints in the RFK assassination case that would lead conspiracists to build a case (albeit, a flimsy one) for CIA involvement in creating a robotic patsy, including Sirhan's strange behaviour before and after he was arrested, the presence of a mysterious girl in a polka-dot dress and the purported presence of CIA agents at the Ambassador Hotel the night Robert F. Kennedy was assassinated.

However, a close examination of the RFK case renders the JFK and RFK mind-control hypotheses specious. RFK assassination conspiracy writers are supported by two hypnosis experts, Dr Milton Kline and Dr Herbert Spiegal, who agreed that Sirhan was hypnotized by others. Kline said, 'It [hypno-programming assassins] cannot be done consistently, but it can be done'. Spiegal believed that, 'It is by no means simple, but under the right circumstances it is definitely attainable . . . Sirhan, being an outstanding hypnotic subject, was probably programmed through hypnosis to shoot Senator Kennedy and to experience a genuine amnesia of the shooting.'[4]

Among the 'evidence' the conspiracy writers assembled to prove Sirhan had been a hypnotized assassin were:

1. Sirhan allegedly suffered memory loss. His last memory before he shot RFK was of leaving the Ambassador Hotel, walking to his car, found himself too drunk to drive, and returned to the hotel for some coffee around 11 p.m.
2. Not one person who was present in the Ambassador Hotel that night reported that Sirhan had been drunk.
3. Sirhan wore a 'stupid' or 'sickly' smile while he was firing his gun. Vincent DiPierro said what most stood out in his mind was Sirhan's 'stupid smile. A very sickly-looking smile.'
4. Mary Grohs, a teletype operator at the Ambassador Hotel, remembered Sirhan standing and staring at the teletype machine in the hotel's Colonial Room in the hours before the assassination. Grohs said, 'I'll never forget his eyes . . . He just kept staring.'
5. Sirhan showed incredible strength when he was being subdued following his shooting spree.
6. Sirhan's eyes were enormously 'peaceful' and he showed complete concentration on what he was doing.
7. Arresting officer Arthur Placencia examined Sirhan and concluded the suspect was 'definitely under the influence of something'.
8. Sirhan remained silent about his identity when he was questioned by police officers following his arrest.
9. Sirhan was unemotional and had complete self-possession when questioned by police.
10. Sirhan got the 'chills' following his arrest and exhibited similar symptoms at the end of his hypnosis sessions with Dr Bernard Diamond. Diamond had been brought into the case to examine Sirhan before the trial.
11. According to family and friends, Sirhan's personality had changed after his fall from the horse at the racetrack where he worked. Some conspiracists speculated that one of the doctors who treated Sirhan could have identified him as a potential hypnosis subject for conspirators.

12. Sirhan's notebook entries showed certain phrases repeated over and over again, a sign of 'automatic writing' which occurs when a subject is hypnotized. After his arrest Sirhan said he could not remember what he had written in his notebooks.

Most conspiracy writers also believe that a notorious hypnotist, Dr William Joseph Bryan Jr, hypnotized Sirhan to commit the assassination. Bryan was famous for having hypnotized the Boston Strangler, Albert DeSalvo, and claimed to have discovered DeSalvo's motive under hypnosis. Bryan also claimed he had worked for the CIA and bragged to two prostitutes that he had hypnotized Sirhan to kill Kennedy.[5]

The Truths of Hypnosis

A number of myths about hypnosis have led most conspiracy writers to make grossly speculative conclusions about Sirhan's purported hypnotic state.

No one really knows how hypnosis works, and scientists, including psychiatrists and psychologists, disagree about not only a definition but also how and why people react when in a trance. They do agree, however, that something unusual happens when a subject is put into a hypnotic state. Most psychologists agree that hypnotic techniques give the hypnotist access to the subconscious and have value as a therapeutic technique in the treatment of mental disorders.[6] However, the notion that a hypnotist has control over a subject is, essentially, a myth. A 1979 study by Coe and Ryken indicated that hypnosis is no more bothersome to subjects than other activities such as taking a college exam and the subject retains the ultimate decision to comply with or refuse the suggestion.[7]

Although hypnosis is a highly controversial subject and leading experts differ in their opinions and research, the academic scientific community has reached the consensus that the popular press has misled the public regarding the nature of hypnosis. Countless movies and books have populated the idea that a human subject can be controlled. Hypnosis expert Robert Baker claims that what we call 'hypnosis' is actually a form of learned social behaviour. The hypnotist and subject learn what is expected of them and reinforce each other's behaviour with their performances. The hypnotist provides the suggestions, and the subject responds to the suggestions. The rest of the behaviour – the hypnotist's repetitious sounds and the subject's trance – are simply window-dressing, part of the drama that makes hypnosis intriguing. Strip away these dramas, Baker argues, and what is left is psyched-up states of suggestibility.[8]

According to psychologist Dr Graham Wagstaff, 'hypnotic subjects do not lose consciousness, control of their behaviour, or their normal scruples'. A definition of hypnosis provided by the American Psychological Association clearly rejects the notion of the hypnotic automaton, and one survey of ten experts on forensic hypnosis, conducted by Vingoe (1995), all rejected the view that 'during hypnosis the control a person normally has over him or herself is in the hands of the hypnotist'.

Wagstaff quoted a similar view expressed by the editors of the contributors to what is probably the most important academic volume on hypnosis to be published that decade, *Theories of Hypnosis* (1991), edited by Lynn and Rhue. They concluded, 'Since the "golden age" of hypnotism (the 1880s and 1890s), the view of the hypnotized subject as a passive automaton under the sway of a powerful hypnotist has faded in popularity. In fact, this rather extreme position is not endorsed by any of the theorists whose ideas are represented in this book.'[9]

Despite the overwhelming evidence that points to the impossibility that a person can be made to commit murder under hypnosis, conspiracists continue to insist there is evidence that such a crime had been committed in the past. In their RFK assassination books conspiracy advocates Philip Melanson, Jon Christian and Lisa Pease, and most recently James DiEugenio and Robert Blair Kaiser, reference Bjorn Nielsen who purportedly hypnotized Palle Hardrup to commit murder in 1951. They used this case as a proven example of how someone can hypnotize another to commit murder. What these conspiracists do not do, however, is inform their readers that Hardrup confessed to making everything up in 1972 in an interview with Soren Petersen of the Danish newspaper *B.T.*[10]

Conspiracists also fail to inform their readers that shortly before he died, Dr Joseph Bryan, Sirhan's alleged hypnotist, confessed to Hollywood reporter Greg Roberts that the Sirhan story was untrue.[11] Bryan's credibility was further damaged when it was discovered he had a history of bragging, consorted with prostitutes and used unethical practices, including having sexual relationships with some of his patients. One associate described him as a 'sexual pervert'.[12]

The CIA and Hypnotism

Conspiracy theorists suggest that the CIA successfully developed drugs and mind-control techniques to manipulate their Cold-War adversaries or to get unwitting persons to do their bidding. Many conspiracists also believe the CIA used these techniques to control Sirhan and then programme him to forget.[13]

However, the agency abandoned the idea that it was possible to turn men into puppets.[14] CIA scientists were also never able to produce 'total amnesia' in a subject. The record shows that the CIA made two attempts to produce a 'Manchurian Candidate Assassin'. The first involved a hypnotist hired by the agency to hypnotize a suspected Mexican double agent. The hypnotist's job was to coax the subject to murder a Soviet KGB agent. Eventually, the hypnotist, code-named 'Mindbender', decided the idea was unrealistic and decided not to continue.

The second attempt occurred in 1966 when the CIA hired a hypnotist to coax a Cuban exile to return to his homeland and assassinate Fidel Castro. The hypnotist tried to coerce three subjects into committing the act – all of the attempts failed.[15]

According to an ARTICHOKE and MKULTRA operative, 'All experiments beyond a certain point always failed because the subject jerked himself back for some reason or the subject got amnesiac or catatonic' and the agency's methods occasionally turned the subjects into vegetables who could not do anything, especially the agency's bidding. A former MKULTRA official told author John Marks that a foolproof way of triggering amnesia could not be found. 'You had to accept,' he stated, 'that when someone is caught, they're going to tell some things'. David Rhodes, a long-serving MKULTRA official, declared, 'Creating a Manchurian Candidate is a total psychological impossibility'.[16]

Conspiracy advocates frequently cite experiments conducted by CIA scientist Morse Allen, who they allege was successful in programming an assassin. Allen hypnotized his secretary, who had a fear and loathing of guns, to pick up a pistol and shoot another secretary. The gun, of course, was unloaded. After Allen brought the secretary out of the trance, she had no memory of what she had done.

Those who promoted this experiment as proof of programmed assassins failed to mention that Allen did not give much credibility to it. Allen believed that he had simply convinced an impressionable young woman volunteer to accept orders from a legitimate authority figure to carry out an order she likely knew would not end in tragedy.[17] Allen also believed there were too many variables in hypnosis for it to be a reliable weapon. And all the participants in such trials knew they were involved in a scientific experiment. An authority figure was always present to remind the subject or some part of the subject's mind that it was only an experiment. The CIA's ARTICHOKE team concluded that it could not effectively hypnotize a subject even though Allen thought it could be possible.[18]

Following years of research into the subject of possible CIA mind-controlled assassin programmes, author John Marks concluded that, '[MKULTRA officials] were not interested in a programmed assassin because they knew in general it would not work and, specifically that they could not exert total control. The CIA had concluded that there were more reliable ways to kill people.'[19]

CIA agent William Buckley, who acted as liaison between the CIA and Ewan Cameron, an MKULTRA psychiatrist who was conducting experiments into the use of hypnosis to build a robotic assassin, said 'MK-ULTRA had become a big, bad, black game which men like Gottlieb and Cameron and others like them played because they wanted to believe. Not actually believe, but wanted to.'[20] Gottlieb confessed to Buckley, 'Nothing worked for me so why should it work for anyone else?'[21]

A leading hypnosis expert, Dr Steve Lynn of Binghamton University, concurs. Lynn believes that a 'trigger [mechanism] that would move someone into a hypnotic state where they would commit murder . . . would [not] really work . . . You do not relinquish your will. You do not become a dupe, a patsy or a mindless automaton despite some public beliefs that this may be the case.'[22]

Sirhan's Hypnotic State

For decades conspiracists have used the robotic assassin theory to get Sirhan off the hook. As recently as May 2008, Sirhan's new attorney, William Pepper, a supporter of Martin Luther King assassination and 9/11 conspiracy theories, reiterated that allegation, stating, 'Sirhan was hypno-programmed'. Pepper provided no real evidence to support his conclusions and simply offered up Sirhan's loss of memory as proof enough.[23]

In his video documentary *RFK Must Die*, Shane O'Sullivan alleges that CIA agents may have been at the Ambassador Hotel the night RFK was assassinated and acted as Sirhan's controllers. That story was successfully debunked not long after the BBC aired it in November 2006.[24]

What the conspiracy writers omit to tell their readers about is the over-whelming and conclusive evidence presented during the 1969 trial and after-wards. This revealed how Sirhan was fully aware of everything around him on the night he killed Robert F. Kennedy and that no credible evidence has ever been discovered that would indicate Sirhan's actions were the product of a hypnotized mind.

During interviews with police officers following his arrest, Sirhan never once asked why he had been arrested. If he had indeed been hypnotized and then came out of the trance in the early hours of 5 June, his most logical first question would have been, 'Why have I been arrested?' Sirhan was also fully alert when he was given a police caution that he need not say anything until he sought legal assistance. He refused to give police officers any details about himself, including his name and address.

In fact, Sirhan played with his interrogators at the police station. The unremorseful assassin kept his identity secret because the arresting officers 'might lose interest in the mystery'.[25] He told arresting officers he wanted to wait 'until I could see what the hell's going on'.[26]

Police tapes further confirm that Sirhan was 'alert and evasive' on the night he was arrested, and this observation was substantiated by all police officers present during Sirhan's questioning. The doctor at the County Jail who examined Sirhan immediately following his arrest also testified to his subject's alertness. He said the suspect was 'self-satisfied, smug and unremorseful'.[27]

Conspiracy advocates point to Sirhan's staring at a teletype machine as evidence that he was hypnotized. Yet Sirhan frequently became strangely fascinated by things around him which provoked him into staring at people or objects. Sirhan told his police interrogators:

> Everything . . . life itself is a challenge . . . When you watch a barber, sir, I just stand and watch that barber for hours. I . . . from the time I'm watching him I want to be nothing but a barber. You know, if I'm watching a dentist, boy, he fascinates me, and I want to be him. I was talking to [LAPD officer] Frank here a while ago.

The way he talked, you know . . . I was very fascinated and, you know, I was sort of superimposing myself in his position for . . . temporarily.[28]

According to Sirhan's mother, her son often experienced trance-like states as a boy growing up in Jerusalem. (Author's note: Robert Blair Kaiser, who came to know Sirhan better than any of the defence lawyers, believed Sirhan knew that the Boston Strangler committed his crimes in a 'disassociated state'. Following his arrest, Sirhan had asked Officer Frank about the Boston Strangler case and how Albert DeSalvo had committed the crimes because he had suffered a deprived childhood. Sirhan told Frank, 'But, correct me if I'm mistaken, is it when . . . the man is self-admitting? He admits that he's, wasn't trying, but they won't believe him? Is this related to it?'[29])

Sirhan's defenders believe the assassin's great physical strength when he was apprehended proves he was in some sort of disassociated state. But friends have testified that Sirhan, although short and slight of build, was very strong despite his size. Conspiracists also claim Sirhan's calm and peaceful state at the time he was apprehended proves he had been in a hypnotic state.

However, as FBI profiler John Douglas discovered, Sirhan's calmness was not at all unusual behaviour for an assassin. With reference to Mark Chapman, who stalked and then murdered John Lennon, Douglas wrote: '[Chapman's unusually calm state] squares with the emotions of so many others . . . Once they decide on their course of action, stress and conflict are lifted.'[30] And, of course, Sirhan was under the influence of the calming effect of alcohol. It has long been established that alcohol greatly reduces inhibitions and often produces a glassy-eyed stare effect as well as, in some people, a trance-like, calm look.

Conspiracists allege that a controller, probably a 'girl in the polka-dot dress', manipulated Sirhan in the Ambassador Hotel – yet they do not explain how, during the weeks preceding the assassination, Sirhan was able to be hypnotized along the lines laid down by their hypnosis experts. These experts believe Sirhan could have become a hypno-programmed assassin only if he was isolated for a considerable amount of time and subjected to brainwashing techniques. According to Dr Herbert Spiegal, who supports the notion that Sirhan was hypnotized at the time of the assassination: '[It could happen if he were] subject to proper programming under control conditions, and subject to some degree of supervision.'[31]

The person many conspiracists say hypnotized Sirhan, Dr William Bryan Jr, also believed the conditioning of the subject would take time and effort before it was successful. In a 1974 broadcast, two years before he died, Bryan stated:

> I am an expert in the use of hypnosis in criminal law, I sure as hell am. You have to have the person locked up physically, to have control over them; you have to use a certain amount of physical torture . . . and there is also the use of long-term hypnotic sugges-tion . . . probably drugs . . . whatever . . . and so on . . . Under these situations where you have all this going for you, like in a prison camp and so on, yes, you can brainwash a person to do just about anything.[32]

However, in Sirhan's case, these brainwashing conditions are unlikely to have been met. Sirhan's movements in the year prior to the assassination leave no unaccountable missing period when the assassin could have been hypnotized and/or indoctrinated along the lines established by the conspir-acists' mind-control experts. Furthermore, family and friends have never indicated Sirhan had ever been under the influence of drugs.

In the year prior to the assassination, waitress Marilyn Hunt had seen Sirhan frequently in Pasadena's Hi-Life Bar. Sirhan also was seen in Pasadena's Shap's Bar during this time, placing illegal bets. In July 1967, Sirhan filed a disability complaint for workmen's compensation. Between July and September 1967, Sirhan's mother and brother Munir said Sirhan often went to the Pasadena Library. Library records confirm he borrowed books during this period.

Sirhan's mother said her son 'stayed at home for over a year [*sic*] with no job' from October 1966 to September 1967. Also, during this period, Sirhan, by his mother's account, often drove her to work. On 9 September 1967, Sirhan began work at John Weidner's health-food store. Weidner reported no long periods of absence up to the time Sirhan left his employ in March 1968.

Sirhan discussed Martin Luther King Jr's murder with Alvin Clark, a Pasadena rubbish collector some days after 4 April 1968. This leaves only eight weeks unaccounted for before Kennedy was murdered. During most of that eight-week period, Sirhan was reported to be in Pasadena. Sirhan's friend, Walter Crowe, said he met Sirhan in Pasadena on the night of 2 May

1968, when they discussed politics. The last time he saw Sirhan was on the Pasadena College campus on 23 May the same year.

Crowe said he was in a Denny's Restaurant when Sirhan entered with a group of friends. Michael Haggarty, a former school friend of Sirhan's, said he last saw him on 23 May, when they discussed Israel. This leaves only a two-week period unaccounted for. In his conversations with Robert Blair Kaiser, Sirhan referred to local newspaper and local radio reports throughout May. Besides, Sirhan was living at 696 East Howard Street, Pasadena and family and friends have never suggested he was missing during this period.

Some conspiracy advocates have referred to an FBI report of an interview with a neighbour of the Sirhans who said Mary Sirhan had told her Sirhan had been missing for some length of time. Mary Sirhan had never said this to her sons or her son's lawyers, and it is likely the neighbour was confused with an incident which occurred many years before the assassination. Sirhan had moved out of the family home and lived in his boss' trailer for two weeks after an altercation with one of his brothers.

The hypnotized assassin theory is also fundamentally flawed. A robotic assassin can never be a guaranteed success; it is an erratic tool. A hypnotist can plant a suggestion in the subject's mind and ask him to forget that suggestion, but there is no foolproof way of preventing another hypnotist from coming along and recovering the memory. How could plotters, for example, be sure that a captured Sirhan would continue to forget about the people who purportedly hypnotized him? How could they be certain he would not give evidence to the authorities in return for immunity? If the plotters' plan was reliant on Kennedy's security to kill Sirhan in the chaos of the shooting, it couldn't have been a very well-thought-out plan. His lawyers could also have built a strong case around the paid-assassin theory, arguing against the imposition of the death penalty that was eventually handed down.

There are additional fundamental flaws in the hypnotized assassin theory. If plotters had successfully hypnotized Sirhan then they would have been equally successful in making sure he didn't do anything to bring attention to himself before the shooting. So why did Sirhan utter contempt for RFK at the Ambassador Hotel that evening to Enrique Rabago and Humphrey Cordero?[33]

There would always have been the possibility these RFK supporters would report Sirhan to the authorities thus putting the plot in jeopardy. And why did conspirators allow Sirhan to use an illegal pistol for the assassination?

Had Sirhan been challenged by police at any time prior to the assassination the whole conspiracy would have collapsed. Conspiracists would also have made sure he was hypnotized not to tell anyone of the purported plot, yet Sirhan did exactly that when he told Alvin Clark of his intention to kill RFK. The testimony of Alvin Clark alone decisively destroys any notion of a hypnotized killer who had been programmed to forget.[34]

Sirhan's Amnesiac State

Sirhan trial prosecutor David Fitts suggested when he cross-examined defence psychiatrist Dr Eric Marcus, 'If he [Sirhan] was suffering from retrograde amnesia [a state induced by emotional shock] he would still be asking questions of the police, like why was he there and what had he done, as if he were suffering from real [organic] amnesia, wouldn't he?' Dr Marcus agreed, and Fitts continued, 'That leaves me with the only working hypothesis – that he was malingering, doesn't it?' Dr Marcus replied, 'Yes, I guess it does.'[35]

Michael McCowan was a private detective who assisted Sirhan's lawyers following the assassin's arrest. He had worked for the LAPD for ten years while attending law school. In the period before Sirhan's trial, McCowan spoke to Sirhan about the shooting. In a response to one of McCowan's questions, Sirhan told how his eyes had met Kennedy's in the moment just before he shot him, before Kennedy had fully turned to his left to shake hands with the kitchen staff.

McCowan asked Sirhan, 'Then why, Sirhan, didn't you shoot him between the eyes?' Without hesitation, Sirhan replied, 'Because that son-of-a-bitch turned his head at the last second.' This statement, not presented at Sirhan's trial, is damning evidence that Sirhan lied when he said he did not remember shooting RFK. When Dan Moldea published part of the McCowan interview in his book, *The Killing of Robert Kennedy* (1995), he was attacked by Sirhan's lawyer, Lawrence Teeter, who claimed McCowan was lying. Moldea quickly had McCowan 'sign a document attesting to this statement'.[36] In 2011, Michael McCowan released his notes to the press, including documentary evidence, in Sirhan's own hand, which revealed the assassin had lied about his amnesia. These notes are discussed later in a subsequent chapter.

McCowan's story is supported by an incident reported in Kaiser's book, *RFK Must Die!* (1970). During Sirhan's trial, hotel workers Jesus Perez and Martin Patrusky both said Sirhan had approached them to ask if Kennedy was coming through the pantry following his speech. Sirhan had insisted he did not remember anything after he collected his gun from his car. However, after the hotel workers presented their testimonies at the trial, Sirhan told McCowan, who was seated next to him, that he had not approached either witness. When McCowan reminded Sirhan that he supposedly remembered nothing of this period before the crime, Sirhan 'nodded and gulped'.[37]

If Sirhan was lying and remembered the assassination, then how was the hypnotic defence constructed in the first place? Sirhan claimed that his lawyers first put forward the idea that he was in a 'hypnotic trance-like state' when he shot Kennedy, but some evidence suggests that Sirhan had knowledge of amnesiac states before he committed the murder.

Sirhan had read Truman Capote's *In Cold Blood*, a book about the murders of a Kansas farmer, his wife and two teenage children. Perry Smith and Richard Hickock committed the murders in 1959, and Capote's book about the murder, manhunt, trial and executions of the killers was published in 1965. Sirhan said he identified with the short and stocky Perry Smith. He felt great empathy for Smith, a man of small stature who had suffered a deprived childhood, had bouts of shivering and trancelike states, and believed in mysticism and fate. According to Capote, Perry Smith 'had many methods of passing [time] . . . among them, mirror gazing . . . every time [he saw] a mirror [he would] *go into a trance*'.[38]

At the conclusion of his book, Capote quoted the opinions of leading psychiatrists Drs Joseph Satten, Karl Menninger, Irwin Rosen and Martin Mayman about why people like Smith and Hickock committed such devastating crimes and what their mental states were during the commission of the murders. The psychiatrists attempted to assess the criminal responsibility of a number of murderers: 'Murderers who seem rational, coherent and controlled and yet whose homicidal acts have a bizarre, apparently senseless qualities.'

In their examinations the psychiatrists found a number of similarities between the murderers, including the fact that the men they studied:

> . . . were puzzled as to why they killed their victims, who were relatively unknown to them, and in each instance the murderer appears to have lapsed into a *dream-like dissociative trance* [italic emphasis added] from which he awakened to suddenly discover himself assaulting the victim . . . Two of the men reported severe disassociate trancelike states during which violent and bizarre

behaviour was seen, while the other two reported less severe and perhaps less well-organized, *amnesiac episodes.*[39]

Sirhan's trancelike state, if it ever existed, could have been caused by his alcohol intake and his intense concentration (the result of his hypnosis self-improvement exercises) rather than any efforts by conspirators to hypnotize him. Alcohol intake frequently causes amnesia, and it is possible that Sirhan's memory was impaired by the Tom Collins drinks he had earlier in the evening. Sirhan confessed he had been drunk, although arresting officers disputed this.

Hans Peter Bidstrup, an electrician at the Ambassador Hotel, said he believed Sirhan was 'half-drunk' at about 10 p.m. on the night of the shooting. Sirhan said he was not accustomed to alcohol and became intoxicated after consuming four Tom Collins drinks. Sirhan said, 'Everybody was – it was like a party – hell, what do people go to parties for? Fun – you know – celebration. So I started drinking.'[40] He also stated: 'I felt I was quite high in my own self, and if I got more drunk, there was nobody to take care of me.'[41]

Sirhan recalled:

> I got into the car, but, hell, I couldn't drive. I was too drunk. The idea of driving in the condition that I was in doesn't appeal to me. Then I said, 'Sober up, try to run around the block if you can, get coffee' and that's what hit me – go and get some coffee at the Ambassador. And I went down again. I don't remember taking the gun with me.[42]

If Sirhan had indeed been telling the truth about his lapse of memory then it was more likely the result of the blocking of his subconscious thoughts because they were too painful at a conscious level. Sirhan's memory lapses were similar to a person who has had a night of heavy drinking and awakes in the morning with the thought, 'What did I do?' In fact, during Sirhan's interview with author Dan Moldea in the 1990s, he said the root of his amnesia might have been his alcohol intake.[43]

Furthermore, if Sirhan did experience memory lapse, his amnesia was not necessarily the result of hypnosis or drunkenness. In North America and Europe, criminals convicted of a violent crime – and 26 per cent of men who have been convicted of manslaughter or murder – frequently claim they cannot recall the actual crime. Some studies indicate that anywhere from

25 to 65 per cent of violent criminals say they do not remember committing manslaughter or murder. With regard to actual amnesia as opposed to feigned amnesia, studies have shown that, 'amnesia is not uncommon in the case of violent crime and in particular homicide where it can occur in 30–40 percent of cases. A related state is "psychogenic amnesia" which is associated with stress'.[44]

Prosecution psychiatrist Seymour Pollack's theory that Sirhan might have deliberately blocked his memory of the shooting has recently received support from research carried out by scientists at Stanford University. The Stanford study found that if people try hard enough, they can forget something they do not want to remember. The study built on Freud's thesis on memory suppression, which suggested that people can be subconsciously influenced by events buried too deeply in their memory to be recalled. The Stanford University scientists found that people in an experiment were able to block certain memories when asked to do so and that scanners could identify which parts of the brain were involved. According to Professor Michael Anderson: 'If you consistently expose people to a reminder of a memory that they don't want to think about and they try not to think about it, they don't remember it as well as memories where they were not presented with any reminders at all.'[45]

Additionally, some research shows that intense stress can cause failure to recall anything learned in a given situation. Experts have concluded that the combination of stress hormones in the brain that occurs during intense trauma results in post-incident amnesia in which, immediately after a critical incident, the majority of information will not be remembered. The greater the trauma, the more likely a subject is to experience post-incident amnesia.

Keith Ashcroft, head of the Centre for Forensic Psychopathology in Manchester, England, agrees and has concluded that, 'there are certain psychological defences which stop people remembering things, and one of those is trauma'.[46]

FBI profiler Russell Vorpagel also supports the notion that traumatic episodes can lead to amnesia. He believes that forgetting 'is a way of subconsciously lying to your conscience'.[47] However, some leading experts are sceptical of criminals who use the amnesia defence. One expert, C. Cantor, believes that, 'Amnesia is easily feigned and difficult to disprove in criminal cases, in the 11-year experience of the author . . . no case of psychological (psychogenic) amnesia in the absence of a psychotic episode, brain tumour, or brain syndrome was ever confirmed'.[48]

The most credible evidence, however, shows that Sirhan was feigning amnesia and lied when he stated he could not remember killing RFK. Sirhan's first demonstrable lie about his memory lapse occurred when he said he could not remember writing in his notebooks, 'RFK must die'. But FBI handwriting analysis concluded that Sirhan had written the entries, albeit haphazardly, jumping around from page to page in the notebook, and that he had not written them when under the influence of a hypnotic trance.[49] It was also clear to ACLU lawyer Abraham Lincoln Wirin that Sirhan remembered that his notebooks contained incriminating evidence. The morning after the shooting, Sirhan had asked him to tell his mother to 'tidy up his room' which Wirin interpreted as asking his mother to get rid of his notebooks which proved premeditation.[50]

In a conversation with Robert Blair Kaiser, Sirhan's amnesiac defence crumbled when he told the defence investigator that he thought Lee Harvey Oswald and James Earl Ray had acted as cowards by shooting their victims from behind. Kaiser asked Sirhan if his act was less cowardly. Sirhan responded, 'Hey, when you shoot a man in the back? There you go! At least Kennedy saw me.' Sirhan quickly and disingenuously added: 'I think, I don't know.'[51]

Sirhan also revealed how disingenuous he was by faking his outbursts in court during his trial. He told his brother Adel he had planned them all along.[52]

Sirhan was also cunning and deceptive with the doctors who hypnotized him before his trial began. He was forthright with defence psychologist Dr Bernard Diamond when he was under hypnosis, yet he refused to answer important questions when prosecution psychologist, Dr Seymour Pollack, hypnotized him. Pollack responded to Sirhan's memory blocking by telling him:

> Whenever we try to get you to talk about these things that are important, you pull away, you fall asleep. We spent a half hour trying to find out where the gun was. How could you carry the gun from your car . . . near Wilshire? How could you carry a gun from there back to the Ambassador Hotel and not know you had it?[53]

The notion that Sirhan Sirhan (or Oswald) had been hypnotically controlled by others does not bear up under close scrutiny. There is no credible evidence that Sirhan was hypnotized by others to murder Robert F. Kennedy, nor is there any credible evidence he was controlled by others during the commission of his crime. Those who believe this to be true have not understood the truths of hypnosis, the CIA secret experiments to create a robotic assassin or the manipulative and cunning nature of the assassin.

There is no doubt Sirhan had been mentally disturbed in some way when he killed Robert F. Kennedy. However, his mental illness was not the product of a hypnotized mind but rather the disturbance created by fanatical anti-Jewish and anti-Israeli propaganda emanating from the hatred that spewed out of the Middle East.

* * *

Commentary 2022

In the years that followed my original research and the publication of the above article I discovered new evidence that addresses Sirhan's purported hypnotic state. In 2018, for example, journalist Ronen Bergman revealed that Israel's Mossad intelligence agency came to the conclusion that hypnotising an assassin was a futile and unreliable way of eliminating a target.

In May 1968, the Israeli Intelligence services were advised by a Swedish-born navy intelligence psychologist, Binyamin Shalit, of the possibility that a hypnotized killer could be used to assassinate Yasser Arafat, the PLO leader. Shalit said a Palestinian prisoner with the 'right characteristics to undergo brainwashing and hypnotism' could be sent across the border to Jordan, join Fatah forces there and attempt to kill Arafat.

Sharit's plan was approved by the Israeli government. The Palestinian selected by Sharit was a 28-year-old, 'solidly built . . . swarthy man . . . not particularly bright, easily influenced, and seemingly not entirely committed to Yasser Arafat's leadership'. However, Rafi Sutton, the Israeli Intelligence operative who was to oversee the plan, said it was a 'foolish, crazy idea'.

After two months of so-called 'brainwashing', the Palestinian was sent to Jordan in December 1968. Although Shalit insisted the assassin was in an 'optimal hypnotic state', the plan ended in failure when the hypnotic killer turned himself into the Katameh, Jordan's police. He told the police officers that Israeli agents had tried to brainwash him into killing Arafat and handed over his pistol. When he was handed over to Fatah he made a 'passionate speech in support of Yasser Arafat'.[54]

Additionally, I discovered an overlooked part of a witness statement in the FBI's RFK files. It was made by one of Sirhan's co-workers at John Weidner's health-food store. Carol Burgess said that Sirhan 'believed in what he called "Witchcraft"'. The FBI report stated:

> And he believed he has the power to do greater things than did others. [Burgess] said he had indicated in words not now recalled, that he 'could do anything that God could do'. She said he seemed not to 'understand our religion', however, he never explained what his religion was. She added he said, 'There are lots of things you can do if you put your mind to it'. Sirhan had once given her a paperback book, title and author not recalled, concerning Witchcraft, for her to read. She said she took it home, did not read it, and brought back the book the next day. She said Sirhan had said he read by candlelight from candles on a table. She said she asked him in connection with his witchcraft what he did, would he lift tables by witchcraft. Sirhan said he did. She said she told him he could not be serious and Sirhan remarked that he was. She said he came back from lunch one day with two red candles and two blue candles apparently to read by or to use in his witchcraft.[55]

A further discovery involved an overlooked tape recording of an interview police held with Merla Stephens. She witnessed Sirhan pretending to be hypnotized by a friend. During his short time as a Pasadena College student Sirhan associated with Arab students. After he flunked college, he continued his associations. Stephens, who worked at a bar/restaurant in Pasadena, told of how Sirhan and a friend she called 'Ali' frequented the place where she worked.

Stephens said at one time Sirhan and his friend acted out a scene in which Ali would pretend to hypnotize Sirhan who then began to behave as though he was a controlled automaton. It is likely Sirhan and his friends were attempting to impress the girls who worked in the bar. Sirhan's unsuccessful ploys to attract young women were apparent to those who knew him. In fact, at one point in his adult years he was so enamoured with a beautiful local young woman, Peggy Osterkamp, he wrote about her in his diaries, but knew, as he confessed to author Robert Blair Kaiser, he did not have any chance of romancing her.[56]

Additionally, the idea arose among conspiracy writers that as Sirhan showed unusual strength when he was apprehended following the shooting it meant he was in a hypnotized state. The idea, however, does not stand up to close scrutiny. According to a friend of Sirhan's:

> Sirhan was strong, of wiry build . . . Sirhan engaged in the normal number of fights with other boys during their early acquaintance and Sirhan indicated he was frequently teased because he was a foreigner. Sirhan told [redacted] that at first he did not fight back when teased and would allow himself to be beaten, but later on learned how to fight and usually won his fights.[57]

Chapter 9

The 'Mystery' of the Polka-Dot Girl

'RFK Assassination: New Revelations from the FBI's "Kensalt" Files', first published by History News Network, 2009

Commentary 2022

Many conspiracy writers relate how Sirhan had been missing for a two-week period – enough time for him to be hypnotized, they say. They often cite a report given to police investigators after the RFK assassination. However, conspiracists fail to tell their readers the 'missing two-week period' occurred in 1963 when Sirhan had an argument with his brother Saidallah. Sirhan called the police because he was afraid to live in the same house as Saidallah. At this point he was working for a gardening business and stayed in his boss' trailer a few blocks away from the Sirhan home..

Unable to pinpoint when this 'missing time' occurred, conspiracists suggest it was during the period when he injured himself after falling from a horse when working as a hotwalker/trainee jockey. Sirhan did indeed have a short stay in hospital, but it occurred in late 1966 and the doctors overseeing his treatment stated Sirhan stayed in a Corona hospital overnight and not a number of weeks as conspiracists allege. The doctors had no reason to lie.

Sirhan's movements in the year prior to the assassination leave no unaccountable missing period when the assassin could have been hypnotized and/or indoctrinated in a way conspiracists allege – a process that is generally accepted, by those who believe it is possible, to take weeks or months.

However, conspiracists continue to claim that a group of conspirators took control of Sirhan and secreted him away for a period of 'brainwashing'. The group allegedly included a woman who had been seen with Sirhan at a gun range and who was allegedly observed at the Ambassador Hotel wearing a polka-dot dress.

* * *

As the US people look back forty years to the tragic assassination of one of their most gifted leaders, conspiracy advocates have once again attempted to prove a conspiracy was behind Robert F. Kennedy's murder. Internet sites and blogs are awash with bogus revelations and the repetition of long-abandoned myths which imply there is proof that RFK's assassin, Sirhan Sirhan, had been aided in his crime.

In the years following the assassination various official investigative bodies concluded there was no credible evidence to link Sirhan with co-conspirators. Yet conspiracy advocates have been persistent in raising issues which cast doubt on those findings.

There were indeed many anomalous pieces of evidence in the case which included problems with the ballistics and forensics evidence and witness statements which raised the possibility that Sirhan had not been alone when he assassinated RFK. This is entirely normal and consistent with most murder investigations, particularly those major investigations where human error is inevitable because of the vast amounts of paperwork and physical evidence accrued. Additionally, forty years ago, police forces were not as careful in securing a murder scene as they are now.

Most of the so-called RFK assassination mysteries were addressed by investigative journalist Dan Moldea, who successfully debunked many allegations by his thorough research and interviews with LAPD officers.[1] Despite the work of Moldea and others, conspiracists have continually resurrected four central areas of contention which they have used to cast doubt on the RFK assassination official investigations:

1. The allegation that Sirhan Sirhan was never close enough to RFK to fire the fatal shot.
2. The presence of a mysterious 'polka-dot-dress girl' and her accomplices who allegedly were the only people who fled the pantry after the shots were fired and were seen on a fire escape, proclaiming they had shot RFK. Conspiracists claim the mystery woman 'controlled' a 'hypnotically-programmed Sirhan'.
3. Allegations that more than eight shots had been fired in the pantry of the hotel proving a second gunman had been present.
4. Witness statements that purportedly established the presence of a second gunman in the pantry of the Ambassador Hotel.

Conspiracists have alleged the second gunman was either security guard Thane Cesar or bookstore clerk Michael Wayne.

However, overlooked evidence in the FBI 'Kensalt' files reveals how conspiracists have constructed their conspiracy scenarios on false assumptions.

Sirhan's 'Point-Blank' Shot

One of the enduring myths of the RFK assassination, repeated ad nauseum by conspiracy writers and documentary makers alike, is the allegation that Sirhan was never less than 3ft away from the Senator thus the assassin was unable to fire the point-blank fatal shot to RFK's head.

One of the most recent allegations to this effect were made by Sirhan's new attorney, William Pepper, conspiracy advocate Robert Joling and author David Talbot. Pepper said: 'There is no account that pushes him any closer than 3 or 4 feet away from Bob Kennedy in front of him.'[2]

Joling stated: 'Sirhan was never in a position where he could shoot Senator Kennedy from behind'. Talbot wrote in his recent book *Brothers*: 'But not one witness saw Sirhan shoot Kennedy in the back of his skull at point-blank range. According to witnesses, Sirhan attacked Kennedy from the front.'[3]

Conspiracists are clearly in error as the 'Kensalt' files prove – 'Kensalt' was the codename for the FBI investigation. Many of the twelve eyewitnesses who were close to RFK when he was shot stated that Sirhan was anywhere from 3 to 12ft away from RFK. However, Dan Moldea established the majority of the twelve witnesses gave estimates of muzzle distance based only on the first shot and did not see Sirhan lunging at the Senator.

Vincent DiPierro clearly saw this happen, as he has often stated. 'It would be impossible for there to be a second gun', DiPierro told reporter Ron Kessler in 1974, 'I saw the first shot. Kennedy fell at my feet. His blood splattered on me. I had a clear view of Kennedy and Sirhan.'[4]

DiPierro recently stated that, 'Sirhan . . . was three feet away but the muzzle of the gun (in his outstretched arm) couldn't be more than 3 to 5 inches away from his head'. According to DiPierro, Sirhan managed to stretch his arm around Karl Uecker who was escorting Kennedy through the pantry. Uecker was facing away from RFK when Sirhan reached around him to place the gun at RFK's head.[5] This is supported by other witness statements, particularly those of Boris Yaro and Juan Romero who had been very close to RFK during the shooting. Boris Yaro stated RFK was shot at 'point-blank range'. Romero, who had been shaking hands with RFK when the shots rang out, initially said the gun was a 'yard away' but in a 2003 *LA Times* interview he said that Sirhan 'put out his hand to the Senator's head . . . Then I see the guy put a bullet in the senator's head.'[6]

The statements of Yaro, Romero and DiPierro can now be supported by a previously overlooked statement in the 'Kensalt' files by the wife of writer George Plimpton, Freddy Plimpton. She 'saw an arm go up towards Senator Kennedy's head, but did not see a gun, heard shots and it was obvious to her that Senator Kennedy had been shot . . . She saw Sirhan very clearly. She saw his arm up toward Senator Kennedy's head.'[7]

Sirhan's Alleged Accomplices

Conspiracy advocates have promoted the idea that Sirhan Sirhan was controlled by a girl in a polka-dot dress when he shot RFK. Witness Sandra Serrano, who conspiracists often cite as proof of a plot to kill RFK, told police that a girl in a polka-dot dress first entered the Embassy Room via a fire escape accompanied by two men. According to Serrano the girl fled with one of her accomplices down the same stairway about 20 minutes after they had arrived proclaiming, 'We shot Kennedy.'

Although there were inherent problems with Serrano's story from the beginning, including testimony by a Fire Department inspector who said she was not on the fire escape at the time she stated, there is overlooked evidence in the FBI files that confirms Serrano may have been telling the truth after all – or at least a version of the truth. This newly discovered evidence buried in the FBI files has been ignored by assassination writers and researchers for nearly forty years and sheds new light on what Serrano actually saw and heard.

Serrano told investigators that the emergency fire stairs she had sat on were located on the south side of the Ambassador Ballroom. Large double doors opened on to the stairway from a hallway adjacent to the ballroom. From this doorway the stairs went down to ground level and up to double fire doors leading into the Embassy Room which was located directly above the Ambassador Ballroom.

According to the FBI files, Geraldine Agnes McCarthy, a Kennedy supporter, had given a statement to FBI agents which described her activities at the time of the shooting. She had been with members of her family in the Ambassador Ballroom. The party consisted of Geraldine McCarthy, Margaret McCarthy, Winnie Marshall, Mary Towley, Eileen Anderson, Phil

Litroh, Chris Marshall and Paul Benedict. They were waiting for the final election results and the victory speech by RFK.

Shortly after midnight on 5 June 1968, she and several members of her family left the stage and went to a small alcove to the left of the stage and near the rear of the ballroom. This alcove had access to a stairway leading up to the Embassy Room and also had access to an outside door opening onto the Wilshire Boulevard parking lot of the hotel. She stated that immediately outside this doorway to the parking lot there was a fire escape leading down from the floor above.

McCarthy and several members of her family were in this alcove attempting to get a breath of fresh air when several people came down the stairway from above and a girl in an orange dress stated, 'Kennedy has been shot.' Shortly after that a girl in a 'beige dress with black dots' came down the outside fire escape and exclaimed, 'Oh my God, Kennedy's been shot.'

Geraldine McCarthy told FBI agents that at no time did she hear anyone make the statement, 'We've shot Kennedy.' She stated that several more people came down the stairway of the fire escape and she asked them questions attempting to verify what they had heard, and it became apparent to her that RFK actually had been shot. McCarthy's story was confirmed by a family member, Mrs Winnie Theresa Marshall.[8]

Given this 'new' evidence it is clear that Serrano had been mistaken in hearing the girl in the polka-dot dress shouting, 'We shot him.' But even if Serrano heard correctly, another explanation is possible without resorting to speculations about conspiracies. Serrano may also have been witness to an innocent cry of 'We [i.e. the US people] shot Kennedy'; a natural response reflecting the intense concern Americans had at that time to the growing senseless violence that had become a societal phenomenon during the 1960s. In fact, a number of Embassy Room witnesses heard people in the crowd shout 'We shot him'.

Albert Victor Ellis, a roommate of John Shamel, the hotel's convention manager:

> . . . heard a female voice state 'We shot him'. He assumed at the
> time this person meant we the people . . . he left the Embassy
> Room . . . and went out into the lobby . . . where numerous peo-
> ple were milling around . . . he heard several other people . . .
> state something to the effect 'We shot him' and from the other

conversations he was able to determine that they meant that the people were the cause of Senator Kennedy being shot.[9]

Laurie Gail Porter, the daughter of California state senatorial candidate Shelley Porter, was in the Embassy Room during RFK's victory speech. After hearing the shots from about 50ft away she heard her friend Robin Casden shout, 'We shot him.' She 'did recall . . . there were several people who shouted, "We shot him" and she attributed the exclamation to the hysterical nature of the situation'.[10]

In fact, Sandra Serrano offered this explanation to FBI agents when she was interviewed. According to an FBI memo, 'Miss Serrano was asked if this woman could have said, "He shot him" or "They shot him" rather than "We shot him". Serrano insisted the word was "we" but volunteered that she realized that "we" could have meant we, meaning we as a group of Kennedy supporters or as we as society in general.'[11]

This overlooked evidence in the case may also place in the correct context a report made by LAPD Sergeant Paul Sharaga that a couple he remembered as the 'Bernsteins' told him shortly after the shooting they had observed a young woman in a polka-dot dress, accompanied by a young man, laughing and shouting, 'We shot him.'[12]

It is clear from the FBI files that a second polka-dot girl, besides Valerie Schulte, had indeed been present in the pantry at the time of the shooting. Howard 'Cap' Hardy, for example, among others, saw a young woman in the pantry at the time of the shooting and she had been wearing a 'sleeveless dress, off-white in color, with navy blue circles on it. The blue circles were of different sizes and the smaller circles had a white peace symbol in them and the larger circles had the word "McCarthy" in lower case white letters . . . she was not with anyone'. Howard said she later joined a group of Kennedy supporters in the Embassy Room.[13]

Unable to give any real meaning to the sightings of a polka-dot-dress girl in the pantry and unable to positively state the girl was with Sirhan, conspiracists have attempted to show her actions in the pantry after the shooting were suspicious. They have, therefore, given some importance to the statements made by witness George Green and Security Guard Jack Merritt to the effect that the polka-dot girl and her accomplice/accomplices were the only people attempting to leave the pantry at the time of the shooting or immediately afterwards.

Conspiracy writers have clearly misunderstood the testimonies of these witnesses. FBI files also show that they have misinterpreted Merritt's statement and of how Green was mistaken in his belief that the polka-dot girl and her accomplices were the only people fleeing the pantry at the time of the shooting. Others who fled the pantry at the time of the shooting or shortly after the shots had been fired include Charles D. White, Boris Yaro, Thomas Perez, Evan Freed, Uno Timanson, Angelo DiPierro, Robin Karen Casden, Barbara Rubin, James W. Lowe, Gonzalo Cetina-Carrillo, Trudy Jennings, Freddy Plimpton and Marcus McBroom.

Richard D. Little recalled that 'one of the Kennedy girls . . . came running out of the kitchen to the lobby of the Embassy Room shouting "They shot him"'.[14] Fred Meenedsen said he saw a 'man calling for a doctor [who] came running out. Next, an unknown woman . . . ran through these kitchen doors and said Kennedy had been shot as she went towards the lobby'.[15]

Furthermore, it is clear the conspiracists have mischaracterized Merritt's original statement. According to the FBI's 'Kensalt' files, 'In the confusion [Merritt] noticed, among others, two men and a woman leave the kitchen through a back exit . . . she was wearing a polka dot dress . . . *other people also left*'.[16]

From the FBI interviews with these pantry witnesses it is evident they had been fleeing the pantry for non-suspicious reasons including running to a phone, looking for police officers, evading gunfire or looking for doctors to attend to the pantry shooting victims.

There were also plenty of deranged individuals around that night to give cause for concern about the behaviour of some individuals at the time of the shooting. The *Daily Express* photographer Harry Benson said that after the shooting he 'went outside the ballroom where there was a white male . . . with a United States flag in his mouth . . . a real nutty guy who said something such as "Thank God, he's been shot"'.[17]

Henrietta Sterlitz and her friend Evelyn Planavsky saw, 'two teenage boys and one teenage girl . . . pop balloons and . . . exclaim "Kennedy's Dead!"', shortly before the assassination.[18] These individuals may have been the teenagers in Sharaga's police report mentioned above.

Conspiracists believe the fact the 'girl in the polka-dot dress' did not come forward after the mystery was publicized is supportive of a sinister interpretation of events. However, there is a more logical explanation. The national media was referring to the girl as a possible accomplice in

RFK's murder. And some newspaper reports were seriously considering the possibility RFK may have been assassinated as the result of a conspiracy. Given these conditions it is natural that the girl and her colleagues would not want to risk being charged as co-conspirators even though their actions that night were entirely innocent.

There is also an inherent illogicality to Serrano's story which appears to be lost on conspiracy advocates – why would escaping plotters immediately proclaim to the world their involvement in the assassination? How could they be sure members of the public wouldn't take them seriously and ask police officers to apprehend them before they could make good their escape?

Allegations That More Than Eight Shots Had Been Fired

The notion that more than eight shots were fired in the pantry of the Ambassador Hotel has gained credence among doubters since the airing of a Discovery Times television documentary in June 2007.

The documentary claimed that a second gunman aided Sirhan in the pantry of the hotel. An audio engineer hired by the Discovery Times Channel had claimed he had detected thirteen shots on an audio tape made by a journalist at the time of the shooting. However, the Discovery Times Channel's claims have proven to be flawed by acoustics experts (Philip Harrison and Professor Peter French).

Additionally, the Discovery Channel's allegation that two shots fired in quick succession had been too close to have been fired by one gunman was also built on erroneous assumptions. The audio engineers quickly discounted a ricochet because the end of the room was too far away to produce a ricochet sound as quickly as it is heard on the tape. However, they never considered the possibility the bullet could have ricocheted off any of the metal surfaces (pots, pans, tray stackers and a metal serving table) anywhere in the pantry, not just off the far wall.

Earwitness testimony had never established a scenario in which thirteen shots had been possible. FBI files show all the pantry witnesses, with the exception of only a few, never heard more than eight shots and those few who guessed they heard further shots did not put the number beyond ten. The FBI files, furthermore, show that no one who had been in the pantry when Robert F. Kennedy was shot told the FBI or LAPD that anywhere near thirteen shots had been fired. Only one witness gave this number, Nina Rhodes, but she never said this at the time she made her original statement in 1968. In 1968 she said she heard 'eight distinct shots'. In 1992 Rhodes told conspiracy authors that she heard between ten and fourteen shots.[19]

According to the FBI files, most of the estimated seventy-seven witnesses in the pantry could not remember how many shots had been fired and described the gunshots in terms of 'a number of shots', 'a series of firecrackers', 'several shots' or 'a number of shots in rapid succession'. However, of those witnesses who ventured an opinion about how many shots had been fired all but a few put the number of shots at eight or less. They included Harold Edward Hughes, Pete Hamill, Ralph Elmore, Joseph A. LaHive, Richard Aubry, David Saul Barrett, Richard L. Cohen, David M. Esquith, Jacqueline Sullivan, James Cummings, Paul Green Houston, Richard Edward Drew, Bob Funk, Roosevelt Grier, Robert Anthony Toigo, Barbara Rubin, Freddy Plimpton, Lon Bruce Rubin, Dun Gifford, Charles Bailey, Jimmy Breslin, Stanley Kawalac, Robert Ray Breshears, Thomas Perez, Uno Timanson and Rafer Johnson.

The 'Second Shooter'

RFK conspiracy advocates believe a second gunman (whom conspiracists claim was security guard Thane Cesar) had been present in the pantry when RFK was shot. They build their case on statements by witnesses who claim they saw someone other than Sirhan carrying a weapon and who fled the pantry before he could be apprehended.

Conspiracists cite the statements of Marcus McBroom, Evan Freed, Don Schulman, Booker Griffin, Patricia Nelson and Dennis Weaver as indicative of a second gunman firing in the pantry. However, as the FBI files show, these statements have been misinterpreted, taken out of context or simply lack credibility. Conspiracy writers have used these statements to infer that Thane Cesar or Michael Wayne or both men had been assisting Sirhan in the pantry. Conspiracy writer James DiEugenio recently named Michael Wayne and Thane Cesar as Sirhan's accomplices and said they both participated in the shooting.[20]

However, the FBI files reveal how conspiracy writers have manipulated the original statements of witnesses to claim there is evidence of a second gunman.

In 1986, nearly twenty years after the assassination, Marcus McBroom told a conspiracy writer that 'a man with a gun under his newspaper ran out in a very menacing way and myself and a man by the name of Sam Strain and the man running the ABC camera drew back instinctively when we saw the gun'.[21]

Marcus McBroom's original interview with FBI agents reveals no mention of a second gun.[22] And McBroom's friend, Sam Strain, did not see a gun, as his statement to the FBI demonstrates. Strain stated that the young man appeared to be carrying 'a package about two feet long and six inches wide which was wrapped in black paper of some type'.[23]

Dr Fred S. Parrott told FBI agents that while he was standing outside the door to the Embassy Room, a man came by carrying a rolled-up newspaper under his arm followed by men shouting 'Stop that man! Stop that man!' He described the man with the newspaper as a white male, dark complexion, dark hair, 25 to 27 years old, 5ft 7in tall, medium build.[24]

This description fits that of Michael Wayne who, at the time of the assassination, was a 21-year-old clerk at the Pickwick Bookstore in Hollywood and an avid collector of political memorabilia. After the shooting Wayne ran out of the pantry area and because someone shouted, 'Get him, he's getting away', Security guard Augustus Mallard grabbed him then put him in handcuffs. Wayne told police he was only running for a telephone to tell friends to turn on their television sets. He was interviewed by the LAPD but was never considered a suspect.[25]

Other witnesses have been used by conspiracists to show a second gunman had been present in the pantry. However, it is clear from the FBI files that the person who these witnesses believed had carried a gun that night was actually Michael Wayne. Patricia Nelson and Dennis Weaver told FBI agents they believed they saw a man with a rolled-up newspaper or poster and that the wooden stock of a rifle had been protruding from it. However, they later stated they were likely mistaken and identified the man as Michael Wayne. Nelson later identified Wayne from film footage of the hotel shown to her. 'That's him. That's the same sweater, the same hair, the same sideburns', she told agents. She also identified the package as the one she saw.[26] Weaver agreed with Nelson.[27] Joseph Klein, who was with them at the time said, 'That's him right there, I'm positive.'[28]

It is clear from these interviews that the man McBroom, Parrott, Strain, Weaver, Nelson and Klein had observed was Michael Wayne, despite the differing descriptions given to agents. Wayne had earlier in the evening been photographed by Bill Eppridge. Eppridge's photo shows RFK autographing Wayne's poster as the Senator walked to the Embassy Room to give his speech. It is clear from Eppridge's photo that the poster in Wayne's hand is too small to hold a pistol let alone a rifle.[29]

Other initial sightings of a second gunman were later found to be the result of misidentification or misunderstanding – or a change of heart many years after the assassination which suggested some witnesses had been heavily influenced by conspiracy buffs. Booker Griffin, for example, told a conspiracy writer in 1987 that he had observed a second gunman. However, in his 1968 interviews with the LAPD he only said the sounds of the shooting appeared to suggest more than one gun.[30]

Evan Freed and Don Schulman are cited by conspiracy writers as having observed a second gunman. In an interview with FBI agents on 14 June 1968, Freed said he saw two men and a woman leave the pantry in a hurry after the shooting. And in 1992 Freed reportedly signed a document to the effect that more than one gunman was present in the pantry and that he had observed another man who looked like Sirhan. However, Freed had inadvertently sent an uncorrected draft of what he described as 'a letter' to lawyer Marilyn Barrett. He amended it to read:

> At about the same time, I saw the 'second man' . . . who I described as resembling Sirhan . . . it is possible he could have been holding a weapon, but I cannot be sure . . . I cannot say how many shots were fired by Sirhan Sirhan or whether any shots came from the 'second man'.[31]

Freed's comments made in 1992 were entirely consistent with his statement to FBI agents on 11 September 1968.[32]Furthermore, his 1992 comments about a 'second man' are entirely consistent with the preponderance of evidence presented above which suggests this was actually Michael Wayne – a Sirhan look-alike.

To this day Freed continues to insist he never saw a second gunman in the pantry of the Ambassador Hotel when RFK was assassinated. His most recent denial was in the DVD documentary *RFK Must Die*. Freed said:

> [In the early 1990s] I was asked a number of times did I see a second shooter? Are you sure you didn't? And I got the feeling that people were trying to convince me that I saw something that I didn't really see. My recollection is I only saw one person shooting that night and that's what I told the police when I was interviewed by

the police. That's what I told the FBI when I was interviewed by the FBI.[33]

However, the conspiracists' favourite 'second gun' witness is Don Schulman, a KNXT-TV news runner. Statements made by Schulman have been used for decades in an attempt to prove Thane Cesar had fired the fatal shot that killed RFK.

Immediately following the shooting Don Schulman was interviewed by Jeff Brent of Continental Broadcasting and said a security guard 'had fired back'. In 1971 Schulman said he did not see Sirhan shoot Kennedy, but he insisted that he saw the 'security guard' fire his gun. He also said he saw wounds erupting on Kennedy's body but refused to make any connection between the two events.

However, Schulman later retracted his statement of having seen a second gunman citing his confusion during the chaotic moments of the shooting. In the mid-1970s Schulman told the Kranz Investigation (which was set up by the Los Angeles authorities to look into allegations made by conspiracy theorists) that immediately following the shooting he was 'tremendously confused' and that the words he used to describe the shooting to reporters in 1968 were the result of 'confusion'. Schulman reported that he meant to tell reporters that, 'Kennedy had been hit three times, he had seen an arm fire, he had seen the security guards with guns, but he had never seen a security guard fire and hit Robert Kennedy.'[34]

Furthermore, new ballistics evidence has eliminated the possibility Cesar had fired his .38 pistol that night.[35] And the idea that Thane Cesar had carried his .22 pistol – Sirhan used a .22 to kill Kennedy – and used it to shoot RFK cannot be supported by either hard evidence or logic.

Thane Cesar carried a .38 pistol on the night of the assassination but he owned an H and R .22 pistol. However, accusing Cesar of having used his .22 pistol to kill RFK appears ridiculous at the outset – why would a murderer, under threat of execution if caught, hang on to the purported murder weapon for three months before he got rid of it? Cesar sold his H&R .22 pistol in September 1968.

For forty years conspiracy theorists have used human error to build their case for a non-existent conspiracy. Conspiracists believe Thane Cesar murdered RFK. Why? Simply because Cesar was standing behind RFK at the time of the shooting and pulled his gun after RFK fell to the floor. Don Schulman saw Cesar pull his gun and Schulman believed he fired it. Schulman later retracted his statement and confessed he had been mistaken. Sandra Serrano thought she heard a girl in a polka-dot dress shout 'We shot Kennedy' but the preponderance of evidence suggests what she heard was entirely benign.

Some witnesses believed people running away from the scene of the crime were co-conspirators but the police investigation proved that many of them were simply running to a telephone or seeking medical assistance or evading gunfire. Some witnesses believed the girl in the polka-dot dress and her companions who were in the pantry during the shooting were the only ones to flee the scene of the crime, thus rendering their actions suspicious. But, as we have seen, others ran out of the pantry at the same time.

The new and overlooked evidence in this case highlights more than anything else the way conspiracists have tortured the evidential record in order to build smokescreens and spread doubt. To paraphrase historian Richard Hofstadter, the RFK conspiracy theorists' procedure is to start with defensible assumptions using heated exaggeration to prove that the unbelievable is the only thing that can be believed.

* * *

Commentary 2022

Following the publication of this article conspiracy theorists continued to claim there was indeed evidence that a girl in a polka-dot dress accompanied Sirhan in the pantry of the Ambassador Hotel and quickly left after the shooting.

In 2016, one conspiracy writer, Ferdinand Faura, claimed he had solved the mystery of the polka-dot girl in his book, *The Polka Dot File on the Robert F. Kennedy Killing: The Paris Peace Talks Connection.* On 12 June 1968, Faura recorded a long interview with John Fahey before the government apparently frightened Fahey into recanting, Faura said. Fahey told Faura he had spent the better part of the day of the assassination with a stranger who turned out to be 'the girl in the polka-dot dress'. She told him her name was Geraldine Oppenheimer.

Faura has a riveting story to tell, full of real-life intrigue and mystery, about how he and a few other dedicated citizens chased down important leads that the LAPD and FBI ignored or sought to suppress. The bulk of his account seems rational and factual especially as it had the benefit of Faura's writing style.

Faura writes of a chance meeting between two strangers; a woman named Gilda Oppenheimer and a man called John Fahey. We read that within a very short time of these two individuals meeting, the woman was confiding in Fahey of a plot to kill RFK; 'they're going to take care of Mr. Kennedy tonight'.

Purportedly, the girl asked for Fahey's name, where he worked, what he did for a living. Fahey answered and asked what she was doing at the hotel. 'I don't want to get you involved,' she said. She then informs Fahey that she doesn't want to tell Fahey what she is doing. '[Fahey's] bigger surprise came with her next question. Could he come to the hotel tonight, to the winning reception, to watch them get Mr. Kennedy?'[36]

As with most conspiracy stories Faura's account collapses once he tries to interject some meaning in Fahey's fantastic tale. With scant evidence, Faura builds his case on baseless accusations and cites dubious sources to bolster his claims which includes promoting New Orleans District Attorney Jim Garrison's bogus JFK investigation.[37]

Most ridiculous is his allegation that a powerful US Senator could have been involved in the assassination conspiracy because he was a 'womanizing heavy drinker'. And, like many a conspiracy theorist that has gone before, Faura is not afraid to name and libel the long-deceased purported Senator/conspiracist who is unable to sue.

However, what Faura fails to tell his readers is the true story of the LAPD and the FBI investigation into Fahey's false story. When interviewed by the FBI Fahey said he had been followed by two men – Sirhan and his brother Munir. He said Munir threatened him. On 6 June Fahey told agents about the threats to investigators based in the Los Angeles office of the FBI. He said that on 4 June 1968 at 9 a.m. he was at the Ambassador Hotel coffee shop to keep an appointment. His expected appointment did not arrive. As he waited, he noticed two men talking in a foreign language and they looked of Latin appearance. He then engaged in a conversation with an 'attractive woman' outside the coffee shop. As they sat in the coffee shop the woman, a complete stranger to Fahey, began to tell her story.

Witnesses who were interviewed by the FBI said they had not seen Fahey at any of the places he visited accompanied by a 'Ms Oppenheimer'. His boss told FBI agents Fahey had mentioned that one of the men in one of two vehicles that followed him after his coffee shop meeting with the girl had pulled a gun on him. Fahey failed to mention that fact to others he told the story to.

On 18 June 1968, Fahey told FBI agents he had told the story to Fernando Faura. Both men were subsequently interviewed by FBI agents and their story began to unravel. Fahey was given a polygraph test on 30 August 1968 and the examiner stated Fahey had been deceptive.

Moreover, the FBI discovered through an independent investigation that Munir Sirhan was at work during the time Fahey alleged he had seen him. Also, Fahey's addition of a second vehicle to the incident he related made a significant change to his story and he contradicted himself each time he met with agents. Most damning to Fahey were the recollections of former employers who described Fahey as 'emotionally unstable' and 'highly irritable and unreliable'.

Due to the many discrepancies in his story Fahey was asked to take a polygraph examination on 5 September 1968. The result was damaging to Fahey's claims. The examiner said Fahey had been untruthful in his answers about meeting a woman who allegedly told him RFK was going to be killed and he was untruthful when he said he had been truthful with LAPD police officers. Fahey also answered honestly when he said he had never seen Munir Sirhan.

On 9 September Fahey asked to speak to FBI agents. At the meeting he confessed to picking up a woman at the Ambassador on 4 June but the rest of his story was a 'figment of his imagination'. He said Fernando Faura had strongly influenced him in his thinking that what he had told the police had actually occurred.[38]

In 2018 two other writers, Tim Tate and Brad Johnson, claimed to have identified the polka-dot-dress girl – a woman named Patricia 'Elayn' Neal, an alcoholic and paranoiac who kept a polka-dot dress in her attic. Every now and again she would get the dress out, put it on and parade around the room with a 'sad face'. And the proof that she was the 'girl in the polka-dot dress' who was purportedly Sirhan's 'trigger' at the Ambassador Hotel? Someone in her high-school class joined the CIA after graduation.

Conspiracy writer Lisa Pease criticizes me for using Geraldine Agnes McCarthy and her family members to rebut Sandra Serranno's story. Pease wrote: 'Ayton misunderstood the placement of a witness he claimed rebutted Serrano, not realizing that his witness was on the Wilshire side of the hotel, not the 8th Street side where Serrano sat.'[39]

The FBI report of Geraldine's mother, Margaret McCarthy, however, states:

> Shortly after midnight the room became very close and stuffy so she and several others went to a small alcove to *the left and rear of the Ambassador Ballroom* [italic emphasis added], where they attempted to get a breath of fresh air. This alcove had a stairway leading up to the next floor where the Embassy Room was located; there was a door leading to the Wilshire Street parking lot with a fire escape leading upstairs directly outside this door.[40]

The left and rear of the Ambassador Ballroom places the McCarthy family outside the south-west fire escape where Serrano was situated. We are thus left with a conundrum. Either the report was correct in placing the McCarthy group on the other side of the building to Serrano or the report was incorrect and the McCarthys were wrong about on which side of the building they were positioned. I believe the report was in error in placing the family at the Wilshire Boulevard side of the building. To believe otherwise means an incredible coincidence occurred – that is, two men with their female partners, both wearing polka-dot dresses, exited the Ambassador Hotel through fire escapes on either side of the building at exactly the same time with both women exclaiming either, 'We shot Kennedy' or, 'They shot Kennedy.'

Chapter 10

The Myths of the RFK Assassination

'A Lie on Every Page – A Review of a Lie Too Big to Fail: The Real History of the Assassination of Robert F. Kennedy by Lisa Pease', first published by Washington Decoded, *2019*

Commentary 2022

Many myths about the assassination of Robert F. Kennedy have been built on the chaotic scenes in the pantry of the Ambassador Hotel, including the number of shots fired, earwitness and eyewitness accounts of the shooting, and the positioning of Sirhan when he fired his pistol.

However, as wounds and ballistics expert Larry Sturdivan stated to this author:

> If anybody . . . tells me he can reconstruct the location and posture of each person in that room at the time of each shot, I would con-clude that he was delusional. If I were there, I would guarantee that my location and posture would change continuously between shots and there would be no way I could remember exact locations or postures at any given moment. Photographs help, but one cannot pinpoint the time of the photograph to the millisecond and that's what one would need to do to reconstruct a trajectory from gun to entry point.[1]

A more rational approach to the anomalies that existed in the collection of evidence regarding the shooting comes from Dan Moldea. He said no witnesses were focusing on Sirhan Sirhan's actions once shots were fired because they instinctively dived for safety, leaving him free to pin Bobby down and force the close-range shots that others claimed no one witnessed.

Moldea said:

Sirhan Sirhan shot Bobby Kennedy and he acted alone. When a civilian investigator is looking for a conspiracy in a highly publicized case like this, he's probably gonna find it, but you have to run through the gauntlet of re-examining the evidence and in this case, all of the large questions that would indicate a second gunman at the crime scene go by the wayside.[2]

In recent years Lisa Pease became the most prominent of the RFK assassination conspiracists who propagated the myths surrounding the assassination. In 2019 she published her book about the case, *A Lie Too Big to Fail*, which attracted media attention. However, readers of her book were probably unaware of how preposterous some of her other conspiracy theories have been over the years. Among her many conspiracy beliefs, for example, is the idea that the US government was behind the 2001 terrorist attack on New York and Washington DC.

The following article critically examines her claims regarding a purported RFK conspiracy.

* * *

Since the publication of *The Forgotten Terrorist* in 2007, Sirhan Sirhan has continued to claim he is innocent of the murder of Robert F. Kennedy. Another shooter was actually responsible, Sirhan asserts, adding, in contradiction, that he has no memory of the event. He was a 'hypnotized assassin' and therefore not responsible.

Sirhan's defenders chime in that he was not in a position to shoot Kennedy in the head, and thus a second assassin in the pantry must have been culpable. They also say an audio tape recording of the shooting 'proves' there was a second gunman.

During these same twelve years, the US media have carefully followed Sirhan's efforts to persuade the courts and the California Parole Board he should be released, after fifty-one years of confinement. These news stories, with very few exceptions, have re-propagated the tall tales of conspiracy advocates. One recurring refrain is that of purported 'assassination witnesses' who disavow their original testimonies and now support the notion that Kennedy was killed by someone other than Sirhan. It goes without saying that vital evidence to the contrary is always omitted during the breathless presentation of such bogus revelations.[3]

There is no doubt the LAPD investigation of the assassination was less than optimal. Some possible leads were not exhausted, some evidence was handled incorrectly and the all-important ballistics investigation was not one for the textbooks.

Yet the same could be said of nearly every major criminal investigation. The likelihood of human error is compounded in high-profile crimes because of the vast amounts of paperwork and physical evidence that must be processed. Anomalies are perhaps the major reason why conspiracy advocates have been able to plant doubt in the minds of the US public, by representing simple or inadvertent mistakes as conspiratorial shenanigans.[4]

Conspiracy advocates have promoted a false history of the RFK assassination (the same as their JFK brethren do) by deliberately skewing evidence in the case to suit their agenda. And unfortunately, in too many cases they have been aided and abetted by gullible journalists who do not know their way around the mountains of evidence collected by the FBI and the LAPD. The media is thereby complicit in leaving the public confused.

These are the six central myths about the Robert F. Kennedy assassination that have been concocted by conspiracy theorists and given credence by a too-credulous mainstream press:

1. Sirhan was never in a position to fire the fatal shot that killed Senator Kennedy in the kitchen pantry of the Ambassador Hotel in Los Angeles on the night of 4–5 June 1968. Conspiracists posit that a security guard positioned behind the Senator fired the fatal shot.

2. An audio recording of the shooting allegedly recorded thirteen or fourteen shots being fired in the pantry. If so, this proves there was a second gunman since Sirhan's revolver held only eight bullets.

3. Sirhan was a hypnotized assassin, programmed to kill. He was also programmed to forget who hypnotized him and the circumstances of the shooting.

4. Sirhan's amnesia about the assassination is genuine.

5. Sirhan was aided by a 'girl in a polka-dot dress', who was seen with Sirhan in the days before the assassination.

6. Sirhan was not interested in politics and therefore had no motive to commit political murder.

The most recent incarnation of these fables appears in Pease's *A Lie Too Big to Fail*. The theories in her book relentlessly recycle just about every fabrication and falsehood conspiracists have managed to dredge up in the five decades since the 1968 assassination, inserting them into public discourse.

Until recently Pease had been a marginalized conspiracy author deservedly ignored by the mainstream media and published by the likes of Feral House. In February 2019, however, that changed when the *Washington Post* touted her findings. Shortly afterwards, Pease's book was featured on a morning television news show in Los Angeles on the KTLA channel. KTLA is not just another LA television station. It began broadcasting in 1947, and for decades was an authoritative source of local news, viz., it was the first station to broadcast the infamous Rodney King tape. The station assiduously covered the 1968 Kennedy assassination with many reporters who were local legends and had great sources inside the LAPD. To feature Pease was to do down KTLA's own contemporary reporting of the assassination.

The *Washington Post* article was written by Tom Jackman, a reporter who had previously written a series of articles to coincide with the fiftieth anniversary of Robert F. Kennedy's assassination. One can find more ludicrous articles about the assassinations of the 1960s. But normally they are found in the *National Enquirer*, while Jackman's recitations of crackpot theories appear in, of all things, the storied *Washington Post*.[5]

The lead 'fake news' in Jackman's account was Pease's allegation that Robert Maheu, an aide to business magnate Howard Hughes, was responsible for Robert F. Kennedy's murder, and that Maheu was acting, moreover, on behalf of the CIA. The allegation rests almost entirely on an unproven, if not improvable, accusation made by another former Hughes aide named John H. Meier in 2015 – in other words, long after everyone concerned was dead and could sue Meier for libel.

The *Washington Post* deceptively published a stiff denial of the allegation by Maheu's son, Maheu himself having died in 2008. Missing from Jackman's reporting, however, was some crucial context, namely that Meier has been labelled a 'conman', a 'multi-million-dollar fraudster' and a 'liar' according to a reputable journalist and other authors who have dealt with him previously.[6]

Nor does Jackman provide much context to Pease and her irrational speculations. She believes the US government was responsible for the 9/11 attacks, and that the CIA/government was responsible for the JFK, Malcolm X and

Martin Luther King Jr assassinations prior to knocking off RFK – and for good measure, was probably guilty of the attempted assassination of George Wallace and John Lennon's murder twelve years later.

Pease's book is chock full of speculation from beginning to end, 'what ifs' she doesn't even pretend to have answers to. An outstanding example of her methodology concerns the lack of evidence that another cheap revolver was present in the pantry. There are reasons another murder weapon wouldn't have been seen, she asserts, '[W]hat if the gun was in . . . a rolled-up poster? . . . What if the gun were hidden under a busboy's towel? . . . Hidden in a pocket? Fired from within a purse . . . what if the gun was disguised in another object?'[7]

A Lie Too Big to Fail creates mysteries where none exist, defaming innocent bystanders in the process. It is nothing more than an army of paranoid speculations moving over the landscape in support of a pre-determined theory: the CIA did it.

Myth No. 1: Sirhan Was Not Close Enough to Fire the Fatal Shot

It comes as no surprise when Lisa Pease puts front and centre the most enduring myth of the RFK assassination, repeated ad nauseam by other conspiracy writers and documentary makers. Pease writes, 'No credible witness ever placed Sirhan close enough to get his gun muzzle within an inch of Kennedy's head'. This falsehood is the allegation that Sirhan was always at least 3ft away from the senator and thus not in a position to fire the point-blank fatal shot to RFK's head. The allegation is voiced by virtually everyone who writes about a purported conspiracy.[8]

A most recent proponent of this view is Robert F. Kennedy Jr, who expressed it during a 2018 interview with the *Washington Post*. 'It's not only that nobody saw that,' he said. 'The people that were closest to [Sirhan], the people that disarmed him all said he never got near my father.'[9]

In their never-ending quest to introduce mystery where no mystery exists, conspiracists omit vital statements made by eyewitnesses who were very close to Kennedy when he was shot.

As eyewitness Vincent DiPierro told the *Washington Post*'s Ronald Kessler in 1974, it is true that Sirhan was standing about 3ft in front and slightly to the right of Kennedy. But a moment before Sirhan whipped out his handgun, Kennedy turned to his left to greet some busboys. Then, while in the act of firing, Sirhan also lunged forward, bringing the muzzle of his Iver Johnson revolver to within inches of Kennedy's head. 'It would be impossible for there to be a second gun,' DiPierro told Kessler. 'I saw the first shot. Kennedy fell at my feet. His blood splattered on me. I had a clear view of Kennedy and Sirhan.'[10]

Decades later, DiPierro's memory had not diminished. During a 2018 radio interview, DiPierro stated:

> I saw the gun come from the right side of my eye and [Sirhan's arm] was outstretched . . . We always talk about the upward trajectory . . . Well, Sirhan was shorter than Robert and he was also stretched out so that his arm was an extended version going in an upward trajectory . . . There was nobody between Robert, Sirhan, and me . . . The first shot was directly to his head . . . I got sprayed with the bullet to his head . . . There was a pause because Robert's hands went up to his head . . . the third bullet hit the top of his jacket . . . and the fourth shot went through my shirt . . . I didn't get hit . . . A lot of people said there were more than eight shots. Well, there was a lot of popping, a lot of banging. I only saw seven shots come out of the gun. There were eight.[11]

Long ago, DiPierro's testimony was essentially corroborated by several witnesses, including the wife of the late writer George Plimpton, Freddy Plimpton. She told the FBI in 1968 that she 'saw an arm go up towards Senator Kennedy's head, but did not see a gun, heard shots and it was obvious to her that Senator Kennedy had been shot . . . She saw Sirhan very clearly. She saw his arm up toward Senator Kennedy's head.'[12]

Not content with ignoring testimony that contradicts a conspiracy, Pease also grievously distorts the observations of witnesses who were at the scene, such as Don Schulman, who described what he saw to two TV crews shortly after the assassination. Although Pease admits to Schulman's confusion about the shooting, she nevertheless believes his initial and confused account that a security guard had shot Kennedy. (Schulman: '[I] saw a man pull out a gun . . . and shoot three times . . . I saw all three shots hit the senator . . . I also saw the security men pull out their weapons . . . the security guards fired back'.[13])

However, Schulman later retracted and clarified this account, explaining that when he made it initially he was 'tremendously confused'. In his corrected account, Schulman said he meant to tell reporters the following:

'Kennedy had been hit three times, he had seen an arm fire, he had seen the security guards with guns, but he had never seen a security guard fire and hit Robert Kennedy.'[14]

Contrary to Pease's beliefs, the real evidence in this case is clear: as Sirhan approached the Senator with an outstretched arm and gun in hand, Kennedy turned his head to the left in a defensive stance. RFK's right arm rose, and his body was bending in a downwards motion at the time he was shot in the head. The arc of the gun was following Kennedy's head as the Senator stooped to avoid his assailant.

Myth No. 2: The Pruszynski Tape Recording

Pease accepts, without reservation, the claims made by an audio engineer that a tape recording of the sounds of the shooting – the Pruszynski tape – contained thirteen or fourteen shots. The tape recording was released in the late 1980s with a batch of documents and other evidence that were part of the LAPD investigation into the shooting. The recording was made by a Polish journalist, Stanislaw Pruszynski, who accidentally left his tape recorder running when the shots were fired.

Conspiracy advocates, including Pease, cite the subsequent research conducted by an audio engineer named Philip van Praag, who concluded thirteen or fourteen shots could be identified on the tape.

At the same time van Praag was researching the audio tape I enlisted the assistance of two acoustics experts, Dr Philip Harrison and Dr Peter French of J.P. French Associates, based in York, England. Dr Harrison conducted the tests and his work was verified by Dr French. Harrison was able to identify seven impulse sounds (which are characterized by a sharp onset and rapid decay) that corresponded to Sirhan's gun being fired to the exclusion of another weapon (the seven impulses all exhibited similar characteristics). An eighth shot could not be clearly identified on the spectrogram made from the tape recording; this sound appeared to be masked by other noise, including loud screams.

Harrison's conclusions were confirmed by a trio of Americans who have spent decades examining the scientific aspects of the JFK assassination. Steve Barber, Michael O'Dell and Chad Zimmerman all independently examined a digital version of the master tape. They concurred with Dr Harrison's conclusion that the tape captured the sound of no more than eight gunshots.[15]

Clearly unable to understand Philip Harrison's acoustics research, Pease has, for years, misinterpreted his report. In her latest comment Pease wrote: 'The expert found seven shot sounds and "three possible locations" for the "eighth shot." To any reasonable, honest person, that means Ayton's expert found ten possible shot sounds – two more than Sirhan's gun could have fired.'[16]

Harrison objects to this characterization of his research, and maintains he has not altered his firm belief that 'no more than eight shots' can be found on the tape. Harrison wrote, 'I haven't heard or seen anything since the work I previously did that would make me change my mind as to it being eight shots or less.'[17]

Despite the controversy over the Pruszynski tape, it is counterintuitive to assume thirteen or fourteen shots were fired when every pantry witness who ventured a guess at the number of shots, with the exception of three, put the number at eight or less.

When RFK was assassinated, approximately seventy-seven people were caught up in the mayhem that followed the shooting. Kitchen utensils were being knocked over, doors were banging, balloons were bursting, and people were shouting and screaming. Of the pantry witnesses who volunteered a guess at how many shots were fired, thirty-five put the number at anywhere between three and seven. A few witnesses claimed there were more than eight shots.

At the time of the assassination and afterwards no witness said they heard anywhere near thirteen or fourteen shots. A very small number changed their minds after talking to conspiracy minded authors, however. Among these witnesses was Nina Rhodes-Hughes, who told CNN reporter Brad Johnson in 2011 there were more than a dozen shots fired. Yet, according to her 1968 FBI interview, she heard 'eight distinct shots'. Rhodes-Hughes explains this discrepancy away by claiming her 1968 statement was falsified by the FBI.[18]

Myth No. 3: The Hypnotized Assassin

Like conspiracy theorists before her, Pease believes that Sirhan was a hypnotized assassin programmed to forget. She takes Sirhan at his word that he cannot remember anything after drinking coffee with a girl at the Ambassador Hotel – until he became aware of being choked as he was subdued by Kennedy's bodyguards in the kitchen pantry.

Falling further down the rabbit hole, Pease argues that a hypnotized Sirhan served as a distraction in front of Kennedy, firing blanks and drawing the crowd's attention, while the actual shooters shot Kennedy from behind and escaped. She cites a number of witnesses who thought the sounds of the shooting were like those of a cap gun emitting shredded paper which fluttered through the air. This is the totality of her proof that Sirhan did not fire real bullets.

Pease cites hypnotists Bjorn Nielsen and Derren Brown as evidence that hypnotized assassins can be created. Nielsen purportedly hypnotized Palle Hardrup to commit murder in 1951. But on 5 August 1972, Palle Hardrup gave an interview to Soren Petersen of the Danish tabloid newspaper *B.T.* He admitted he had not been hypnotized into committing the murders. Presaging Sirhan's imaginative defence in 1968, Hardrup told the *B.T.* journalist that when the police had suggested that hypnotism had caused the crimes, he realized he 'might get off the hook' if he agreed.[19]

Pease also naively alleges a show-business hypnotist, Derren Brown, had successfully 'programmed' a 'Manchurian Candidate-style' assassin during one of his television shows. The entertainer himself, however, has scorned these claims. In 2018 Brown said:

> The more bewildered we are, the more susceptible we become . . . I'm quite open about how the whole thing I do happens in inverted commas, so not to believe everything you see or hear. It's a form of entertainment. Some of it's real and some of it isn't. Hopefully, part of the fun is trying to unpick that.[20]

Pease also accepts without reservation the conclusions of Dr Daniel Brown, who has asserted that Sirhan 'did not act under his own volition and knowledge at the time of the assassination and is not responsible for actions coerced and/or carried out by others'. According to Brown, Sirhan was a 'true "Manchurian Candidate," hypno-programmed into carrying out a violent political act without knowing it'.[21]

Brown is a proponent of 'recovered memory syndrome' which postulates that some patients who have suffered trauma in their lives have, over the years, suppressed memories of it – and yet it is possible to revive these memories through proper treatment. The existence of repressed memory recovery has not been accepted by mainstream psychology, including by the

Royal College of Psychiatrists in Britain, the British Psychological Society and the American Psychological Association. According to the latter, it is not possible to distinguish repressed memories from false ones without corroborating evidence. Some experts in the field of human memory believe that no credible scientific support exists for the notions of repressed/recovered memories. The mechanism(s) by which both of these phenomena happen are not well understood.[22]

Many conspiracy advocates believe the CIA used hypnosis to control Sirhan and then programmed him to forget. The agency, however, had long before abandoned the idea that it was possible to turn men into puppets. CIA scientists were also never able to produce 'total amnesia' in a subject, and a CIA scientist named Morse Allen came to the conclusion there were too many variables in hypnosis for it to be a reliable tool for such a sensitive activity. The Israeli Mossad came to the same conclusion. Their officers once attempted to hypnotize a Palestinian into killing Yassir Arafat but the plot failed when they discovered that hypnosis was unsuccessful in creating the desired results.[23]

It seems clear Sirhan himself was the original propagator of this fantasy. There is compelling evidence, as already stated, that Sirhan used his knowledge of Perry Smith, a real-life murderer portrayed in Truman Capote's 1965 book *In Cold Blood*, to promote the fable that he, too, had been in a hypnotic state when he shot RFK. Sirhan, an avid reader, identified and felt great empathy with Smith, according to author Robert Blair Kaiser. Smith had bouts of 'shivering', 'amnesia' and 'trance-like states', and like him, Sirhan engaged in 'mirror-gazing' and fell into 'trances'.[24]

The hypnotized assassin theory is fundamentally flawed because a robotic assassin can never be a guaranteed success. A hypnotist can plant a suggestion in the subject's mind and ask him to forget that suggestion, but there is no foolproof way of preventing another hypnotist from coming along and recovering the memory. How could plotters, for example, be sure that a captured Sirhan would continue to forget about the people who purportedly hypnotized him? How could they be certain he would not give evidence to the authorities in return for immunity?

It should come as no surprise, then, that California courts have roundly rejected Brown's 'hypnotized assassin' theory.[25]

Myth No. 4: Sirhan's 'Amnesia'

Pease devotes an entire chapter of her book to the illusion that Sirhan's behaviour on the night of the assassination indicated he had been hypnotized to act as a patsy, shooting blanks as a cover for the real assassins, and then programmed to forget.

Many leading hypnosis experts are sceptical of criminals who use the amnesia defence. One expert has written, 'Amnesia is easily feigned and difficult to disprove in criminal cases . . . [I]n the 11-year experience of the author . . . no case of psychological (psychogenic) amnesia in the absence of a psychotic episode, brain tumour, or brain syndrome was ever confirmed.'[26]

There is ample evidence showing Sirhan's amnesia defence is bogus. Readers do not need to take a course in psychiatry and 'repressed memory' to judge whether or not Sirhan has been lying when he says he cannot remember shooting Robert F. Kennedy.

Alcohol intake frequently causes amnesia, and it is possible that Sirhan's memory was impaired by the Tom Collins drinks he had earlier in the evening. Still, the first demonstrable lie about his memory lapse occurred when he said he could not remember writing in his notebooks, 'RFK Must Die'. It was clear to American Civil Liberties Union lawyer A.L. Wirin, who visited the accused assassin in jail shortly after the shooting, that Sirhan in fact remembered his notebooks contained incriminating evidence. The morning after the assassination, Sirhan asked Wirin to tell his mother to 'tidy up his room', which Wirin interpreted as asking his mother to get rid of the notebooks that proved premeditation.[27]

In a subsequent conversation with Robert Blair Kaiser, Sirhan's amnesiac defence crumbled again when he told the defence investigator that he thought Lee Harvey Oswald and James Earl Ray had acted as cowards by shooting their victims from behind. Kaiser asked Sirhan if his act was less cowardly. Sirhan responded, 'Hey, when you shoot a man in the back? There you go! At least Kennedy saw me.' Sirhan quickly and disingenuously added, 'I think, I don't know.'[28]

Sirhan's explanation of having no memory of the shooting was also in direct contradiction to documentary evidence compiled by Michael McCowan, another Sirhan defence investigator during the 1969 trial. In 1995, Dan Moldea reported that Sirhan told McCowan of the moment when his eyes met Kennedy's just before he shot him. Shocked by what Sirhan had just admitted, McCowan asked, 'Then why, Sirhan, didn't you shoot him between the eyes?' With no hesitation and no apparent remorse, Sirhan replied, 'Because that son of a bitch turned his head at the last second.'[29]

In 2011 McCowan produced a manuscript of notes Sirhan made in his own hand. This new evidence effectively destroyed the amnesia defence Sirhan continually raised at his parole hearings. The historically important manuscript shows, clearly and vividly, that Sirhan did in fact remember the events of 4–5 June 1968, directly refuting his defence that he suffered from amnesia and/or was hypnotized and then programmed to not remember. Though he perhaps drank too much that night, the behaviour described in this manuscript was controlled and intentional.[30]

Myth No. 5: The 'Girl in the Polka-dot Dress'

Conspiracy minded authors have long promoted the notion that Sirhan's 'handler' that evening was a young woman wearing a polka-dot dress. The myth has been repeated for decades despite compelling evidence to the contrary that emerged, indicating that Sandra Serrano, the 'star witness' for the polka-dot story, simply heard outraged expressions of distress at the assassination of yet another Kennedy or, alternatively, embellished her story. The polka-dot-girl story is, essentially, a red herring. The LAPD had no choice but to investigate the story lest the police be accused of a cover-up. Unfortunately, that decision gave the story unwarranted credence.

Evidence in the FBI files confirms that even if Serrano was telling the truth about her encounter – hearing the exclamation 'We shot him!' right after the assassination – this statement amounted to nothing more than an innocent cry of anguish. Serrano's well-publicized story is a glaring example of how easily twisted words can often distort the truth.

The words Serrano heard do not necessarily suggest co-conspirators acted in concert with Sirhan. According to the FBI's interview of eyewitness Albert Victor Ellis, who also heard a female voice state, 'We shot him', Ellis immediately assumed this person collectively meant 'the American people' when she said 'we'. Ellis then went out into the lobby of the Ambassador Hotel, according to the FBI, where numerous people were milling around, and heard others say something to the same effect, viz., that 'We shot him' meant people in general were the cause of Senator Kennedy being shot.[31]

Similarly, Laurie Gail Porter, the daughter of California state senatorial candidate Shelley Porter, was in the Embassy Room during RFK's victory speech. After hearing the shots from about 50ft away, according to her FBI interview, she heard her friend Robin Casden shout, 'We shot him.' Porter in fact recalled 'several people shouted "We shot him" and she attributed the exclamation to the hysterical nature of the situation'. For that matter, even Serrano herself admitted to police officers that the polka-dot-dress girl's outcry could have meant that 'we the people' assassinated Kennedy.[32]

Putting aside the interpretation of the overheard exclamation, RFK assassination investigators also discovered many flaws in Serrano's story. On 8 June 1968, FBI agents questioned her parents, Manuel and Amparo Serrano, who said their daughter had not said anything about a girl in a polka-dot dress claiming responsibility for the assassination. When asked later why she did not mention the polka-dot-dress girl to her mother, Serrano explained that she had always had trouble talking to her mother.[33]

Other aspects of Serrano's story were also challenged by two government workers, deputy district attorney John J. Ambrose and fire-department captain Cecil R. Lynch. Ambrose had been approached by Serrano shortly after the shooting. He told FBI investigators a few days after the assassination that Serrano said she had been, '*walking down the hall* [italic emphasis added] when a man and woman approached her from the opposite direction. Both were walking and the girl stated "We just shot him." Serrano then inquired what the girl meant by this and the girl stated, "We just shot Senator Kennedy".'

Serrano later changed her story to say she had been *sitting on the stairs of a fire escape* [italic emphasis added] when the couple said they had shot Kennedy.[34]

Serrano's later account was also contradicted by Lynch, the fire-department captain, who had been on duty at the Ambassador checking fire escapes and exits. He had inspected the stairs Serrano claimed she had been sitting on. He said no one was on the stairs at the time she indicated.[35]

Additionally, an FBI agent took Serrano to the Embassy Room and told her:

> On television, with [NBC correspondent] Sandy Vanocur, you didn't say anything about seeing a girl and two men going up the fire stairs. You only said you saw a girl and a man coming down. And later you told the police you saw two men and a girl going up together and one of them was Sirhan Sirhan. That was

the most significant thing you had to tell the police and yet you
didn't say anything about this in your first interview, your interview on television.

Serrano replied, 'I can't explain why.'[36]

The lack of veracity in Serrano's polka–dot–girl story did not prevent Pease
from repeating it and adding further mystery by claiming the polka–dot girl
had met Sirhan at a shooting range the day before the assassination. The
range master, Everett Buckner, had originally told police that a 'blonde'
woman at the range had spoken to Sirhan and said, 'God damn you, you son
of a bitch. Get out of here or they will recognize us.'[37]

The 'blonde girl' was Claudia Williams; she was a barmaid in the San
Gabriel Valley with a husband and two children. Police tracked her down
and interviewed her. She said Sirhan had simply shown her how to use her
new gun. Police then confronted Buckner with her story and he retracted it
saying he heard a woman say something to Sirhan but he didn't know what
it was.[38]

Pease attempts to prove that Williams was not the woman who allegedly
spoke to Sirhan in order to bolster Buckner's original story. Her attempts
to promote the idea, however, that Buckner was correct all along fail.
Witness statements by Henry Carreon, Ronald and Claudia Williams, David
Montellano and Charles Kendall match with what the police said about the
time Sirhan spent at the gun range and that he was there at the same time as
the Williamses.[39]

Myth No. 6: The Non-Political Sirhan

Pease's attempts to portray Sirhan as a mild-mannered, non-violent and
apolitical individual destroys what's left of her credibility. She quotes six
acquaintances of Sirhan – including his gas-station boss, Jack Davies, a
co-worker at the station, Sidney McDaniel, and his landscape-gardener boss,
William Beveridge – all of whom characterize Sirhan as non-violent, polite
and mild-mannered. The same selective and sentimentalized characterization could be applied to just about every assassin in US history.

Pease's description of Sirhan is risible. The author wilfully ignores the
statements made by many of Sirhan's family, friends and work colleagues
who painted a completely different picture of the assassin. These witnesses
unequivocally describe Sirhan as a 'highly political' person.

Among the many descriptions of Sirhan by those who knew him well include those of his brothers Munir, Sharif and Adel, friends Walter Crowe, William A. Spaniard, Lou Shelby, William Divale and John and Patricia Strathmann, as well as his former boss John Weidner and a former teacher, assistant professor of anthropology Lowell J. Bean. They all agreed that Sirhan was quick-tempered, hated Jews and was intense and emotional whenever he discussed the Arab–Israeli conflict. They all agreed he was vehemently critical of US foreign policy regarding Israel.

His brother Munir said Sirhan was 'stubborn' and had 'tantrums'. Sirhan was anti-Semitic in his political views and also espoused a belief in violent action as a political tool. He admired the Black Panthers and the Black Muslims and wanted to join their organizations. According to his brother Munir, Sirhan attended the Black Muslim Temple in central Los Angeles until he was told he could not join the organization because he was not black. He did, however, purchase some Black Muslim literature.[40]

William A. Spaniard, a 24-year-old Pasadena friend of Sirhan's, said the young Palestinian was 'a taciturn individual'. Fellow students at Pasadena College concurred – sort of. They characterized Sirhan as not only 'taciturn' but also 'surly', 'hard to get to know' and 'withdrawn and alone'. One of his professors saw Sirhan and another student have an argument that 'almost became a fist fight'. He said Sirhan had 'an almost uncontrollable temper'.[41]

As a young adult, Sirhan sought meaning by embracing anti-Semitism, anti-Americanism and Palestinian nationalism. Sirhan's parents taught him the Jews were 'evil', 'stole their home' and they also taught him to hate, despise and fear Jews. As a part-time gardener Sirhan came to hate the Jews whose gardens he tended.[42]

Sirhan's brother Adel said his sibling became angry with television reports of the Arab–Israeli conflict and would 'walk across the room with a sour face very fast and get away'. Another brother, Sharif, told Egyptian journalist Mahmoud Abel-Hadi that, following the broadcast of an RFK pro-Israel speech on television, 'he [Sirhan] left the room putting his hands on his ears and almost weeping'.[43]

Walter Crowe, who had known Sirhan from the time they were teenagers, said Sirhan was virulently anti-Semitic and also espoused a belief in violent action as a political tool. Crowe said Mary Sirhan propagated these views to Sirhan.[44]

Crowe believed al-Fatah's terrorist acts were justified and that Palestinian terrorists had gained the respect of the Arab world. He said Sirhan spoke of 'total commitment' to the Palestinian cause and took a left-wing position on issues such as racism and the Vietnam War. However, Crowe said, Sirhan was a 'reactionary' when it came to the Arab-Israeli conflict. Crowe believed that Sirhan saw himself as a 'committed revolutionary' willing to undertake 'revolutionary action'. Sirhan was for 'violence whenever, as long as it's needed'. Later Crowe came to feel guilty about the part he may have played in putting ideas of terrorist acts into Sirhan's head and reinforcing Sirhan's resolve to commit a violent political act.[45]

Lou Shelby was Adel's boss and the owner of the Fez Club in Hollywood. He knew the Sirhan family intimately and described Sirhan as 'intensely nationalistic with regard to his Arab identity'. According to Shelby:

> We had a really big argument on Middle East politics . . . we switched back and forth between Arabic and English. Sirhan's outlook was completely Arab nationalist – the Arabs were in the right and had made no mistakes. I tried to reason with him and to point out that one could be in the right but still make mistakes. But he was adamant. According to him, America was to blame for the Arabs' misfortunes – because of the power of Zionism in this country. The only Arab leader he really admired was Nasser and he thought Nasser's policies were right. The Arabs had to build themselves up and fight Israel – that was the only way.[46]

John and Patricia Strathmann had been 'good friends' with Sirhan since high school. According to John, Sirhan was an admirer of Hitler, especially his treatment of the Jews, and was impressed with Hitler's *Mein Kampf* and the Nazi leader's 'hypnotic control over people'. John also said Sirhan became 'intense' and 'mad' about the Arab-Israeli Six-Day War just a year earlier. Sirhan's friend Elsie Boyko said Sirhan had always been fervent and emotional whenever he discussed the Arab-Israeli conflict and was critical of US foreign policy regarding Israel.[47]

Sirhan discussed politics, religion and philosophy with his boss, John Weidner, a committed Christian. Weidner was honoured by Israel for his heroism in saving more than 1,000 people from the Nazis. Sirhan worked for Weidner from September 1967 to March 1968. It was Sirhan's touchiness, arrogance, feelings of inadequacy and inferiority, and resentment of authority that caused friction between employer and employee. Weidner described Sirhan as 'a hot-tempered man' with 'fantasies'. 'He had strong patriotic feelings for his country [Palestine]', Weidner recalled.[48] Weidner also confirmed that Sirhan 'hated Jews . . . because of their power and their material wealth . . . they had taken his country from his people who were now refugees'.[49]

The notion that Sirhan never held any animus towards Robert F. Kennedy is entirely without foundation as Sirhan's friends and Sirhan himself revealed. According to one of his lawyers at the trial, '[Sirhan] was disturbed that both his mother and his brothers did not see Senator Kennedy as the same destructive and malevolent and dangerous person as Sirhan perceived him to be; and I gather that he and his family, his mother and brothers, had some arguments about this.'[50]

Sirhan thought RFK would be:

> . . . like his brother the president, and help the Arabs but, 'Hell, he f ***** up. That's all he did . . . He asked for it. He should have been smarter than that. You know, the Arabs had emotions. He knew how they felt about it. But, hell, he didn't have to come out right at the f ****** time when the Arab-Israeli war erupted.[51]

Sirhan also expressed hatred for Robert F. Kennedy to John Shear, an assistant to trainer Gordon Bowsher at the Santa Anita Racetrack. Shear recalled that the newly hired Sirhan heard a co-worker read aloud a newspaper account of Robert F. Kennedy recommending the allocation of arms to Israel. 'Sol [Sirhan] just went crazy,' Shear said. 'He was normally very quiet, but he just went into a rage when he heard the story.'[52]

No Decency
Lisa Pease adheres closely to the conspiracists' playbook: admit to none of the available, credible evidence while spewing uncorroborated speculation as fact, all in the service of fingering a preferred and predetermined culprit.

To help persuade readers of an immense conspiracy, the reputations of innocent people are besmirched, yet that is of no consequence. Thane Eugene Cesar was an armed security guard in the pantry caught up in the mayhem of the shooting as he stood behind RFK. In Pease's hands, though, Cesar was likely the assassin hired by Maheu and the CIA because he also allegedly worked for Hughes Aircraft, including in the 1970s. That seems awfully tiny compensation for a supposedly successful assassin: Good job Thane, and here's some more security guard work for you.[53]

Pease is not the first to make unfounded allegations about Cesar, of course, in keeping with the derivative nature of the recycled material in her book. Still, her treatment is so noxious one is reminded of the Boston lawyer Joseph N. Welch, who spontaneously confronted Senator Joseph McCarthy with these words, 'Have you no sense of decency, sir, at long last? Have you left no sense of decency?'

Pease has none, of that there is no doubt. What is truly disconcerting though is that her ridiculous book and bullying tactics have won her an undeserved hearing in the *Washington Post* and on KTLA in Los Angeles. That is nothing short of astonishing.

* * *

Commentary 2022

Lisa Pease is the author of one of two books that received widespread publicity on the fiftieth anniversary of RFK's assassination in 2018. The second book was written by British author Tim Tate and CNN journalist Brad Johnson. Their book recycles just about every myth conspiracists have managed to place in the public mind over the past fifty years.

One example of their many errors is their treatment of an alleged co-conspirator who accompanied Sirhan to a gun range where the assassin practised his shooting skills.

Like Lisa Pease, the authors state that in the first stages of the LAPD police investigation, officers were told by a shooting range instructor, Everett Buckner, that a young woman had approached Sirhan at a shooting range. 'Around 12 hours before Kennedy was shot', Tate and Johnson wrote:

> Sirhan was spotted at the San Gabriel Valley Gun Club, where he rapid-fired more than 350 bullets from his .22 caliber Iver Johnson revolver. Here at last, thought the police and FBI, was evidence of an assassin practicing for his lone night's work. They were less sanguine after interviewing Everett Buckner, the club's range master, who'd been on duty all that day. He said a blonde woman in her 20s had arrived a little while after Sirhan. After they began shooting, Sirhan offered to help her get her shots on target. According to

Buckner, she said: 'Get away from me, you son of a bitch – they'll recognize you.'[54]

However, the authors never tell their readers who this 'blonde girl' was. As readers will have discovered in the review of Pease's book above, her name was Claudia Williams. Police tracked her down and interviewed her. Williams told police that she had been approached by a young man she had never seen before who offered to show her how to shoot her new gun. Police confronted Buckner with Claudia Williams. Buckner recognized her and then police officers asked him was he sure he heard her say to Sirhan 'get away'. Buckner responded: 'No, I do not know what she said to him. But she said something.'[55]Claudia Williams said her only connection with Sirhan was when he offered to show her how to shoot her new pistol.

Tate and Johnson also have no interest in informing their readers that four other witnesses at the range that day – Henry Carreon, Claudia Williams' husband Ronald Williams, David Montellano and Charles Kendall – told police officers that Sirhan was alone. In building their case for conspiracy Tate and Johnson also need to portray Sirhan as non-violent. Thus, they describe him as a young man who 'quickly adjusted to his new life in America'. At school, they write, he was remembered as a 'quiet, well-mannered student'.

This statement is in direct contradiction with the true facts of Sirhan's life as readers will have discovered in previous chapters. Additionally, I subsequently discovered more information about Sirhan's violent tendencies. When Sirhan was employed as an exercise boy/trainee jockey, two exercise girls who worked at the Grande Vista Ranch said Sirhan treated the horses 'cruelly'. Del Mar Racetrack foreman Larry Peters also saw Sirhan kick a horse in the belly and after he remonstrated with him, he was taken aback at the vitriol that emanated from the young employee. Peters said Sirhan's temper had been unusually violent when he was told he would never become a jockey.[56]

Furthermore, another horse trainer at the Grande Vista Ranch saw Sirhan mistreat a horse, 'kicking and hitting it with his fists'. Sirhan, he said, 'was in a rage of temper'. By way of explanation Sirhan told him the horse 'provoked him'.[57] In fact, Sirhan had used this 'provocation' excuse at his trial when he testified that Robert F. Kennedy, by his support of Israel, had 'provoked' him, which led to his decision to assassinate the Senator.[58]

To bolster their claims that Sirhan was never in a position to have fired the fatal shot at RFK and that a second shooter was responsible, Tate and Johnson distort the comments of Don Schulman, who spoke to TV crews after the shooting. Tate and Johnson write that Don Schulman said he, 'saw a man pull out a gun . . . and shot three times. "I saw all three shots hit the Senator . . . I also saw the security men pull out their weapons . . . the security guards fired back".'[59]

However, Tate and Johnson are being less than candid with their readers. Schulman retracted his statement about having observed a second shooter or a security guard having fired his pistol after he gave evidence to an independent panel of investigators in 1976. He said that immediately following the shooting he was 'tremendously confused' and that the words he used to describe the shooting to reporters in 1968 were the result of 'confusion'.

Schulman reported that he meant to tell reporters that, 'Kennedy had been hit three times, he had seen an arm fire, he had seen the security guards with guns, but he had never seen a security guard fire and hit Robert Kennedy'. From Schulman's original reports conspiracy advocates began to construct a second-gun scenario, a scenario built on confused statements made just upon emerging from the chaos that enveloped the pantry area the night of the shooting.[60]

The authors also fail to inform their readers that an LA Channel 2 film editor named Frank Raciti told author Robert Blair Kaiser that Schulman was with him and a fellow film editor named Dick Gaither in the Embassy Room at the time of the shooting. In other words – Schulman was not even in the pantry at the time he allegedly witnessed a second shooter.[61]

Like conspiracy theorists before them, Tate and Johnson believe Sirhan had been a hypnotized assassin programmed to forget. They take Sirhan at his word that he could not remember anything after drinking coffee with a girl at the Ambassador Hotel. To support this myth the authors reference Dr Daniel Brown, a proponent of 'recovered memory syndrome'. Brown said Sirhan 'did not act under his own volition and knowledge at the time of the assassination and is not responsible for actions coerced and/or carried out by others'. *Washington Post* journalist Tom Jackman reported that Sirhan 'was, Brown said, a true "Manchurian Candidate," hypno-programmed into carrying out a violent political act without knowing it'.[62]

According to the American Psychological Association it is not possible to distinguish repressed memories from false ones without corroborating evidence, nor are they unequivocally proven to exist, and some experts in the field of human memory feel that no credible scientific support exists for the notions of repressed/recovered memories. The mechanism(s) by which both of these phenomena happen are not well understood and, at this point it is impossible, 'without other corroborative evidence, to distinguish a true memory from a false one'.[63]

Accordingly, it should come as no surprise to those who reject Brown's 'hypnotized assassin' theory that the California courts did not accept his missives about how Sirhan had been hypnotized then programmed to forget.[64]

Chapter 11

Case Closed

'The Robert Kennedy Assassination – The Final Truth', *first published in* Crime Magazine, *2021*

Commentary 2022

This following article published in 2021 examines the latest attempts by Sirhan to gain his freedom. In seeking Sirhan's release, defence lawyers argued in the California courts between 2011 and 2015 that Sirhan should be given a second trial and that he had not been physically in position to fire the fatal shot, and that a second shooter and gun may have been responsible.

In rejecting Sirhan's bid for freedom, Judge Beverley Reid O'Connell accepted an August 2013 recommendation by US Magistrate Judge Andrew Wistrich. 'Though petitioner advances a number of theories regarding the events of June 5, 1968, petitioner does not dispute that he fired eight rounds of gunfire in the kitchen pantry of the Ambassador Hotel,' O'Connell wrote. 'Petitioner does not show that it is more likely than not that no juror, acting reasonably, would have found him guilty beyond a reasonable doubt.'[1]

In 2021 Sirhan was granted parole but his freedom was denied by California Governor Gavin Newsom in January 2022.

In the following article I cite the most recent acoustic examination of the RFK assassination audio tape by Ed Primeau, an audio forensic expert with thirty-five years' experience.

* * *

It has been decades since Palestinian immigrant Sirhan Sirhan assassinated Senator Robert F. Kennedy in the pantry of the Ambassador Hotel in Los Angeles. During the past six decades Sirhan has insisted he had no knowledge of having fired the shots that killed the senator and that he had been a 'hypnotized patsy' enlisted by unknown conspirators.

Numerous conspiracy authors and supporters of the assassin have enjoined him in promoting the notion that a second gunman fired the lethal shot that took Kennedy's life and that the LAPD, the FBI and the CIA covered up the purported conspiracy. For over fifty years, Sirhan's representations before the California courts and the California Parole Board have also elicited the support of many mainstream media organizations in publicizing Sirhan's alleged innocence. Their 'news' stories have done nothing except place the truth about the Robert F. Kennedy assassination in eternal obfuscation.

During his parole-board hearings, Sirhan has been represented by his lawyer, William Pepper, who acted as James Earl Ray's attorney at the time of Ray's death in 1998. Ray was the convicted assassin of Dr Martin Luther King Jr who claimed that the US government had framed him. In his conviction that Ray had been telling the truth, Pepper named an innocent former soldier as the real assassin.

It had a devastating effect on the soldier's reputation and that of his family. Pepper also brought a 'fantasist', Lloyd Jowers, to the civil trial in 1999 as a co-conspirator in the case, even though the man's family insisted Jowers had repeatedly lied about his purported involvement in the King assassination.

Shelby County Assistant District Attorney John Campbell said he had, 'spent four years on Mr. Pepper's theories . . . After you've watched them change [so frequently] you just don't want to hear any more of them. It's so bizarre that it's hard to take it seriously any more. It's a tragedy. This should be taken seriously, but it's become almost comical.'[2]

Pepper's defence of Sirhan included the promotion of purported RFK assassination witnesses who altered their original testimonies in favour of new claims that Kennedy had been killed by more than one gunman. However, without exception, the media stories about these witnesses have omitted vital evidence in the case which had been readily available at the time of their publication. This is called 'lazy journalism'. Lazy journalism happens when journalists don't do their homework, and don't check the accuracy of the information they find.

Today, it comes as little surprise, given the absence of any editorial vetting on the Internet, to find many websites and blogs saturated with bogus revelations about the RFK assassination and mindless repetition of supposed 'facts' that were, in actuality, refuted or rationally explained years ago. However, what may shock many people is the way in which a number of mainstream media outlets have mimicked the editorial vetting styles of Internet publications.

Three examples of media 'trust-in-me-style lazy journalism' which circulated within mainstream media were the BBC's 2006–8 story of CIA agents allegedly being present at the scene of Robert F. Kennedy's assassination, CNN's reporting of the assassination between 2011 and 2016, and the *Washington Post*'s story about Sirhan's 2016 parole hearing. In all three cases the journalists and television producers abrogated their professional responsibility in favour of biased reporting, allowing no wider context to the stories let alone serious counter-claims to the conspiracy stories promoted by various writers and Sirhan's lawyer.

In November 2006, the BBC aired a *Newsnight* story about Shane O'Sullivan, who sought to promote a book and documentary about the Robert F. Kennedy assassination. O'Sullivan alleged CIA agents had been skulking around the Ambassador Hotel in Los Angeles on the night of the assassination with the alleged intent to assassinate the presidential candidate. The producers omitted to include any challenge to O' Sullivan's spurious allegations.[3]

The *Newsnight* producers eventually recognized their mistake after an article I wrote was published on History News Network's website. The article revealed how O'Sullivan's book and documentary were seriously flawed and that the author had erred in naming innocent individuals of having participated in the assassination (they turned out to be innocent Bulova watch salesmen). I was later asked to appear on the BBC programme to discuss O'Sullivan's errors. Nevertheless, O'Sullivan shamelessly continued to promote purported CIA involvement in the assassination by 'exploring the possibility' that these men were using Bulova as cover for 'another agency'.[4]

The BBC also ignored the work of leading Robert F. Kennedy assassination expert Dan Moldea, an investigative journalist whose 1995 book on the assassination was highly acclaimed by *Newsweek*, *Time*, the *New York Times* and many other responsible reviewers.[5] Had they done so they would have been able to understand the dynamics of the pantry shooting and thus contributed a note of scepticism to O'Sullivan's bogus shooting scenario.

In 2011, CNN interviewed assassination witness Nina Rhodes-Hughes, in which she claimed she heard more than eight shots fired in the Ambassador Hotel pantry, and an audio engineer who said that after examining an audio recording of the assassination he concluded that thirteen or fourteen shots were fired.[6]

The CNN journalists accepted, without challenge, Rhodes-Hughes' belief that she heard between ten and fourteen shots. They did not query her original 1968 FBI interview transcript which stated she heard 'eight distinct shots', which she now claimed, without proof, had been falsified.

Of the seventy-seven pantry witnesses who gave an opinion about the number of shots fired the report cited the very small number who said there were more than eight shots. The journalists had clearly ignored the statements of numerous witnesses who said there had been eight shots or less fired in the pantry. It begs the question – why would the CNN journalists choose to cite only a few witnesses who thought they heard more than eight shots against the vast majority who put the number at eight or less?[7]

The CNN journalists also failed to put the shooting in the correct context with regard to the statements made by earwitnesses and eyewitnesses. After the first shot had been fired the crowd acted as one would expect. Some witnesses reacted out of fear for their own safety and attempted to avoid the gunman who was firing wildly into the crowd after he had succeeded in placing his gun against Kennedy's head and firing. Others fell about after hearing gunshots and observing flashes coming from the muzzle of Sirhan's gun.

Consequently, the pantry was in such a turmoil it is no wonder the witness statements were contradictory and fraught with speculation as to what exactly happened. As nationally acclaimed wounds ballistics expert Larry Sturdivan stated:

> If anybody . . . tells me he can reconstruct the location and posture of each person in that room at the time of each shot, I would conclude that he was delusional. If I were there, I would guarantee that my location and posture would change continuously between shots and there would be no way I could remember exact locations or postures at any given moment. Photographs help, but one cannot pinpoint the time of the photograph to the millisecond and that's what one would need to do to reconstruct a trajectory from gun to entry point.[8]

CNN also revealed its own bias by favouring the research conducted by audio engineer Philip van Praag and his team alleging thirteen or fourteen shots could be identified on the Pruszynski audio tape of the shooting and ignoring acoustic expert Philip Harrison's detailed study. The CNN story merely reported that the California Attorney General had said the audio engineer's report was an 'interpretation or opinion that is not universally accepted by acoustic experts'.[9]

A trained acoustic engineer, Harrison had worked on more than a thousand cases for one of the leading forensic firms of its kind in the world. Van Praag is actually an audio engineer by profession, which is quite a different thing, and his experience is simply not comparable to Harrison's; nor is the rest of van Praag's team. It could also be argued that the vast majority of earwitness testimony comports with Harrison's analysis and contradicts van Praag's assertions. It also begs the question – why didn't Sirhan's lawyers hire an acoustics company to examine the Pruszynski tape? No other acoustics company in the world has examined the tape in the decade or so since Harrison published his report.

Harrison was able to identify seven impulse sounds (which are characterized by a sharp onset and rapid decay) that corresponded to Sirhan's gun being fired to the exclusion of another weapon (the seven impulses all exhibited very similar characteristics). An eighth shot could not be clearly identified on the spectrogram made from the tape recording; this sound appeared to be masked by other noise, including screams.

A trio of Americans who have spent decades examining the scientific aspects of the JFK assassination – Steve Barber, Michael O'Dell and Chad Zimmerman – independently examined the RFK audio tape which was a digital version of the master tape. Steve Barber had already begun to analyse the Pruszynski recording even before Philip Harrison became involved. He concurred with Harrison's finding. Their analyses were published on History News Network's website in March 2007. Michael O'Dell, one of the leading experts on the JFK acoustics evidence, worked independently of Barber and Zimmerman and his specific findings were very similar to Harrison's in that he concluded there were 'seven similar sounds and an eighth obscured by noise'.[10]

In 2016, the *Washington Post* reported Sirhan's fifteenth parole hearing, citing the Prusynski tape and research carried out by van Praag's team of audio engineers while failing to acknowledge counter-arguments based on Harrison's acoustics study or the Steve Barber-led study.[11]

In recent years, research by Harrison and others has been confirmed by another acoustics expert, Ed Primeau, an audio forensic expert with thirty-five years' experience. He analysed the Pruszynski recording and was able to isolate the sound of gunfire. 'I can confirm based on observation at the [assassination] site by witnesses as well as my scientific observation in the lab that there was one shooter and there were eight shots fired,' he said.

Primeau used a sophisticated computer programme called iZotope RX, which isolated the sounds of gunshots from the cacophony of the crowd that night. 'When the crowd murmur is removed, it's pretty clear to hear those pops,' Primeau said. 'As poor as this recording is, it still gives us valuable perspective and scientific foundation to the fact that there were eight shots fired.' Primeau said the use of this sophisticated computer software, which has only become available in the last few years and is used by the FBI, solves the mystery as to how many people were involved in the RFK assassination.[12]

The flawed BBC, CNN and *Washington Post* stories not only raised questions about editorial standards of two of the world's largest news organizations. It also highlighted the way conspiracy advocates have acted irresponsibly in their reporting of the story. Not only were innocent individuals wrongly named as assassins in mainstream media, but other stories insinuated Kennedy's bodyguard Bill Barry and Kennedy aide John Seigenthaler had participated in the conspiracy.[13]

Sirhan has been denied parole fifteen times since his incarceration. Today he is held in the Richard J. Donovan Correctional Facility in San Diego. At all his parole hearings, the most recent in 2016, Sirhan has testified that he continued to have no memory of the assassination. His lawyers also repeated claims that Sirhan was 'hypno-programmed' and his memory of being programmed was 'wiped' by unknown conspirators which is why the assassin had no recollection of the murder. In support of Sirhan's claims, Dr Daniel Brown of Harvard Medical School testified he spent more than 60 hours with Sirhan in an attempt to recover his memory of both the shooting and having been put under hypnosis. The parole boards rejected these claims and Sirhan's parole has been denied on the grounds that he continued not to understand the full ramifications of his crime.

Sirhan's explanation to the parole board of having no memory of the shooting was in direct contradiction of historical and damning documentary evidence provided by one of his defence investigators who worked for Sirhan's lawyers at the time of the 1969 trial.

Michael McCowan, who acted as an investigator for the Sirhan trial defence team, produced a manuscript of notes he made with Sirhan present. This new evidence in the case effectively destroyed the amnesia defence Sirhan continually used at his parole hearings. The manuscript also included an intricate map of the Ambassador Hotel ballroom. The map, drawn from a bird's eye view, includes both captions of people he encountered and personal details he remembered – 'Danish Electrician', '2 Mexicans', 'Section of Bar I bought drinks at'. The manuscript was accompanied by a Letter of Authenticity from McCowan as well as a copy of a letter signed by both Sirhan Sirhan and McCowan, giving McCowan 'the right to write a book about his investigation into my case'.[14]

The historically important document shows, clearly and vividly, in Sirhan's own hand, that he did in fact remember the events of 4–5 June 1968, directly refuting his defence that he suffered from amnesia or was hypnotized and then programmed to not remember. Though he perhaps drank too much that night (which he would later say contributed to his crime), his behaviour described in this manuscript is controlled and intentional.[15]

Sirhan's insistence he could not remember shooting Kennedy was also contradicted by statements made by McCowan to Dan Moldea. During Moldea's early 1990s investigation into the assassination, McCowan told the investigative journalist he had reconstructed the crime with Sirhan during the 1969 trial. In the midst of their conversation, McCowan said, Sirhan started to explain the moment when his eyes met Kennedy's just before he shot him. Shocked by what Sirhan had just admitted, McCowan asked, 'Then why, Sirhan, didn't you shoot him between the eyes?' With no hesitation and no apparent remorse, Sirhan replied, 'Because that son of a bitch turned his head at the last second.'[16]

In a 2011 email to the author, Dan Moldea stated that the newly published collection of McCowan documents 'completely annihilates Sirhan's long-standing position that he has never remembered the details of his actions that night . . . Just to be clear, you and I were right on target.'[17]

The most important development in the case occurred in 2015 when, after a long history of delays, the US District Court in Los Angeles ruled on a request by Sirhan and his lawyers that he be released, retried or granted a hearing on alleged new evidence. The purported new evidence included van Praag's analysis of the Pruszynski tape, Nina Rhodes-Hughes' declaration that more than eight shots had been fired during the shooting, a number of issues dealing with the ballistics evidence, the positioning of Sirhan and Kennedy when the shooting started and other issues pertaining to Sirhan's purported 'hypnotic programming' and the existence of a 'second shooter'.[18]

In 2013, Magistrate Judge Andrew J. Wistrich produced a sixty-seven-page 'Report and Recommendation' for the United States District Court,

Central District of California, opining that the case 'may be the final chapter in an American tragedy'. In January 2015, District Court Judge Beverly Reid O'Connell approved and adopted Wistrich's factual findings and legal conclusions, but also independently rejected Sirhan's conspiracy claims and dismissed his habeas petition with prejudice. The Ninth Circuit Court of Appeals declined to hear Sirhan's appeal in 2016.

After considering objections by Sirhan's lawyers, a final judgment was eventually handed down in 2015. Having reviewed the evidence in the case, the court agreed with Judge Wistrich's report that Sirhan and his attorneys failed to meet the showing required for actual innocence.[19]

Judge Wistrich acknowledged there were, to be sure, apparent anomalies in the evidence which Sirhan's lawyers chronicled, including problems with the ballistics and forensic evidence. In addition, some eyewitness statements, if taken completely at face value, at least raised the possibility that Sirhan had not acted alone in the pantry of the Ambassador Hotel. But such incongruities are entirely normal in most murder investigations. It is particularly true of major investigations, where the possibility of human error is compounded because of the vast amounts of paperwork and physical evidence that must be processed. Then, too, police departments fifty years ago were simply not as careful about securing a murder scene as they are trained to be now.

Judge Wistrich's report addressed one of the enduring myths of the Robert F. Kennedy assassination which has been repeated ad nauseam by conspiracy writers, journalists and Sirhan's attorneys for nearly five decades. It is the notion that Sirhan was never less than 3ft away from the Senator and was always facing Kennedy – thus unable to fire the point-blank fatal shot to his head.

Sirhan's attorney William Pepper said, 'There is no account that pushes him any closer than three or four feet away from Bob Kennedy in front of him'.[20] David Talbot wrote in his book *Brothers*, 'But not one witness saw Sirhan shoot Kennedy in the back of his skull at point-blank range. According to witnesses, Sirhan attacked Kennedy from the front'.[21] Conspiracy advocate Shane O'Sullivan in his 2008 book wrote, 'not one witness placed Sirhan's gun close enough to Kennedy and in the correct firing position to inflict the wounds observed in the autopsy'.[22]

In 2016, RFK shooting victim Paul Schrade said, 'The evidence clearly shows [Sirhan was] not the gunman who shot Robert Kennedy . . . Sirhan fired in front of Kennedy but the candidate was struck in the back by three bullets, including a fatal shot to the back of the head.'[23]

Pepper, Talbot, O'Sullivan and Schrade are clearly in error as I demonstrated in a History News Network article in 2008 titled 'RFK Assassination: New Revelations from the FBI's "Kensalt" Files'. The article was based on further discoveries I had made since the publication of *The Forgotten Terrorist* regarding witness statements given to the FBI after the assassination.[24]

Many of the twelve eyewitnesses who were close to Kennedy when he was shot stated that Sirhan was anywhere from 3 to 12ft away from the Senator. However, Dan Moldea established the majority of the twelve witnesses gave estimates of muzzle distance based only on the first shot and most of them did not see Sirhan lunging at Kennedy.[25]

Vincent DiPierro, a waiter at the Ambassador Hotel, however, clearly saw this happen as he has often stated. According to DiPierro, who was standing some 5ft behind the Senator in the pantry and had an unobstructed view of the shooting, Sirhan managed to stretch his arm around Karl Uecker who was escorting Kennedy through the pantry. Uecker was facing away from Kennedy when Sirhan reached around him to place the gun at his head.

As DiPierro told the *Washington Post*'s Ronald Kessler in 1974, it was true that Sirhan was standing about 3ft in front, and slightly to the right, of Kennedy. But a moment before Sirhan whipped out his handgun, Kennedy turned to his left to greet some busboys. As Sirhan began firing, he lunged forward, bringing the muzzle of his Iver Johnson revolver to within inches of Kennedy's head. 'It would be impossible for there to be a second gun,' DiPierro told Kessler. 'I saw the first shot. Kennedy fell at my feet. His blood splattered on me. I had a clear view of Kennedy and Sirhan.'[26]

Many years later, in a 2018 radio interview, DiPierro's memory had not diminished with the passage of time. In 2006 he had stated, 'Sirhan . . . was three feet away but the muzzle of the gun [in his outstretched arm] couldn't be more than 3 to 5 inches away from his head'.[27]

In 2018 DiPierro said:

> I saw the gun come from the right side of my eye and [Sirhan's arm] was outstretched . . . We always talk about the upward trajectory . . . well, Sirhan was shorter than Robert and he was also stretched out so that his arm was an extended version going in an upward trajectory . . . no one ever really brought it up . . . there was nobody between Robert, Sirhan and me . . . I heard popping of balloons . . . the first shot was directly to his head . . . I got sprayed with the

bullet to his head . . . there was a pause because Robert's hands went up to his head . . . the third bullet hit the top of his jacket and hit Paul Schrade in the head . . . the fourth shot went through my shirt . . . I didn't get hit . . . A lot of people said there were more than 8 shots. Well, there was a lot of popping, a lot of banging. I only saw seven shots come out of the gun. There were 8.[28]

DiPierro's recall of the shooting is supported by other witness statements, particularly those of Boris Yaro and Juan Romero who had been very close to Kennedy. Boris Yaro stated the senator was shot at 'point-blank range'. Romero, who had been shaking hands with Kennedy when the shots rang out, initially said the gun was a 'yard away' but in a 2003 *LA Times* interview he said, '[Sirhan] put out his hand to the senator's head . . . Then I see the guy [Sirhan] put a bullet in the senator's head.'[29]

There is a further statement corroborating DiPierro's account that Sirhan, and no one else, shot Kennedy at point-blank range. I found the previously overlooked witness statements in the FBI files after my book *The Forgotten Terrorist* was published. It was made by Freddy Plimpton, the wife of writer George Plimpton. She 'saw an arm go up towards Senator Kennedy's head, but did not see a gun, heard shots and it was obvious to her that Senator Kennedy had been shot . . . She saw Sirhan very clearly. She saw his arm up toward Senator Kennedy's head.'[30]

In his 2013–15 report, Magistrate Judge Wistrich stated that the evidence did indeed show that Sirhan had been able to position his gun near to RFK's head, leaving powder burn marks on the Senator's body. In his adjudication he stated that Sirhan and his attorneys failed 'to address the chaos that ensued once [Sirhan] began shooting and the subsequent movements of the senator and [Sirhan] in reaction to the shooting. Establishing that [Sirhan] was initially in front of Senator Kennedy does not preclude him from firing the fatal shot.'[31]

Wistrich went on to explain his reasoning:

First, eyewitness testimony supports a finding that Senator Kennedy moved during or after the first shot. In fact, Mr. Uecker's testimony described Senator Kennedy as turning his head just as the shots were fired. Second, none of the eyewitnesses saw Senator Kennedy sustain the fatal shot. Any estimates of muzzle distance or the angle of [Sirhan's] gun were based on the position of the gun either before the shooting began or at the time of the first shot. While each statement initially places [Sirhan] in front of Senator Kennedy, they vary in describing the direction and distance between the two individuals . . . Third, eyewitness statements paint a chaotic picture, which would undoubtedly make it difficult for eyewitnesses to gauge the exact locations of [Sirhan] and the senator . . . Due to the overwhelming testimony identifying [Sirhan] as a shooter, and [Sirhan's] own admission regarding the use of his gun, a reasonable jury could conclude that [Sirhan] fired the fatal shot.[32]

Later in his report, Wistrich expanded on his conclusions that there was no evidence to prove that Sirhan had been unable to fire the lethal shot to the Senator's head: 'Perhaps most importantly, the eyewitness testimony consistently described Senator Kennedy as turning his head just as the shots were fired. That explains how the bullet could have struck the back of his head even if petitioner was technically "in front" of Senator Kennedy.'[33]

In his *Report and Recommendations*, Judge Wistrich made reference to an examination of the 'Pruszynski audio recording' which had been used by Sirhan and his attorneys as evidence of a second gunman. Wistrich rejected the claim that van Praag's analysis of the audio recording proved that more shots were fired than Sirhan's gun could hold. Wistrich wrote:

Mr. Van Praag's opinions do not disprove the conclusions of the 1975 Wenke commission regarding the ballistics evidence. [Sirhan] himself undermined the second shooter theory at his 1985 parole hearing when he stated, 'If anybody else was involved, wouldn't I help myself after all these years, by telling authorities who else was in on it?' Mr. Van Praag's expert opinion is not sufficient to show actual innocence or to undermine the reliability of evidence so as to make a showing of actual innocence . . . Van Praag's opinion is far from 'conclusive' evidence of a second gunman because other experts analyzing the Pruszynski recording have reached contrary conclusions.[34]

Sirhan and his lawyers had argued that a bullet had been substituted for another; that the bullet identified as consistent with being shot from Sirhan's gun was not the same as the one removed from Senator Kennedy's neck. However, Judge Wistrich disagreed:

> The issues raised by [Sirhan] have been rejected previously. In 1975, a court-appointed panel of experts extensively reviewed the ballistics evidence and heard testimony from witnesses . . . The panel was unable to confirm that three bullets were fired from [Sirhan's] gun due to 'barrel fouling' and a potential loss of fine detail in the intervening years; the commission did find, however, that the bullets were consistent with having been fired from the same gun. The panel concluded that '[there was] no substantive or demonstrable evidence to indicate that more than one gun was used to fire any of the bullets examined.' Accordingly, the Court does not find merit in [Sirhan's] objections pertaining to his substitution theory . . .
>
> In sum, [Sirhan] has pointed out some gaps in the ballistics evidence. At best, however, [Sirhan] has raised a question whether the bullet shown to [LAPD ballistics expert DeWayne] Wolfer that he testified matched bullets fired from [Sirhan's] gun was the same bullet that had been removed from Senator Kennedy's neck. [Sirhan], however, must do more. Nothing [Sirhan] has presented affirmatively shows that the bullet was in fact substituted for another, that the bullet identified as consistent with being shot from petitioner's gun was not the same as the one removed from Senator Kennedy's neck, or that there actually was an additional bullet. . . . Instead, the discrepancies that [Sirhan] points out are equally likely to be the result of innocent mistakes or negligence, rather than a complex conspiracy involving numerous governmental officials and agencies.[35]

In 2012, California Attorney General Kamala Harris rejected the hypno-programming claim made by Sirhan's attorneys. She wrote, 'The theory that a person could be hypnotized into planning and committing a murder against his will is a controversial (if not fantastic) one, and has not been adopted by most of Brown's peers, including the American Psychological Association.'[36]

Adjudicating on the hypno-programming claims of Sirhan's lawyers and the counter-claims of the California Attorney General, Judge Wistrich noted how Sirhan's attorneys had hired Dr Daniel Brown and Professor

Alan Schein as experts in hypnosis to examine Sirhan. 'Roughly 40 years after the incident,' Wistrich continued, 'Dr. Brown opines that a third party used a combination of drugs, hypnosis, sensory deprivation, and suggestive influence to exert coercive persuasion over [Sirhan], causing him to commit the acts at issue here.'

However, Wistrich argued:

> . . . psychiatrists and psychologists often disagree on patient assess-ments, particularly with diagnoses of mental illness . . . [Sirhan's] mere presentation of new psychological evaluations . . . does not constitute a colourable showing of actual innocence . . . the opin-ions of Brown and Schein are inconsistent with, and substantially contradicted by, the various psychiatrists who examined [Sirhan] 40 years earlier, contemporaneously with the crime. Unlike the psychological experts who testified at [Sirhan's] trial, Brown and Schein were unable to personally observe and examine petitioner in 1968 to render opinions about his then-current mental state. Thus, Brown's retrospective opinion based upon tests assessing (Sirhan's) mental condition 40 years after the fact is of negligible weight.[37]

With regard to the so-called 'new witness evidence' provided by Sirhan, Wistrich was dismissive, concluding that, 'there are no contemporaneous statements by Rhodes-Hughes that corroborate her current recollection of events now 45 years in the past'.[38]

As per his appearances before the parole board, Sirhan thought only of himself. At his fifteenth parole hearing in 2016, he said at its conclusion, 'This is such a traumatic . . . horrendous experience, that for *me*, to keep dwelling on it is harmful to *me* . . . [italic emphasis added]'.[39]

If caught in a lie, conspiracists shamelessly manufacture a new one. Facts do not matter, because their conspiracy mongering is seldom, if ever, about the facts. However, the tactics and gambits employed by conspiracists are now becoming readily identifiable as the public becomes increasingly aware of the dangers of falsehoods spread by the Internet and social media. Additionally, the public have become aware of how 'fake news' is becoming problematic for the mainstream media.

Despite the presence of questionable journalistic practices and con-spiracy mongering it can now be established beyond any reasonable doubt that Sirhan Sirhan wilfully, and with premeditation, assassinated Senator

Kennedy and acted alone when he fired his gun in the pantry of the Ambassador Hotel.

There is overwhelming evidence to show that Sirhan had repeatedly lied when he stated he could not remember shooting Senator Kennedy. Sirhan not only admitted he could remember the shooting, as revealed in the notes provided by Michael McCowan, but he also admitted as much in a threatening letter he sent to his lawyer, Grant Cooper. In the letter, Sirhan wrote: 'If [author Robert Blair Kaiser] gets his brains splattered he will have asked for it like Bobby Kennedy did. Kennedy didn't scare me; don't think that you or Kaiser will: neither of you is beyond my reach.'[40]

There is no credible evidence to show that Sirhan had been hypnotized beyond his own 'Rosicrucian' hypnotic self-development exercises. Sirhan had long been fascinated with hypnosis and made reference to it frequently in the years before the assassination. Additionally, no credible evidence supports the notion that a purported 'girl in a polka–dot dress' acted as Sirhan's accomplice and 'trigger' on the night of the assassination.[41]

There is also no credible evidence to show that Sirhan had been accompanied by a second shooter on the night of the assassination. As Judge Wistrich observed: 'Since the fatal shot was at point-blank range, it seems highly unlikely that the unknown second shooter could have approached Senator Kennedy that closely, shot him, and then escaped a crowded room essentially unnoticed.'[42]

The evidence establishing Sirhan's motives, as delineated in *The Forgotten Terrorist*, is also becoming clearer to a US public weaned on nightly news stories of Middle-East violence and Arab fanaticism. As Harvard law professor Alan Dershowitz observed, 'I thought of [the RFK assassination] as an act of violence motivated by hatred of Israel and of anybody who supported Israel. It was in some ways the beginning of Islamic terrorism in America. It was the first shot. A lot of us didn't recognize it at the time.'[43]

And, as *Guardian* reporter Stephen Kinzer once wrote:

> Decades must often pass before shattering historic events can be truly understood . . . Mel Ayton [is] one of the few analysts who has fully grasped the crime's Middle East connection . . . The source of [Sirhan's] rage, bitterness, and anger at 'Jews' was not explained in most news stories. Far from being a 'maniacally absurd' crime, as *Newsweek* concluded, the Robert Kennedy assassination was in

fact an eminently political act. It was the first 'blowback' attack the United States suffered as a result of its Middle East policies.[44]

Case closed.

* * *

Commentary 2022

In 2017 Robert F. Kennedy Jr visited his father's assassin at the Robert J. Donovan Correctional Institution in San Diego, California. He was accompanied by Sirhan's attorney, Laurie Dusak. Pease wrote, 'Bobby hugged Sirhan, told him he knew he hadn't killed his father, and that he considered him as much a victim as his father. "He's a sweet man", Bobby told me after his visit.'[45]

RFK Jr's characterization of Sirhan as a 'sweet man' seriously contradicts the statements the assassin made over the years about his victim:

1968:   'I saw that bastard [RFK] as a mass murderer. He was to the Arabs what Hitler was to the Jews.'

1968:   Following his arrest, a police officer asked if he was ashamed of what he did. Sirhan replied, 'Hell, No!'

1968:   'A fucking politician, who would have been a killer if he had been elected, he would have sent those fucking jets, I don't think I should be convicted at all.'

1969:   'The bastard isn't worth the bullets.'

1969:   'That bastard is not worth my life.'

1969:   'Kennedy got what was coming to him.'

RFK Jr told the *Washington Post* journalist Tom Jackman he had spent months of research into the assassination, including speaking with witnesses and reading the autopsy and police reports. Kennedy Jr alleged that:

1. His father was shot four times at point-blank range from behind, including the fatal shot behind his ear. But Sirhan, a 24-year-old Palestinian immigrant, was standing in front of him.

2. RFK Jr said that nobody saw Sirhan get close enough to his father to fire at point-blank range. 'It's not only that nobody saw that,' Kennedy said. 'The people that were closest to [Sirhan], the people that disarmed him all said he never got near my father.'

3. 'There were too many bullets,' Robert Kennedy Jr said. 'You can't fire 13 shots out of an eight-shot gun.'

4. RFK Jr also said that, 'the case never went to a full trial because that would have compelled the press and prosecutors to focus on the glaring discrepancies in the narrative that Sirhan fired the shots that killed my father'.[46]

As readers of this book will have discovered, those claims are entirely spurious. Most egregious of Robert Kennedy Jr's claims is his allegation that a security guard who had accompanied Senator Kennedy through the Ambassador Hotel pantry killed his father. He made the allegations shortly after Eugene Thane Cesar died in 2019, clearly aware that you cannot libel deceased persons.

'Cesar waited in the pantry as my father spoke in the ballroom,' RFK Jr said, 'then grabbed my father by the elbow and guided him toward Sirhan'. RFK Jr also claimed that it was Cesar who fired the fatal shot. 'Cesar was a bigot who hated the Kennedys for their advocacy of Civil Rights for blacks', he said and also believed that Sirhan 'to this day, has no memory of the assassination'.[47]

The 26-year-old Cesar worked on the assembly line at Lockheed Aircraft. Early in 1968 he had applied for the position of security guard at Ace Guard Service because he was desperate to earn extra money and the additional $3 an hour wage was enticing. He worked part time for Ace on occasion, and in the late afternoon of 4 June he received a call to report to the Ambassador Hotel for duty. Cesar said that he was called late because another guard had called at the last minute to say he could not show up for work and that he was not there as a 'bodyguard' but for 'crowd control'.

At 11.15 p.m. he was assigned to check credentials at the Colonial Room doorway and clear the way for the Kennedy entourage en route. As the crowd entered through the kitchen pantry food-service area, he took up his duty and followed Senator Kennedy closely behind and to the right. Seconds later, when the shooting began, Cesar hit the floor and drew his weapon only as he began to get up. He insisted he did not fire it.

Cesar was interviewed during a reinvestigation of the assassination by the Los Angeles Special Counsel Thomas Kranz in the mid-1970s. He told investigators that he could have left the Ambassador without talking to anyone about the incident as no one seemed to be interested in taking his statement. He told LAPD officers that he had been inside the pantry at the time of the shooting, and they took him to Ramparts Police Station, where he was questioned. However, officers failed to examine his .38 pistol. Cesar also told the Kranz team that Ted Charach, who had filmed him for a documentary, *The Second Gun*, had taken his statements out of context and exaggerated them.[48]

Conspiracy advocates alleged that the only armed man witnesses saw close enough to Kennedy to fire and cause powder burns was Cesar. Did Cesar shoot RFK point blank behind the ear while they were both standing, then fall to the floor?

For more than thirty-five years Cesar has had to live with the accusation that he was Robert F. Kennedy's real killer. Every anniversary of the assassination produced more allegations and 'conclusive proof' that Cesar had lied about his involvement in the 'conspiracy' and that he had been hired as the second gunman. Over time Cesar consulted two lawyers who both said he had an excellent case for libel action. However, they refused to represent him as there was 'no money in it'. According to one lawyer, 'The case you've got is with people who have no money'.[49]

Investigative journalist Dan Moldea researched Cesar's background thoroughly and found no sinister connections with groups or organizations that had an animus toward Kennedy. Cesar was initially evasive when LAPD investigators questioned him about his political views. He was a supporter of 1968 presidential candidate George Wallace after the Watts Riots of 1965. He held radical right-wing views and disliked the Kennedys.

However, Moldea found no evidence that Cesar had worked for the Mafia, the CIA, billionaire Howard Hughes, as conspiracists have alleged, and he had not worked as freelance hit man or been a member of a right-wing political organization. Moldea also discovered that Cesar had never been a wealthy man, and there was no evidence that he had received any funds from conspirators. According to Moldea:

> At the time of my first interview with him, Cesar had only $2,500 in his bank account and still owed the bulk of the $88,000 mortgage on his house. He owed $8,000 on a truck and $5,000 for another personal loan. Also, on December 9th, 1986, Cesar married his

third wife, Eleanor, a Filipino woman, and began taking care of her and helping to support her family.[50]

According to Cesar:

No matter what anybody says or any report they come up with, you know, I know, I didn't do it. The police department knows I didn't do it. There're just a few people out there who want to make something out of something that isn't there – even though I know that some of the evidence makes me look bad.[51]

Moldea arranged for Edward Gelb, a former president and executive director of the American Polygraph Association, who had over thirty years' experience in the field, to give Cesar a polygraph test. According to Gelb, 'Based upon the polygraph examination and its numerical scoring, Thane Eugene Cesar was telling the truth when he answered [questions about his alleged role in the shooting] . . . In other words, Cesar did not fire a weapon the night Robert Kennedy was killed nor was he involved in a conspiracy to kill Kennedy.'[52]

Accusing Cesar of being the second gunman appears ridiculous at the outset. He would have had to put his gun very close to Kennedy's head at the same time Sirhan was firing rapidly in his direction, and he would have run a considerable risk of being shot. The Cesar-as-second-gunman theory is thus rendered highly improbable.

There is an additional ridiculous component to the conspiracy advocates' attempts to link Cesar to the shooting – why would a murderer, under threat of execution if caught, hang on to the purported murder weapon for three months before he got rid of it? Cesar sold the weapon in September 1968 – think about it – he sold it instead of throwing it in a river![53]

There are three people who have spoken with Sirhan over the years and their accounts of their meetings with him have often been overlooked or dismissed out of hand by conspiracy theorists over the past four decades. However, I believe their accounts will leave the reader convinced of Sirhan's guilt – beyond any reasonable doubt.

In 1978 a British journalist had a 'terrifying' experience when he interviewed Sirhan in Soledad Prison. According to Paul Callan, who interviewed Sirhan in his cell, the assassin 'coiled his fingers around an imaginary .22 calibre revolver – and aimed it at my head. It was terrifying . . . I have never doubted that he was the man who took the senator's life'.

Sirhan told him:

'I have a hazy memory of that day . . . I am deeply remorseful at having killed another human being. I have a deep hatred, in principle, of killing anyone . . . [but] I was not regretful about killing a man who was threatening me, my life, my country, my Palestine, my beloved homeland . . . What I did was a political act. I was the instrument . . . Some of that time was hazy. But I remember I was greatly agitated and in a highly nervous condition . . .'

'Then I read in the *Los Angeles Times* that a Zionist organisation [Callan said Sirhan 'spat out the word "Zionist"'] was planning to hold a victory march in the vicinity of the hotel where Kennedy was speaking. It was that march that compelled me to go down – my lovely Palestine was emotionally in my heart. Like most Arabs, I do not drink alcohol, so my body was not used to it. I remember returning unsteadily to my car to rest. I had to get my mind straight. I also had to go and get the gun because I was afraid the Jews would steal it.'

As we parted, he showed no real contrition and quoted Nietzsche: 'One should guard against being spiritually disturbed after committing a great act.'

Callan thought, 'A great act? The brutal murder of Robert Kennedy?'[54]

Carmen Falzone was a friend of Sirhan's when the assassin spent part of his prison time in PHU 1 at California's Soledad Prison.

I asked Sirhan, if you were angry because the U.S. supported Israel, why didn't you kill the president, kill LBJ? He started to tremble, those dark eyes popping, and he said, 'Don't you understand, I did kill the president. Kennedy would have been president. And if he was that pro-Israel when he wasn't president, imagine how he would be as president. So I decided to change history.' Sirhan is saner than you or me. He told me he made up all that trance and hypnosis stuff . . . He told me the love for the Kennedys was declining, so now he wanted to make himself look more sympathetic in the media . . . I found out Sirhan was highly intelligent, one-directional, emotionless, and suspicious, the perfect terrorist.[55]

Investigative journalist Dan Moldea interviewed Sirhan three times. He said that until Lawrence Teeter became his lawyer, years after his initial trial, Sirhan never mentioned the possibility of being hypnotized and 'just claimed he was drunk and couldn't remember that night'.

Moldea added:

> [Sirhan] was heavily influenced by Teeter, who believed that the CIA was responsible for anything that went wrong in society and was a real conspiracy buff. Sirhan was a kid, an average guy who was 24 and the same age as Lee Harvey Oswald. He was checking out girls that day at PCC, and before that was even practicing firing his weapon at a firing range. He went to the Ambassador because there were three different election-night parties there, had several Tom Collinses when he got there, and it was hot, and he got drunk.
>
> Sirhan and I are the same religion, Eastern Orthodox, and he's a very nice guy now . . . He's not the same person he was then, when he was young and full of anger. He claims he can't remember but he has a very good recollection of that night except when it goes to motive, means or opportunity. But I don't think Sirhan ever said anything he didn't want to say, under hypnosis or not.[56]

Dan Moldea said no witnesses were focusing on Sirhan Sirhan's actions once shots were fired because they instinctively dived for safety, leaving him free to pin Bobby down and force the close-range shots that others claimed no one witnessed. Moldea wrote:

> Sirhan Sirhan shot Bobby Kennedy and he acted alone. When a civilian investigator is looking for a conspiracy in a highly publicized case like this, he's probably gonna find it, but you have to run through the gauntlet of re-examining the evidence and in this case, all of the large questions that would indicate a second gunman at the crime scene go by the wayside.[57]

Notes

Introduction

1. William Klaber and Philip H. Melanson, *Shadow Play – The Murder of Robert F. Kennedy, The Trial of Sirhan Sirhan and the Failure of American Justice* (St Martin's Press, 1997), xiii.
2. Robert Blair Kaiser, *RFK Must Die! A History of the Robert Kennedy Assassination and Its Aftermath* (1st edn, E.P. Dutton, 1970), 145.
3. See John McAdams, 'The Kennedy Assassination', http://mcadams.posc.mu.edu/oliver.html.
4. US News and World Report, 'A Curious Conspiracy' by Chitra Ragavan, 20 December 1999.
5. Daryl F. Gates, *Chief – My Life in the LAPD* (Bantam Books, 1993), 153.
6. Michael Baden and Marion Roach, *Dead Reckoning – The New Science of Catching Killers* (Arrow, 2002), 227.
7. 'Final Report, House Select Committee on Assassinations, James Earl Ray Fired One Shot at Dr. Martin Luther King, Jr., the Shot Killed Dr. King', https://www.maryferrell.org/showDoc.html?docId=800#relPageId=317.
8. 'Sirhan Sirhan and the RFK Assassination: Part I: The Grand Illusion', http://jfk.hood.edu/Collection/Weisberg%20Subject%20Index%20Files/D%20Disk/DiEugenio%20James/Item%2004.pdf.
9. Klaber and Melanson, *Shadow Play*, 179.
10. *History Today*, 'Lone Assassins' by Andrew Cook, November 2003, https://www.historytoday.com/archive/lone-assassins.
11. US National Library of Medicine, 'The Cognitive Impact of Past Behavior: Influences on Beliefs, Attitudes, and Future Behavioural Decisions' by Dolores Albarracin and Robert S. Wyer, July 2000, https://www.ncbi.nlm.nih.gov/pmc/articles/PMC4807731/.
12. *New Scientist*, 'The Lure of the Conspiracy Theory' by Dr Patrick Leman, re-published, 11 July 2007.
13. *CounterPunch*, 'Who Killed MLK?' by Douglas Valentine, 2000, https://www.counterpunch.org/2017/01/16/who-killed-mlk-jr/.
14. LeBeau's Le Blog, 'Oliver Stone: Stoned Again', https://lebeauleblog.com/2017/11/08/oliver-stone-stoned-again/2/.
15. *New York Sun*, '[Michael Barkun on] Old Conspiracies, New Beliefs' by Daniel Pipes, 13 January 2004, https://www.danielpipes.org/1439/michael-barkun-on-old-conspiracies-new-beliefs.

Chapter 1

1. Patricia Lambert, *False Witness* (M. Evans and Co., 1998), 41.
2. Commentary, 'Yes, Oswald Alone Killed Kennedy' by Jacob Cohen, June 1992, https://www.commentarymagazine.com/articles/jacob-cohen/yes-oswald-alone-killed-kennedy/.

3. See John McAdams, 'The Kennedy Assassination', https://mcadams.posc.mu.edu/home.htm.

4. See John McAdams, 'The Kennedy Assassination, Testimony of Larry Sturdivan, Physical Scientist, Aberdeen Proving Ground Vulnerability Laboratory, Aberdeen, MD', http://mcadams.posc.mu.edu/russ/jfkinfo/hscastur.htm.

5. Warren Commission, Hearings, Vol. 5, Testimony of Marina Oswald, https://mcadams.posc.mu.edu/russ/testimony/oswald_m1.htm.

6. PBS Frontline, 'Who Was Lee Harvey Oswald?', 1993, William Cran and Ben Loeterman BBC, 1993, https://www.pbs.org/wgbh/frontline/film/oswald/transcript/.

7. Jean Davison, *Oswald's Game* (W.W. Norton, 1983), 212.

8. Rolling Stone, 'This is Where Oliver Stone Got His Loony JFK Conspiracies From' by Tim Weiner, 22 November 2021, https://www.rollingstone.com/politics/politics-features/jfk-oliver-stone-conspiracy-theory-russian-disinformation-1260223/.

Chapter 2

1. Truman Capote, *In Cold Blood* (Penguin Books, 1967), 274.

2. Norman Mailer, *Oswald's Ghost* (Random House, 1995), 789.

3. FBI File, Date 11/26/63, Interview with Airman Second Class Palmer E. McBride, http://mcadams.posc.mu.edu/russ/exhibits/ce1386.html.

4. PBS Frontline, 'Who Was Lee Harvey Oswald?'.

5. Warren Commission Report – Testimonies, Testimony of Mahlon Tobias, https://www.gutenberg.org/files/44010/44010-h/44010-h.htm.

6. National Archives, Warren Report, Lee Harvey Oswald: Background and Possible Motives, https://www.archives.gov/research/jfk/warren-commission-report/chapter-7.html.

7. FBI File, Date 11/26/63, Interview with Airman Second Class Palmer E. McBride, http://mcadams.posc.mu.edu/russ/exhibits/ce1386.html.

8. Newspapers.com, 'I'm A Marxist, Oswald Said in a 1959 Interview' by Aline Mosby, https://www.newspapers.com/clip/30112316/dayton-daily-news/.

9. John McAdams, 'The Kennedy Assassination', Testimony of Mrs Lee Harvey Oswald, http://mcadams.posc.mu.edu/russ/testimony/oswald_m1.htm.

10. PBS Frontline, 'Who Was Lee Harvey Oswald?'.

11. John McAdams, 'The Kennedy Assassination', Testimony of Nelson Delgado, https://mcadams.posc.mu.edu/russ/testimony/delgado.htm.

12. John McAdams, 'The Kennedy Assassination', Testimony of Kerry Thornley, https://mcadams.posc.mu.edu/russ/testimony/thornley.htm.

13. Davison, *Oswald's Game*, 254.

14. Abe Books, https://www.abebooks.co.uk/book-search/title/four-days/author/united-press-international-american-heritage-magazine/.

15. Davison, *Oswald's Game*, 254.

16. National Archives, Warren Report, Chapter 7: Lee Harvey Oswald: Background and Possible Motives, 414, https://www.archives.gov/research/jfk/warren-commission-report/chapter-7.html.

17. John McAdams, 'The Kennedy Assassination', Warren Commission, Testimony of Michael Paine, http://mcadams.posc.mu.edu/russ/testimony/paine_m1.htm.

18. Priscilla Johnson McMillan, *Marina and Lee* (Collins, 1978), 380.

19. Ibid., 259.

200   The Kennedy Assassinations

Chapter 3

1. National Archives, Biography of Jack Ruby, https://www.archives.gov/research/jfk/warren-commission-report/appendix-16.html.
2. *True Detective*, 'The Jack Ruby I Knew' by Melvin Belli, June 1964, 44.
3. Gerald Posner, *Case Closed – Lee Harvey Oswald and the Assassination of JFK* (Warner Books, 1993), 356.
4. Ibid.
5. Ibid., 402.
6. Ibid., 383.
7. Gary Wills and Ovid Demaris, *Jack Ruby: The Man Who Killed the Man Who Killed Kennedy* (Ishi Press, 2011), 53.
8. National Archives, Biography of Jack Ruby, https://www.archives.gov/research/jfk/warren-commission-report/appendix-16.html.
9. HSCA, https://www.archives.gov/research/jfk/select-committee-report/summary.html.
10. *True Detective*, 'The Jack Ruby I Knew' by Melvin Belli, June 1964, 44.
11. *Texas Monthly*, 'Who Was Jack Ruby by Gary Cartwright', November 1975, http://www.texasmonthly.com/story/who-was-jack-ruby.
12. John McAdams, 'The Kennedy Assassination', Testimony of Santo Trafficante, https://mcadams.posc.mu.edu/russ/jfkinfo2/jfk5/traff.htm.
13. Seth Kantor, *Who was Jack Ruby?* (Everest House, 1978), 210.
14. HSCA, Report 5, Possible Associations Between Jack Ruby and Organised Crime, https://www.archives.gov/research/jfk/select-committee-report/summary.html.
15. Posner, *Case Closed*, 361.
16. Ibid.
17. Ibid., 353.
18. Ibid., 354.
19. Ibid., 360.
20. Warren Commission Report, Appendix 17: Polygraph Examination of Jack Ruby, https://www.archives.gov/research/jfk/warren-commission-report/appendix-17.html.
21. John McAdams, 'The Kennedy Assassination', Mobster, Intelligence Agent, or Small-time Hustler?, https://mcadams.posc.mu.edu/russ/testimony/ruby_j1.html.
22. John McAdams, 'The Kennedy Assassination', Warren Commission, Testimony of Harry Holmes, http://mcadams.posc.mu.edu/russ/testimony/holmes1.html.
23. John McAdams, 'The Kennedy Assassination, Mobster, Intelligence Agent, or Small-time Hustler?', https://mcadams.posc.mu.edu/russ/testimony/ruby_j1.html.
24. Capitol Records, EMI Records, *The Controversy: The Voices of President John F. Kennedy Warren Report*, produced by Lawrence Schiller, 1967, https://www.discogs.com/Various-The-Controversy/release/2924828.
25. John McAdams, 'The Kennedy Assassination', Testimony of Napoleon J Daniels, https://mcadams.posc.mu.edu/russ/testimony/daniel_n.htm.
26. The Portal to Texas, JFK/Dallas Police Reports, https://texashistory.unt.edu/ark:/67531/metapth340441/.
27. Warren Commission Hearings, copy of a radio call sheet of the Dallas Police Department, dated November 24, 1963, https://www.govinfo.gov/content/pkg/GPO-WARRENCOMMISSIONHEARINGS-20/pdf/GPO-WARRENCOMMISSIONHEARINGS-20.pdf.
28. The Portal to Texas, JFK/Dallas Police Reports, https://texashistory.unt.edu/ark:/67531/metapth340441/.

29. KenRahn.com, http://www.kenrahn.com/JFK/History/The_deed/Sneed/Ewell.html.
30. PBS Frontline, *Who Was Lee Harvey Oswald?*.
31. Capitol Records, EMI Records, *The Controversy*, https://www.discogs.com/Various-The-Controversy/release/2924828.
32. John McAdams, 'The Kennedy Assassination', Testimony of Curtis Laverne Crafard, https://mcadams.posc.mu.edu/russ/testimony/crafard.html.
33. John McAdams, 'The Kennedy Assassination', Testimony of Mrs Lee Harvey Oswald, http://mcadams.posc.mu.edu/russ/testimony/oswald_m1.html.
34. *True Detective*, 'The Jack Ruby I Knew' by Melvin Belli, June 1964, 44.
35. Posner, *Case Closed*, 376–8.
36. Ibid.
37. Wills and Demaris, *Jack Ruby*, 36.

Chapter 4

1. Vincent Bugliosi, *Reclaiming History* (W.W. Norton, 2007), 1009.
2. John McAdams, 'The Kennedy Assassination', 'Mark Lane – Smearing America's Soldiers in Vietnam' by Neil Sheehan, http://mcadams.posc.mu.edu/smearing.htm.
3. Norman Mailer, Jefferson Morley, G. Robert Blakey, Gerald Posner and Anthony Summers et al., 'JFK's Assassination', *New York Review of Books*, 18 December 2003.
4. Mel Ayton, 'Still Guilty After All These Years: Sirhan B. Sirhan', *Washington Decoded*, 11 May 2008; Mel Ayton, 'Did the CIA Kill Bobby Kennedy? The BBC's Blunder', History News Network, 7 December 2006; Mel Ayton, 'Shane O'Sullivan's Who Killed Bobby?', History News Network, 9 July 2008; Dan Moldea, 'SOS's Comments About My Work', moldea.com, 3 July 2008.
5. Bugliosi, *Reclaiming History*, 1189, 1214.
6. Bayard Stockton, *Flawed Patriot: The Rise and Fall of CIA Legend Bill Harvey* (Potomac Books, 2006), 228.
7. John McAdams, 'The Single Bullet Theory'; John McAdams, 'The Medical Evidence'. Lane also makes much of the testimony of Dallas Police Officer Joe M. Smith, who 'believed' he confronted a Secret Service agent behind the 'picket fence' on the infamous 'grassy knoll'. Smith's allegations were researched extensively by Vincent Bugliosi. He concluded the 'probability was substantial' that the 'Secret Service agent' was James W. Powell, who was part of the 112th Military Intelligence Group that frequently assisted the Secret Service in its protective duties. Powell identified himself to police officers in the parking lot area behind the picket fence as a 'special agent'. And, as John McAdams has pointed out, 'There is one final fact that conspiracy books always omit. The alleged Secret Service agent remained in the parking lot and helped Smith and Deputy Sheriff Seymour Weitzman check out cars.' Bugliosi, *Reclaiming History*, 868–9; John McAdams, *JFK Assassination Logic: How to Think About Claims of Conspiracy* (Potomac Books, 2011), 16.
8. Bugliosi, *Reclaiming History*, 1001, 1002–11.
9. Davison, *Oswald's Game*, 17–19; David Von Pein, Charles Brehm. Lane also omitted the statements of key eyewitnesses. Bugliosi, *Reclaiming History*, 1003.
10. Neil Sheehan, a prominent journalist and critic of US involvement in Vietnam, examined Mark Lane's *Conversations with Americans: Testimony from 32 Vietnam Veterans* (Simon & Schuster, 1970), and found most of his claims to be bogus; Sheehan, 'Mark Lane: Smearing America's Soldiers in Vietnam', *New York Times Book Review*, 27 December 1970.
11. HSCA, Final Report (Government Printing Office, 1979), 424, fn. 16.

12. McAdams, *JFK Assassination Logic*, 198.
13. Lane does not source the 'top secret' minutes. However, he probably is referring to a document entitled 'Warren Commission Executive Session', 30 April 1964.
14. Mark Lane, *Last Word* (Skyhorse Publishing, 2011), 43, 113, 143; Mel Ayton, *The Forgotten Terrorist: Sirhan Sirhan and the Assassination of Robert F. Kennedy* (Potomac Books, 2007), 80.
15. Lane, *Last Word*, 103, 111, 126–7, 129, 134–5, 137, 139, 195, 230.
16. Ibid., 113; Michael, O'Dell, 'The Acoustic Evidence in the Kennedy Assassination', http://mcadams.posc.mu.edu/odell/.
17. John McAdams, 'JFK Assassination – a Hobo Hit? The Three Tramps', http://mcadams.posc.mu.edu/3tramps.htm.
18. Mark Lane, *Plausible Denial: Was the CIA Involved in the Assassination of JFK?* (Thunder's Mouth Press, 1992), 322.
19. Stephen K. Doig, 'Hunt-JFK Article "Trash" But Not Libelous, Jury Finds', *Miami Herald*, 7 February 1985.
20. Lane repeats the story of how Hunt confessed on his deathbed to his alleged knowledge of the conspiracy. He allegedly confessed to his son, St John Hunt, and this bogus revelation was published in *Rolling Stone* magazine.
21. E. Howard Hunt with Greg Aunapu, *American Spy: My Secret History in the CIA, Watergate, and Beyond* (John Wiley and Sons, 2007), 126–47.
22. John McAdams, 'The Kennedy Assassination', Jean Hill: The Lady in Red, https://mcadams.posc.mu.edu/jhill.htm, David Perry, 'Roger Craig: The Rambler Man', https://mcadams.posc.mu.edu/craig.htm.
23. JFK Assassination System, HSCA Record Number 180 – 10070 – 10273, Agency File Number 004825, https://www.archives.gov/files/research/jfk/releases/docid-32244215.pdf.
24. In 1964, Bolden was prosecuted and convicted of conspiring to sell official information in a counterfeiting case and was sentenced to six years in prison.
25. John McAdams, Ed Dolan and Jean Davison, 'Implausible Assertions – Marita Lorenz: Tying Hunt to a Conspiracy', http://mcadams.posc.mu.edu/denial.htm.
26. Posner, *Case Closed*, 407.

Chapter 5
1. John McAdams, 'The Kennedy Assassination', 'Texas in the Imagination' by Dave Perry, http://dperry1943.com/browns.html and John McAdams, 'The Kennedy Assassination', 'The British JFK Producer Who Brought Shame on the History Channel' by Max Holland, http://mcadams.posc.mu.edu/holland3.htm.
2. John McAdams, 'The Kennedy Assassination', The Assassin From Blockbuster – The James Files 'Confession', https://mcadams.posc.mu.edu/files.htm.
3. Der Spiegel, 'Did Castro Kill Kennedy?' by Michael Scott Moore, 4 January 2006, https://www.spiegel.de/international/jfk-assassination-did-castro-kill-kennedy-a-393540.html.
4. PBS Frontline, *Who Was Lee Harvey Oswald?*, https://www.pbs.org/wgbh/pages/frontline/shows/oswald/etc/script.html.
5. *The Times*, '$6,500 to Kill a President: Did Oswald Sell his Soul to Cuba?', https://www.thetimes.co.uk/article/dollar6500-to-kill-a-president-did-oswald-sell-his-soul-to-cuba-jjlknwbnfjx.
6. Findings of the HSCA, Assassination of JFK, https://mcadams.posc.mu.edu/russ/jfkinfo/hscareport.htm.

7. Ibid.
8. Ibid.
9. Gus Russo, *Live by the Sword – The Secret War Against Castro and the Death of JFK* (Bancroft, Press, 1998), 456.
10. David W. Belin, *Final Disclosure* (Charles Scribner's Sons, 1998), 217.
11. James P. Hosty Jr, *Assignment Oswald* (Arcade Publishing, 1996), 225.
12. Bugliosi, *Reclaiming History*, endnotes, 1288.
13. Anthony Summers, email to the author, 9 January 2006.
14. Ibid.
15. NPR, 'Using Modern Ballistics to Crack "Cold Case JFK"', 22 November 2013, https://www.npr.org/2013/11/22/246734533/using-modern-ballistics-to-crack-cold-case-jfk?t=1622027094904.
16. *Washington Post*, 'Opinions, Meet the Respectable JFK Conspiracy Theorists' by Philip Shenon, 19 September 2014, 4.
17. *The Guardian*, 'Fidel Castro May have Known of Oswald Plan to Kill JFK, Book Claims' by Richard Luscombe, 18 March 2012.
18. *Miami Herald*, 'Fresh Meat for JFK Assassination Hounds' by Glen Garvin, 17 March 2012, http://www.miamiherald.com/2012/03/17/2700191/fresh-meat-for-jfk-assassination.html.
19. Ibid.
20. Warren Report, 21.
21. HSCA, Final Report, 1, 1979.
22. 'The Conversation, JFK Conspiracy Theory is Debunked in Mexico 57 Years After Kennedy Assassination' by Gonzalo Soltero, 19 November 2020, https://theconversation.com/jfk-conspiracy-theory-is-debunked-in-mexico-57-years-after-kennedy-assassination-148138.
23. Thomas Mallon, *Mrs. Paine's Garage: And the Murder of John F Kennedy* (Pantheon Books, 2002), 44.

Chapter 6

1. Robert Blair Kaiser, *RFK Must Die! A History of the Robert Kennedy Assassination and Its Aftermath* (2nd edn, Grove Press, 1970), 422.
2. Mohammed Taki Mehdi, *Kennedy and Sirhan: Why?* (New World Press, 1968), 88.
3. *The Progressive Conservative*, Alan Caruba, 'The Dogs of War and the Winds of Change in the Middle East', 5:235, 22 September 2003.
4. *New York Review of Books*, 'Israel and the Palestinians' by Sana Hassan, 14 November 1974.
5. 'Maverick Christians, The Testimony of a Palestinian Muslim Turned Christian in Israel' by A. Dokimos, www.dokimos.org/shepherdsvoice, accessed 20 June 2003.
6. Godfrey H. Jansen, *Why Robert Kennedy Was Killed: The Story of Two Victims* (Third Press, 1970), 80.
7. National Christian Leadership Conference for Israel, 'Palestinian Textbooks: Selections', www.nclci.org/issues/palestinian-textb, accessed 25 July 2004.
8. Kaiser, *RFK Must Die! A History* (1st edn), 363.
9. Ibid.
10. Jansen, *Why Robert Kennedy Was Killed*, 138.
11. Ibid.
12. Ibid., 135.
13. Ibid., 134.

14. Ibid., 135.
15. Ibid., 138.
16. Ibid., 139.
17. Robert Blair Kaiser, *RFK Must Die! Chasing the Mystery of the Robert Kennedy Assassination* (3rd edn, Overlook Press, 2008), 106.
18. Ibid., 189.
19. Kaiser, *RFK Must Die! A History* (1st edn), 200.
20. Robert A. Houghton, *Special Unit Senator: The Investigation of the Assassination of Senator Robert F. Kennedy* (Random House, 1970), 165–6.
21. Kaiser, *RFK Must Die! Chasing the Mystery* (3rd edn), 128.
22. Houghton, *Special Unit Senator*, 232.
23. Jansen, *Why Robert Kennedy Was Killed*, 134.
24. Houghton, *Special Unit Senator*, 232.
25. *Newsweek*, 'Sirhan Takes the Stand', 17 March 1969, 17.
26. Ibid.
27. Houghton, *Special Unit Senator*, 222.
28. Kaiser, *RFK Must Die! A History* (1st edn), 181.
29. *Time*, 'The Least Unreasonable Arab', 14 July 1967, http://www.time.com/time/magazine/article/0,9171,899627,00.html.
30. Kaiser, *RFK Must Die! A History* (1st edn), 257.
31. *New York Times*, 'Sirhan Trial—It Stirs Deep and Conflicting Emotions' by Lacey Fosburgh, 19 January 1969.
32. *New York Times*, 'Sirhan Trial Seen Plodding Along in World of Own', Douglas E. Kneeland, 2 February 1969.
33. Jansen, *Why Robert Kennedy Was Killed*, 221.
34. Kaiser, *RFK Must Die! A History* (1st edn), 166.
35. Ibid.
36. John Seigenthaler, *A Search for Justice* (Aurora Publishers, 1971), 258.
37. Ibid.
38. Ibid., 255.
39. Mary Ferrell Foundation, 'Trial of Sirhan Bishara Sirhan', https://www.maryferrell.org/php/showlist.php?docset=1659.
40. Jules Witcover, *85 Days: The Last Campaign of Robert Kennedy* (Putnam, 1969), 218.
41. Kaiser, *RFK Must Die! A History* (1st edn), 164.
42. Jansen, *Why Robert Kennedy Was Killed*, 148.
43. Kaiser, *RFK Must Die! A History* (1st edn), 515.
44. Jansen, *Why Robert Kennedy Was Killed*, 134–5.
45. Kaiser, *RFK Must Die! A History* (1st edn), 515.
46. Klaber and Melanson, *Shadow Play*, 328.
47. *Pasadena Weekly*, 'The Real Manchurian Candidate' by *Pasadena Weekly* staff, 16 November 2006, https://pasadenaweekly.com/the-real-manchurian-candidate/.
48. LAPD Summary Report, 58.
49. Jansen, *Why Robert Kennedy Was Killed*, 134.
50. LAPD Summary Report, 909.
51. Kaiser, *RFK Must Die! A History* (1st edn), 514.
52. Ibid., 214.
53. Ibid., 217.
54. Ibid.
55. Ayton, *Forgotten Terrorist*, Appendix C, Sirhan diary entries.

56. *Pasadena Weekly*, 'The Real Manchurian Candidate', by *Pasadena Weekly* staff, 16 November 2006, https://pasadenaweekly.com/the-real-manchurian-candidate/.
57. *New York Times*, 6 June 2008, https://www.moldea.com/Response-SOS.html.

Chapter 7

1. Janet M. Knight (ed.), *3 Assassinations: The Deaths of John & Robert Kennedy and Martin Luther King* (Facts on File, 1971), 205.
2. Ibid.
3. Ibid.
4. The first book to thoroughly debunk the supposed mysteries of the RFK assassination was Dan E. Moldea, *The Killing of Robert F. Kennedy: An Investigation of Motive, Means, and Opportunity* (W.W. Norton, 1995).
5. Houghton, *Special Unit Senator*, 292.
6. Lambert, *False Witness*, 124.
7. *Washington Monthly*, 'Was Sirhan Sirhan on the Grassy Knoll?' by Tom Bethell, March 1975, 4.
8. Kaiser, *RFK Must Die* (1st edn); William W. Turner and Jonn G. Christian, *The Assassination of Robert F. Kennedy: A Searching Look at the Conspiracy and Cover-up, 1968–1978* (Random House, 1978). In the late 1960s, Turner, a disgruntled former FBI agent, was the author of several articles in *Ramparts* magazine that extolled the virtues of Garrison's probe.
9. 'Lawrence Teeter', *Washington Post*, 5 August 2005; *National Post*, 'Kennedy's Killer Demands Retrial: Sirhan Sirhan Claims He Was a Victim of Hypnotic Programming' by Isabel Vincent, 11 June 1003.
10. *The Guardian*, 'Did the CIA Kill Bobby Kennedy?' by Shane O'Sullivan, 20 November 2006. Morales, a senior officer, was the paramilitary chief of operations; Joannides served as chief of psychological warfare operations; and Campbell was a former army colonel serving as a contract agent.
11. In his article, O'Sullivan had noted that Tom Clines, a retired senior CIA officer, had disputed the identifications when presented with the same evidence. But O'Sullivan dismissed Clines' denials as an effort to 'blow smoke'. *The Guardian*, 'Did the CIA Kill Bobby Kennedy?' by Shane O'Sullivan, 20 November 2006.
12. Via Bohning, I contacted Lieutenant Colonel Manuel Chavez, an air force intelligence officer, who had known Morales in Venezuela in the late 1950s and later in Miami; Grayston Lynch, the CIA officer present during the Bay of Pigs invasion, who knew Morales and Gordon Campbell from the CIA Miami station; and Luis Rodriguez, an army officer seconded to the Miami station when Morales worked there.
13. Mel Ayton, 'Did the CIA Kill Bobby Kennedy? The BBC's Blunder', History News Network, 27 November 2006, updated 4 December 2006. Wayne Smith, a former foreign service officer, is known to believe, as he once put it, that 'the [JFK] assassination was carried out by the "cowboys" of the CIA—men like David Morales'. He would hardly qualify as an objective eyewitness regarding Morales' alleged involvement with RFK's murder. Eric Hamburg, *JFK, Nixon, Oliver Stone & Me: An Idealist's Journey from Capitol Hill to Hollywood Hell* (Public Affairs, 2002), 273.

    The credibility of Bradley Ayers, who served in the CIA's JMWAVE station in Miami with Morales, is also suspect. Ayers has long sought to profit from his association with JMWAVE station; his first book on the subject was a sober account, but his second, self-published book was sensational, and even contradicted the first one – a sure sign of unreliability. Compare Bradley E. Ayers, *The War That Never Was: An Insider's Account of CIA Covert Operations Against Cuba* (Bobbs-Merrill, 1976) with Ayers, *The Zenith Secret: A CIA Insider Exposes the Secret War Against Cuba and the Plot That Killed the Kennedy Brothers* (Vox Pop, 2006).

14. Although their joint article flatly called the BBC report 'erroneous', Talbot's book claimed, 'Morley and I unearthed new evidence that tied Morales and other JMWAVE veterans to the assassination of President Kennedy, and possibly to the killing of Bobby Kennedy as well.' Talbot's 'new evidence' included old and discredited allegations about former CIA officers H. Howard Hunt and David Atlee Phillips. David Talbot, *Brothers: The Hidden History of the Kennedy Years* (Simon and Schuster, 2008), 398–406.

15. Jefferson Morley and David Talbot, 'The BBC's Flawed RFK Story', Mary Ferrell Foundation; Talbot, *Brothers*, 397–8. Edwin Lopez, a New York lawyer who served as a researcher for the HSCA, was O'Sullivan's sole source for the identification of Joannides, who served as a liaison to HSCA from the agency. But Lopez is also a conspiracy theorist regarding CIA involvement, and his HSCA colleague, Don Hardway, who spent just as much time with Joannides, did not think the grainy photograph depicted Joannides.

16. *RFK Must Die: The Assassination of Bobby Kennedy*, written, directed and produced by Shane O'Sullivan, Soda Pictures, 2007.

17. ABC News, 'Two Guns Used in RFK Assassination, Experts Say' by Pierre Thomas, 27 March 2008.

18. Ibid.

19. A real 'magic bullet' would have been one that disappeared after striking JFK. For if it didn't wound Connally after exiting the president's throat, where did it go?

20. *Washington Post*, 'Expert Discounts RFK 2d-Gun Theory' by Ronald Kessler, 19 December 1974.

21. Ayton, *Forgotten Terrorist*, 277–8. For the Americans' analysis, see Steve Barber, 'The Robert F. Kennedy Assassination: The Acoustics Evidence', History News Network, 26 March 2007.

22. Mel Ayton, 'How the Discovery Channel Duped the American Public about the RFK Assassination Acoustics Debate', History News Network, 19 November 2007.

23. Ibid.

24. *Arizona Republic*, '"Bob Kennedy's Assassin Acted Alone", Lawyer Says' by Don Bolles, 28 November 1971.

25. Emails from Lieutenant Colonel Manuel Chavez, 1–3 December, 2006, 9 December 2006; Grayston Lynch, email to the author, 2 December 2006; Don Bohning, email to the author, 1 December 2006.

Chapter 8

1. *RFK Must Die: The Assassination of Bobby Kennedy*, written, directed and produced by Shane O'Sullivan. National Geographic Channel, *CIA Secret Experiments*, written, produced and directed by Tria Thalman, 2008. Conspiracists also believe RFK was murdered because he was about to end the war in Vietnam thus he was working against the interests of the military industrial complex.

2. Lincoln Lawrence and Kenn Thomas, *Mind Control, Oswald & JFK: Were We Controlled?*, 2nd edn (Adventures Unlimited Press, 1997); Jerry Leonard, *The Perfect Assassin: Lee Harvey Oswald, the CIA and Mind Control* (AuthorHouse, 2002); Ion Mahai Pacepa, *Programmed to Kill: Lee Harvey Oswald, the Soviet KGB and the*

Kennedy Assassination (Ivan R. Dee, Inc., 2007); Dick Russell, *The Man Who Knew Too Much*, 2nd edn (Carroll and Graf, 2003); http://mcadams.posc.mu.edu/nagell3.htm.
3. *New York Times*, 'In Short; Non-Fiction' by David Binder, 3 January 1988.
4. Philip H. Melanson, *Who Killed Robert Kennedy?* (Odonian Press, 1993), 75.
5. *Hollywood Reporter*, 'RFK Assassination Conspiracy Theory Hypnotist Found Dead in Las Vegas' by Greg Roberts, 21 March 1977.
6. Robin Waterfield, *Hidden Depths: The Story of Hypnosis* (Macmillan, 2002), xxiv.
7. *American Psychologist*, 'Hypnosis and Risks to Human Subjects' by W.C. Coe and K. Ryken, 10:6, August 1979, 23.
8. 'They Call it Hypnosis' by Robert Allen Baker, 1990, 23–7.
9. Dr Graham Wagstaff, letter to the author with attachment, *Hypnosis and Forensic Psychology*, 15 March 2003.
10. Dominic Streatfeild, *Brainwash – The Secret History of Mind Control* (Thomas Dunne Books, 2007), 177; Black Op Internet Radio, show 376, 29 May 2008, James DiEugenio and the Palle Hardrup case, http://www.blackopradio.com/archives2008.html.
11. *Hollywood Reporter*, 'RFK Assassination Conspiracy Theory Hypnotist Found Dead in Las Vegas' by Greg Roberts, 21 March 1977.
12. Melanson, *Who Killed Robert Kennedy?*, 204.
13. Washington Decoded, 11 May 2008, http://www.washingtondecoded.com/site/.
14. John Marks, *The Search for the Manchurian Candidate: The CIA and Mind Control* (Norton, 1979), 110; Robert Todd Carroll, 'Hypnosis, The Skeptic's Dictionary', 27 November 2006, http://skepdic.com/hypnosis.html.
15. Marks, *The Search for the Manchurian Candidate*, 154.
16. Ibid., 200.
17. Ibid., 196.
18. Ibid., 198.
19. Ibid., 223.
20. Gordon Thomas, *Secrets and Lies: A History of CIA Mind Control and Germ Warfare*, (J.R. Books Ltd, 2008), 264.
21. Ibid., 321.
22. National Geographic Channel, *CIA Secret Experiments*, written, produced and directed by Tria Thalman.
23. Ibid.
24. Ibid.
25. Houghton, *Special Unit Senator*, 51.
26. Kaiser, *RFK Must Die! A History* (1st edn), 293.
27. Ibid., 86.
28. Houghton, *Special Unit Senator*, 52.
29. *RFK Must Die! A History* (1st edn), 70.
30. John Douglas and Mark Olshaker, *The Anatomy of Motive* (Pocket Books, 1999), 240.
31. *The Assassination of Robert Kennedy* produced by Chris Plumley, Exposed Films Production for Channel 4 in association with the Arts and Entertainment Network, UK, 1992.
32. Ibid.
33. Houghton, *Special Unit Senator*, 275.
34. Seigenthaler, *A Search for Justice*, 239.
35. Ibid., 285.
36. Dan E. Moldea, 'Re: DiEugenio's 'The Curious Case of Dan Moldea', http://www.moldea.com/2000june3.html.

37. Kaiser, *RFK Must Die! A History* (1st edn), 388.
38. Capote, *In Cold Blood*, 13.
39. Ibid., 292 n.; *German Journal of Psychiatry*, 'I Can't Remember, Your Honor: Offenders Who Claim Amnesia' by M. Cima, H. Merckelbach, H. Nijman, E. Knauer and S. Hollnack, 25 February 2001.
40. Kaiser, *RFK Must Die! A History* (1st edn), 250.
41. Seigenthaler, *A Search for Justice*, 263.
42. Kaiser, *RFK Must Die! A History* (1st edn), 251.
43. Carol Burgess put the lie to the conspiracists' oft-stated remarks that Sirhan never drank. She said one day Sirhan came back from lunch with whiskey on his breath and made some remark that he would have to stay away from the boss that afternoon. She said she therefore assumed he drank a little. FBI Interview with Carol Burgess, 14 June 1968.
44. Daniel L. Schacter, *Searching for Memory: The Brain, the Mind, the Past* (Basic Books, 1997), 227.
45. *The Independent*, 'Freud Was Right: Mind Can Block Memories if They are Too Painful', 9 January 2004.
46. *Guardian Weekly*, 'Murder in Mind' by Clint Witchalls, 15 April 2004, 20.
47. Russell Vorpagel, *Profiles in Murder: An FBI Legend Dissects Killers and Their Crimes* by (Dell, 1998), 142.
48. Alan J. Parkin, *Memory and Amnesia* (Psychology Press, 1997), 175.
49. *Newsweek*, 'Sirhan's Trance', 7 April 1969, 31.
50. Kaiser, *RFK Must Die! A History* (1st edn), 94.
51. Ibid., 518.
52. Ibid., 469.
53. Philip H. Melanson, *The Robert F. Kennedy Assassination: New Revelations on the Conspiracy and Cover-up* (Shapolsky, 1991), 163.
54. Ronen Bergman, *Rise and Kill First – The Secret History of Israel's Targeted Assassinations* (Random House, 2018), 120.
55. FBI Interview with Carol Burgess, 14 June 1968.
56. LAPD Files, CSAK183, Merla Stephens, Unidentified woman I-4565 No # Nov. 11, 1968.
57. FBI Files, RFK-LA-56-156-Sub X- 01-Vol. 03.

Chapter 9

1. See Moldea, *The Killing of Robert F. Kennedy*.
2. National Geographic Channel, *CIA Secret Experiments*, written, produced and directed by Tria Thalman.
3. Talbot, *Brothers*, 373.
4. *Washington Post*, 'Experts Discount Second-Gun Theory' by Ron Kessler, 19 December 1974.
5. *RFK Must Die: The Assassination of Bobby Kennedy*, written, directed and produced by Shane O'Sullivan, Vincent DiPierro interviewed.
6. *Los Angeles Times*, 'Ex-Busboy Will Never Forget Bobby Kennedy' by Steve Lopez, 1 June 2003.
7. FBI 'Kensalt' Files, RFK LA 56 – 156 – 1968-1978, FBI Interview with Mrs Freddy Plimpton, 1 July 1968.
8. FBI 'Kensalt' Files, Interviews with Geraldine Agnes McCarthy, 24 June 1968 and Winnie Theresa Marshall, 27 June 1968.

9.   FBI 'Kensalt' Files, Interview with Albert Victor Ellis, 20 June 1968.
10. FBI 'Kensalt' Files, Interview with Laurie Gail Porter, 14 June 1968.
11. FBI 'Kensalt' Files, Interview with Sandra Serrano, 8 June 1968.
12. Klaber and Melanson, *Shadow Play*, 157.
13. FBI 'Kensalt' Files, Interview with Howard 'Cap' Hardy, 2 July 1968.
14. FBI 'Kensalt' Files, Interview with Richard D. Little, 2 October 1968.
15. FBI 'Kensalt' Files, Interview with Fred Meenedsen, 8 November 1968.
16. FBI 'Kensalt' Files, Interview with Jack Merritt, 13 June 1968.
17. FBI 'Kensalt' Files, Interviews with Harry Benson, 31 October 1968, and Henrietta Sterlitz, 2 October 1968.
18. Ibid.
19. FBI 'Kensalt' Files, Interview with Nina L. Rhodes, 15 July 1968.
20. Black Op Radio, show 355, 3 January 2008.
21. Klaber and Melanson, *Shadow Play*, 146.
22. FBI 'Kensalt' Files, Interview with Marcus McBroom, 11 July 1968.
23. FBI 'Kensalt' Files, Interview with Samuel S. Strain, 1 July 1968.
24. FBI 'Kensalt' Files, Interview with Dr Fred S. Parrott, 21 June 1968.
25. Thomas F. Kranz, *Robert F. Kennedy Assassination: Report Consisting of the Los Angeles County Board of Supervisors Independent Investigation*, Section 2, p. 49.
26. FBI 'Kensalt' Files, Interview with Patricia Elizabeth Nelson, 8 June 1968.
27. FBI 'Kensalt' Files, Interview with Dennis Steven Weaver, 8 June 1968.
28. FBI 'Kensalt' Files, Interview with Joseph Thomas Klein, 8 June 1968.
29. Bill Eppridge and Hays Gorey, *Robert Kennedy – The Last Campaign* (Harcourt, 1993), 90 and FBI 'Kensalt' Files, Interview with Bill Eppridge, 19 June 68.
30. FBI 'Kensalt' Files, Interview with Booker Griffin, 11 June 1968.
31. Klaber and Melanson, *Shadow Play*, 144.
32. FBI 'Kensalt' Files, Interviews with Evan Freed, 14 June 1968, 11 September 1968.
33. *RFK Must Die: The Assassination of Bobby Kennedy*, written, directed and produced by Shane O'Sullivan, interview with Evan Freed.
34. Thomas F. Kranz, *Robert F. Kennedy Assassination: Report Consisting of the Los Angeles County Board of Supervisors Independent Investigation*, Section 2, p. 3.
35. See Ayton, *Forgotten Terrorist*, Appendix – A Report on RFK's Wounds by Ballistics Expert Larry Sturdivan.
36. John McAdams, 'The Kennedy Assassination, New Orleans and the Garrison Investigation', https://mcadams.posc.mu.edu/garrison.htm.
37. Ibid.
38. SUS Final Report, John Fahey, RFK LAPD Microfilm, Volume 76, https://www.maryferrell.org/showDoc.html?docId=99762&search=John_Fahey#relPageId=184&search=John_Fahey.
39. Lisa Pease, *A Lie Too Big to Fail: The Real History of the Assassination of Robert F. Kennedy* (Feral House, 2019), 501.
40. FBI 'Kensalt' Files, Interview with Margaret McCarthy, June 24, 1968.

Chapter 10

1.   Larry Sturdivan, email to the author, 22 June 2007.
2.   *Pasadena Weekly*, 'The Real Manchurian Candidate' by *Pasadena Weekly* staff, 16 November 2006, https://pasadenaweekly.com/the-real-manchurian-candidate/.
3.   Mel Ayton, 'RFK Assassination: New Revelations from the FBI's "Kensalt" Files', History News Network, 23 May 2008; Mel Ayton, 'It's Good to See the Mainstream

Media Debunking Conspiracy Claims, But Where were They Years Ago When RFK's Death became Fodder for Nutty Stories?', History News Network, 17 September 2017; Mel Ayton, 'Who Killed RFK? Sirhan Sirhan Did It', History News Network, 4 June 2018.

4. Most of the anomalies in the collation and collection of the evidence in the case, particularly with regard to the ballistics evidence and alleged evidence that extra bullets had been discovered in the pantry door frames, were cleared up by Dan E. Moldea in his highly acclaimed book *The Killing of Robert F. Kennedy*. See also moldea.com on the fiftieth anniversary of Senator Kennedy's murder.

5. *Washington Post*, 'CIA May Have Used Contractor Who Inspired "Mission: Impossible" to Kill RFK, New Book Alleges' by Tom Jackman, 9 February 2019. Earlier, Jackman wrote credulous, conspiracy themed articles about the assassination, including one about RFK Jr's assassination theories. See *Washington Post*, 'The Assassination of Bobby Kennedy: Was Sirhan Sirhan Hypnotized to be the Fall Guy?' by Tom Jackman, 4 June 2018; *Washington Post*, 'Who Killed Bobby Kennedy? His Son RFK Jr. Doesn't Believe It Was Sirhan Sirhan' by Tom Jackman, 5 June 2018; *Washington Post*, 'Did L.A. Police and Prosecutors Bungle the Bobby Kennedy Assassination Probe?' by Tom Jackman, 5 June 2018. Before these articles appeared Jackman interviewed me for an hour over the telephone, and I patiently explained to him the context for each issue raised by conspiracy theorists. Very little of what I told him was included in the articles. Pease cites two additional sources, besides Meier, to support the allegation that Maheu was involved in the assassination. Both corroborations amount to hearsay three times removed.

6. See Charles Roberts, *Tax-Haven Tales: Kooks, Crooks, and Con Men in the Offshore World* (Laissez Faire Books, 2012). Roberts' characterization of Meier is seconded and corroborated by an investigative journalist for *Maclean's*, a leading Canadian magazine, and two authors, Sally Denton and Roger Morris, in *The Money and the Power: The Making of Las Vegas and Its Hold on America, 1947–2000* (Alfred A. Knopf, 2001).

7. Pease, *A Lie Too Big to Fail*, 285.

8. Ibid., 140.

9. *Washington Post*, 'Who Killed Bobby Kennedy?' by Tom Jackman, 26 May 2018, https://www.washingtonpost.com.news.

10. *Washington Post*, 'Expert Discounts RFK 2d-Gun Theory' by Ron Kessler, 19 December 1974.

11. KTLA Television, *Vincent DiPierro, RFK Assassination Witness* by Frank Buckley, 3 January 2018.

12. FBI 'Kensalt' Files, Interview with Mrs Freddy Plimpton, 1 July 1968.

13. Thomas F. Kranz, *Robert F. Kennedy Assassination: Report Consisting of the Los Angeles County Board of Supervisors Independent Investigation*, Section, 2, 3: Conspiracy Theories, Analysis, Investigation, Recommendations, 5. Additionally, one witness disputes whether Schulman was even in the pantry at the time of the shooting. See Kaiser, *RFK Must Die! Chasing the Mystery* (3rd edn), 361.

14. Thomas F. Kranz, *Robert F. Kennedy Assassination: Report Consisting of the Los Angeles County Board of Supervisors Independent Investigation*, Section 2, 3: Conspiracy Theories, Analysis, Investigation, Recommendations, 5. Additionally, one witness disputes whether Schulman was even in the pantry at the time of the shooting. See Kaiser, *RFK Must Die! Chasing the Mystery* (3rd edn), 361.

15. Michael O'Dell was a technical adviser to the National Academy of Science's so-called 'Ramsey Panel', which investigated the JFK acoustics evidence. O'Dell believes van Praag's conclusions that thirteen or fourteen gunshots can be identified on the audio

tape cannot be accepted as 'scientific proof'. Michael O'Dell, 'Review of Philip van Praag's Declaration Regarding the Pruszynski Tape', 20 November 2011; O'Dell, email to author, 28 May 2018. O'Dell's criticisms of van Praag's research are seconded by Steve Barber in 'The Robert F. Kennedy Assassination: The Acoustics Evidence', *History News Network*, 25 March 2007.

16. Pease, *A Lie Too Big to Fail*, 502.
17. Philip Harrison, email to author, 31 May 2018.
18. History News Network, 'CNN's Conspiracy Bias in the Robert F. Kennedy Assassination' by Mel Ayton, 7 May 2012.
19. Streatfeild, *Brainwash*, 177.
20. *Mail on Sunday*, 'Magic? It Can Make You Go Mad' by Cole Moreton, 11 March 2018, 7.
21. *Washington Post*, 'The Assassination of Bobby Kennedy' by Tom Jackman, 4 June 2018.
22. *Psychological Science*, 'Planting False Childhood Memories: The Role of Event Plausibility' by Kathy Pezdek, Kimberly Finger and Danelle Hodge, Vol. 8, No. 6, November 1997, 437–41; S. Porter et al., 'Memory for Murder: A Psychological Perspective on Dissociative Amnesia in Legal Contexts', *International Journal of Law & Psychiatry*, 2001, Jan.–Feb.: Vol. 24, No. 1, 23–42.
23. Marks, *The Search for the Manchurian Candidate*; Bergman, *Rise and Kill First*, 120.
24. Kaiser, *RFK Must Die! A History* (1st edn), 514.
25. *Report and Recommendations of Magistrate Judge Andrew J. Wistrich*, 28 December 2012.
26. Parkin, *Memory and Amnesia*, 175.
27. Kaiser, *RFK Must Die! A History* (1st edn), 94.
28. Ibid., 518.
29. Moldea, *The Killing of Robert F. Kennedy*, 326.
30. *Los Angeles Times*, 'Handwritten Notes by Robert F. Kennedy Assassin Sirhan Sirhan Shed New Light on Killer', 7 April 2011.
31. FBI 'Kensalt' Files, Interview with Albert Victor Ellis, 20 June 1968; FBI interview with Laurie Gail Porter, 14 June 1968; Kaiser, *RFK Must Die! A History* (1st edn), 125.
32. FBI 'Kensalt' Files, Interview of Laurie Gail Porter, 14 June 1968
33. Kaiser, *RFK Must Die! A History* (1st edn), 125.
34. FBI 'Kensalt' Files, Interview of John J. Ambrose, 10 June 1968.
35. Houghton, *Special Unit Senator*, 123.
36. Kaiser, *RFK Must Die! A History* (1st edn), 125.
37. Pease, *A Lie Too Big to Fail*, 119.
38. Kaiser, *RFK Must Die! A History* (1st edn), 156.
39. Houghton, *Special Unit Senator*, 114, 115, 208; Kaiser, *RFK Must Die! A History* (1st edn), 214.
40. Kaiser, *RFK Must Die! A History* (1st edn), 214.
41. Jansen, *Why Robert Kennedy Was Killed*, 121–3; FBI 'Kensalt' Files, Airtel to LA (56-156) from SAC (62-5481), 21 June 1968.
42. Ayton, *Forgotten Terrorist*, 49–71.
43. Kaiser, *RFK Must Die! A History* (1st edn), 214.
44. Houghton, *Special Unit Senator*, 165.
45. Kaiser, *RFK Must Die! A History* (1st edn), 254.
46. Jansen, *Why Robert Kennedy Was Killed*, 138–9.
47. Houghton, *Special Unit Senator*, 231–2.
48. Jansen, *Why Robert Kennedy Was Killed*, 134.
49. *Daily Mirror*, 'Merchant Played Hero Role in War', Los Angeles, 23 June 1957.

50. Jansen, *Why Robert Kennedy Was Killed*, 195.
51. Kaiser, *RFK Must Die! A History* (1st edn), 270.
52. *Orange County Register*, 'Guard Has a Leg Up on Opening Day' by Larry Bortstein, 24 December 2006.
53. Pease, *A Lie Too Big to Fail*, 7, 11, 16–17, 37–8, 213–21, 272–6, 306, 311–15, 339, 345–6, 493–8.
54. *Daily Mail*, 'Why the Man Who's Spent 50 Years in Jail for Killing Bobby Kennedy Couldn't Have Done It', by Tim Tate and Brad Johnson, 26 May 2018.
55. Kaiser, *RFK Must Die! A History* (1st edn), 156.
56. Houghton, *Special Unit Senator*, 191.
57. FBI 'Kensalt' Files, Interviews, 7 June 1968, Inglewood, Ca LA-56-156 and 8 June 1968, Corona, Ca LA-56-156.
58. Seigenthaler, *A Search for Justice*, 256.
59. Tim Tate and Brad Johnson, *The Assassination of Robert F. Kennedy: Crime, Conspiracy and Cover-Up – A New Investigation* (Thistle Publishing, Kindle Locations 2719-2721 3032).
60. Thomas F. Kranz, *Robert F. Kennedy Assassination: Report Consisting of the Los Angeles County Board of Supervisors Independent Investigation*, Section 2, 3: Conspiracy Theories, Interviews and Investigation, 5. Thomas F. Kranz, 'Robert F Kennedy Assassination – (Summary) – "Report consisting of the Los Angeles County Board of Supervisors Independent Investigation"', https://vault.fbi.gov/ Robert%20F%20Kennedy%20(Assassination)%20/Robert%2F%20Kennedy%20 (Assassination)%20Part%201%20of%203 https://foia.fbi.gov/foiaindex/rfksumm. htm).
61. Kaiser, *RFK Must Die! Chasing the Mystery* (3rd edn), 36.
62. *Washington Post*, 'The Assassination of Bobby Kennedy: Was Sirhan Sirhan Hypnotized to be the Fall Guy?' by Tom Jackman, 4 June 2018, https://www.washingtonpost.com/news/true-crime/wp/2018/06/04/the-assassination-of-bobby-kennedy-was-sirhan-sirhan-hypnotized-to-be-the-fall-guy/?utm_term=.6ba7d417a18a).
63. Memories of childhood abuse, evidence, see K. Pezdek and D. Hodge, 'Planting False Childhood Memories: The Role of Event Plausibility', *Child Development*, 70 (4) (July–August 1999), 887–95; S. Porter et al., 'Memory for Murder. A Psychological Perspective on Dissociative Amnesia in Legal Contexts', *International Journal of Law Psychiatry*, 24 (1) (2001), 23–42, doi:10.1016/S0160-2527(00)00066.
64. *Report and Recommendations of Magistrate Judge, Judge Andrew J. Wistrich*, https:// www.leagle.com/decision/infdco20150106770 15/48.

Chapter 11

1. *Report and Recommendations of Magistrate Judge, Judge Andrew J. Wistrich*, https:// www.leagle.com/decision/infdco20150106770 15/48.
2. *The Guardian*, 'Who Killed Martin Luther King?' by Tony Stark, 28 November 1999, https://www.theguardian.com/theobserver/1999/nov/28/life1.lifemagazine1.
3. See Chapter 8 and History News Network, 'Did the CIA Kill Bobby Kennedy? The BBC's Blunder' by Mel Ayton, http://historynewsnetwork.org/article/32193.
4. Shane O'Sullivan, *Who Killed Bobby? The Unsolved Murder of Robert F. Kennedy* (Union Square Press, 2008), 471.
5. Preparing for the blatant exploitation of the upcoming 50th anniversary of Senator Robert Kennedy's murder, http://www.moldea.com/RFKcase.html, Memorandum, http://www.moldea.com/Response-SOS.html.

6. CNN, http://edition.cnn.com/2012/04/28/justice/california-rfk-second-gun/index. html and CNN, http://edition.cnn.com/videos/crime/2012/03/02/bs-rfk-assassination.cnn.

7. History News Network, 'CNN's Conspiracy Bias in the Robert F. Kennedy Assassination', 5 July 2012, http://historynewsnetwork.org/article/146031.

8. Larry Sturdivan, email to the author, 22 June 2007.

9. CNN, 'RFK assassination witness tells CNN: There was a second shooter' by Michael Martinez and Brad Johnson, 30 April 2012, http://edition.cnn.com/2012/04/28/justice/california-rfk-second-gun/index.html.

10. Ayton, *Forgotten Terrorist*, 277–8. For the American Team's analysis, see History News Network, 'The Robert F. Kennedy Assassination: The Acoustics Evidence' by Steve Barber, 26 March 2007, http://historynewsnetwork.org/article/36915. Steve Barber was instrumental in debunking the sound recording of the JFK assassination. His work on the JFK audio recording was praised by the National Academy of Scientists.

11. *Washington Post*, 'Sirhan Sirhan Denied Parole Despite a Kennedy Confidant's Call for the Assassin's Release' by Peter Holley, 11 February 2016, https://www.washingtonpost.com/news/post-nation/wp/2016/02/10/this-kennedy-confidant-has-spent-decades-calling-for-the-release-of-rfks-killer/?utm_term=.09acl84c6669.

12. LaCorte News, 'The RFK Assassination – Modern-day Audio Technology Concludes Sirhan Acted Alone' by Carole McKinley, 4 June 2019, https://www.lacortenews.com/n/the-rfk-assassination-modern-day-audio-technology-concludes-sirhan-acted-alone.

13. FPP, 'A false Wikipedia "biography"' by John Seigenthaler, http://www.fpp.co.uk/online/07/07/False_Wikipedia.html; Washington Decoded, 'Mark Lane: The Original Shyster' by Mel Ayton, 11 May 2012, http://www.washingtondecoded.com/site/2012/05/lane.html.

14. Michael McCowan on Sirhan's knowledge of killing Robert Kennedy, https://www.moldea.com/McCowanLetter.html.

15. *Los Angeles Times*, 'Handwritten Notes by Robert F. Kennedy Assassin Sirhan Sirhan Shed New Light on Killer', 7 April 2011, http://latimesblogs.latimes.com/lanow/2011/04/handwritten-notes-by-rfk-assassin-sirhan-sirhan-shed-new-light-on-killer.html.

16. Moldea, *The Killing of Robert F. Kennedy*, 312–13, 326.

17. Dan Moldea, email to the author, 7 April 2011.

18. Public Intelligence, 'Sirhan Sirhan Plea', 20 November 2011, https://info.publicintelligence.net/SirhanSirhanPlea.pdf.

19. *Report and Recommendations of Magistrate Judge, Judge Andrew J. Wistrich*, https://www.leagle.com/decision/infdco20150106770 15/48.

20. National Geographic Channel, *CIA Secret Experiments*, written, produced and directed by Tria Thalman.

21. Talbot, *Brothers*, 373.

22. O'Sullivan, *Who Killed Bobby?*, 78.

23. Reuters.com, 'Robert Kennedy Assassin, Sirhan Sirhan, Denied Parole: Official', 10 February 2016, https://www.reuters.com/article/us-usa-crime-sirhan/robert-kennedy-assassin-sirhan-sirhan-denied-parole-official-idUSKCN0VJ1PN.

24. See History News Network, 'RFK Assassination: New Revelations from the FBI's "Kensalt" Files', 23 May 2008, http://historynewsnetwork.org/article/50532.

25. *Washington Post*, 'Expert Discounts RFK 2nd Gun Theory' by Ron Kessler, 19 December 1974.

26. See Ayton, *Forgotten Terrorist*, Chapter 4, 'The Shooting'.

27. *RFK Must Die: The Assassination of Bobby Kennedy*, written, directed and produced by Shane O'Sullivan and KTLA 5, *Vincent DiPierro, RFK Assassination Witness* by Frank Buckley, 3 January 2018, http://ktla.com/2018/01/03/vincent-dipierro-rfk-assassination-witness/.
28. KTLA 5, *Vincent DiPierro, RFK Assassination Witness* by Frank Buckley, 3 January 2018, http://ktla.com/2018/01/03/vincent-dipierro-rfk-assassination-witness/.
   In 2016 another assassination witness came forward and his recollections of the tragedy corroborate DiPierro's account. Former political strategist Dick Tuck also observed a bullet going into RFK's head. In June 2016, he told news 4 Tucson (KOVA), he was one of Bobby Kennedy's campaign advisors and was just outside the pantry doors when Sirhan Sirhan fired the fatal shots, '. . . I saw the bullet go in right behind the ear and the bullet go into his head,' said Tuck. 'A lot of people were thinking that he would recover and it was obvious to me that he would never recover.' News 4 Tucson (KOVA), *Anniversary of RFK Assassination Brings Haunting Memories Back to Tucsonan* by Sean Mooney, 9 June 2016, http://www.kvoa.com/story/32179759/anniversary-of-rfk-assassination-brings-haunting-memories-back-to-tucsonan.
29. *Los Angeles Times*, 'Ex-Busboy Will Never Forget Bobby Kennedy' by Steve Lopez, 1 June 2003.
30. FBI 'Kensalt' Files, Interview with Mrs Freddy Plimpton, 1 July 1968.
31. *Report and Recommendations of Magistrate Judge, Judge Andrew J. Wistrich*, https://www.leagle.com/decision/infdco20150106770 15/48.
32. Ibid.
33. Ibid.
34. Ibid.
35. Ibid.
36. CNN, 'Prosecutors Rebut Jailed RFK Assassin's Claims in Freedom Quest' by Michael Martinez and Brad Johnson, 5 February 2012, http://edition.cnn.com/2012/02/04/justice/california-sirhan-rfk/index.html.
37. *Report and Recommendations of Magistrate Judge, Judge Andrew J. Wistrich*, https://www.leagle.com/decision/infdco20150106770 15/48.
38. Ibid.
39. *National Post*, 'Sirhan Sirhan Denied Parole at Emotional Hearing', 11 February 2016, http://nationalpost.com/news/world/sirhan-sirhan-denied-parole-for-robert-f-kennedy-assassination-at-emotional-hearing.
40. Moldea.com, http://www.moldea.com/Sirhan-HeyPunk.html.
41. See Chapter 8 Hypnotized Assassin? here and John McAdams, 'The Kennedy Assassination', 'The JFK and RFK Assassinations and the Bogus 'Manchurian Candidate' Theories' by Mel Ayton, http://mcadams.posc.mu.edu/Manchurian.htm.
42. *Report and Recommendations of Magistrate Judge, Judge Andrew J. Wistrich*, https://www.leagle.com/decision/infdco20150106770 15/48.
43. *Boston Globe*, 'RFK's Death now Viewed as First Case of Mideast Violence Exported to U.S.' by Sasha Issenberg, 8 June 2008, http://legacy.sandiegouniontribune.com/uniontrib/20080608/news_1n8rfk.html.
44. *The Guardian*, 'Shot Heard Round the World' by Stephen Kinzer, 13 June 2008, https://www.theguardian.com/commentisfree/2008/jun/13/israelandthepalestinians.usa.
45. Pease, *A Lie Too Big to Fail*, 500.
46. *Washington Post*, 'Who Killed Bobby Kennedy? His Son, RFK Jr., Doesn't Believe it was Sirhan Sirhan' by Tom Jackman, 26 May 2018, https://www.washingtonpost.com/gdpr-consent/?next_url=https%3a%2f%2fwww.washingtonpost.

com%2fnews%2fretropolis%2fwp%2f2018%2f05%2f26%2fwho-killed-bobby-ken-nedy-his-son-rfk-jr-doesnt-believe-it-was-sirhan-sirhan%2f).

47. Mail Online, 'Robert F Kennedy was Assassinated by Thane Eugene Cesar, Declares RFK Jr' by Chris Spargo, 12 September 2019, https://www.dailymail.co.uk/news/article-7456521/Robert-F-Kennedy-assassinated-Thane-Eugene-Cesar-Sirhan-Sirhan-says-RFK-Jr.html.

48. Thomas F. Kranz, *Robert F. Kennedy Assassination: Report Consisting of the Los Angeles County Board of Supervisors Independent Investigation*, Section 2, 7.

49. Moldea, *The Killing of Robert F. Kennedy*, 205.

50. Ibid., 202.

51. Ibid., 216.

52. Ibid., 289.

53. Author's note: I spoke with Eugene Thane Cesar a year before his death in a telephone conversation during a dinner I had with investigative journalist Dan Moldea. Cesar thanked me for bringing out the truth about his innocent connection to the RFK assassination. Cesar died one year later, in 2019.

54. *Mirror*, 'Sirhan DID shoot Bobby Kennedy . . .' by Paul Callan, 30 May 2018, https://www.mirror.co.uk/news/world-news/sirhan-shoot-bobby-kennedy-held-12623836.

55. *Washington Post*, 'Sirhan by Cynthia Gorney', 20 August 1979, 4.

56. *Pasadena Weekly*, 'The Real Manchurian Candidate' by *Pasadena Weekly* staff, 16 November 2006, https://pasadenaweekly.com/the-real-manchurian-candidate/.

57. Ibid.

Bibliography

JFK

Report of the President's Commission on the Assassination of President John F. Kennedy, 26 accompanying volumes of Hearings and Exhibits, US Government Printing Office, 1964.

Warren Report, without supporting volumes, foreword by Louis Nizer and afterword by Bruce Catton, Doubleday, 1964

The Investigation of the Assassination of President John F. Kennedy, conducted by the Senate Select Committee to Study Governmental Operations, US Government Printing Office, 1976, US Senate Select Committee on Intelligence, http://www.history-matters.com/archive/contents/hsca/contents_hsca_repo rt.htm

Report to the President by the Commission on CIA Activities Within the United States, Vice President Nelson A. Rockefeller, Chairman, US Government Printing Office, June 1975, p. 262, http:// www.history- matters.com/archive/church/rockcomm/html/Rockefeller_0137b.htm

Investigation of the Assassination of President John F. Kennedy, conducted by the Select Committee on Assassinations of the US House of Representatives, US Government Printing Office, 1979, http://www.history-matters.com/archive/contents/hsca/contents_hsca_report.htm

Final Report of the Assassination Records Review Board, September 1998, http://www.fas.org/sgp/advisory/arrb98/

National Archives, JFK Assassination Records, Assassination Records Review Board, Series 4: Research and Analysis 4.0.2 Subject Files SOLO SAC New York to Director, FBI, June 12 1964, NARA 124-10274-10338 released March 30 1995 and 4.0.2 Subject Files Cuba, Castro's Knowledge http://www.archives.gov/research/jfk/review- board/series-04.html

Books

Aynesworth, Hugh (with Stephen G. Michaud), *JFK: Breaking the News*, International Focus Press, 2003

Baden, Michael and Roach, Marion, *Dead Reckoning – The New Science of Catching Killers*, Arrow, 2002

Baker, Robert Allen, *They Call It Hypnosis*, Prometheus Books, 1990

Belin, David W., *Final Disclosure*, Charles Scribner's Sons, 1998

Brennan, Howard, *Eyewitness to History*, Texian Press, 1987

Brown, Walt, *Treachery in Dallas*, Carroll and Graf, 1996

Bugliosi, Vincent, *Reclaiming History*, W.W. Norton, 2007

Davis, John H., *Mafia Kingfish – Carlos Marcello and the Assassination of John F. Kennedy*, McGraw-Hill Publishing Company, 1989

Davison, Jean, *Oswald's Game*, W.W. Norton, 1983

Demaris, Ovid and Willis, Gary B., *Jack Ruby*, Ishi Press, 2011

DiEugenio, James and Pease, Lisa, *The Assassinations*, Feral House, 2012

Epstein, Edward J., *Inquest: The Warren Commission and the Establishment of Truth*, Viking, 1966

—, *Legend: The Secret World of Lee Harvey Oswald*, Hutchinson, 1976

Gates, Daryl, *Chief – My Life in the LAPD*, Bantam Books, 1993

Giancana, Sam and Chuck, *Double Cross – The Story of the Man Who Controlled America*, MacDonald, 1992

Gordon, Thomas, *Secrets and Lies: A History of CIA Mind Control and Germ Warfare*, J.R. Books Ltd, 2008

Helms, Richard, *A Look Over My Shoulder*, Random House, 2003

Hosty, James P., Jr, *Assignment Oswald*, Arcade Publishing, 1996

Hunt, E. Howard with Aunapu, Greg, *American Spy: My Secret History in the CIA, Watergate, and Beyond*, John Wiley and Sons, 2007

Kantor, Seth, *Who was Jack Ruby?*, Everest House, 1978

Klaber, William and Melanson, Philip H., *Shadow Play – The Murder of Robert F. Kennedy, The Trial of Sirhan Sirhan and the Failure of American Justice*, St Martin's Press, 1997

Lambert, Patricia, *False Witness*, M. Evans and Co., 1998

Lane, Mark, Rush to Judgment, Holt Rinehart, 1966

—, *Plausible Denial: Was the CIA Involved in the Assassination of JFK?*, Thunder's Mouth Press, 1992

—, *Last Word*, Skyhorse Publishing, 2011

Latell, Brian, *Castro's Secrets*, Palgrave Macmillan, 2012

Lawrence, Lincoln and Thomas, Kenn, *Mind Control, Oswald & JFK: Were We Controlled?*, 2nd edn, Adventures Unlimited Press, 1997

Leonard, Jerry, *The Perfect Assassin: Lee Harvey Oswald, the CIA and Mind Control*, AuthorHouse, 2002

McAdams, John, *JFK Assassination Logic: How to Think About Claims of Conspiracy*, Potomac Books, 2011

McMillan, Priscilla Johnson, *Marina and Lee*, Collins, 1978

Mailer, Norman, *Oswald's Tale*, Random House, 1995

Mallon, Thomas, *Mrs. Paine's Garage: And the Murder of John F Kennedy*, Pantheon Books, 2002

Marks, John, *Search for the Manchurian Candidate*, Norton, 1979

Mellen, Joan, *A Farewell to Justice*, Potomac Books, 2005

Melanson, Philip H., *The Robert F. Kennedy Assassination – New Revelations on the Conspiracy and Cover-up*, Shapolsky, 1991

Nechiporenko, Oleg M., *Passport to Assassination: The Never-Before-Told Story of Lee Harvey Oswald by the KGB Colonel Who Knew Him*, trans. Todd P. Bludeau, Birch Lane, 1993

Oswald, Robert L. with Land, Myrick and Land, Barbara, *Lee: A Portrait of Lee Harvey Oswald*, Coward-McCann, 1967

Pacepa, Ion Mahai, *Programmed to Kill: Lee Harvey Oswald, the Soviet KGB and the Kennedy Assassination*, Ivan R. Dee, Inc., 2007

Pepper, William, *An Act of State*, Verso Books, 2003

Posner, Gerald, *Case Closed – Lee Harvey Oswald and the Assassination of JFK*, Warner Books, 1993

—, *Killing the Dream*, Little Brown and Company, 1998

Quirk, Robert E., *Fidel Castro*, W.W. Norton and Co., 1993

Russell, Dick, *The Man Who Knew Too Much*, 2nd edn, Carroll and Graf, 2003

Russo, Gus, *Live by the Sword – The Secret War Against Castro and the Death of JFK*, Bancroft, Press, 1998

—, *Brothers in Arms*, with Molton, Stephen, Bloomsbury Publishing PLC, 2008

Sabato, Larry J., *The Kennedy Half Century – The Presidency, Assassination, and Lasting Legacy of John F Kennedy*, Bloomsbury, 2013

Shenon, Philip, *A Cruel and Shocking Act – The Secret History of The Kennedy Assassination*, Little, Brown, 2013

Stockton, Bayard, *Flawed Patriot: The Rise and Fall of CIA Legend Bill Harvey*, Potomac Books, 2006

Streatfeild, Dominic, *Brainwash – The Secret History of Mind Control*, Thomas Dunne Books, 2007

Sturdivan, Larry, *The JFK Myths: A Scientific Investigation of the Kennedy Assassination*, Paragon House Publishers, 2005

Summers, Anthony, *The Kennedy Conspiracy*, Sphere Books, 1998

Thomas, Gordon, *Secrets and Lies – A History of CIA Mind Control and Germ Warfare*, Konecky & Konecky, 2007

Willens, Howard P., *History Will Prove Us Right Inside the Warren Commission Report on the Assassination of John F. Kennedy*, Overlook Press, 2013

Wills, Gary and Demaris, Ovid, *Jack Ruby: The Man Who Killed the Man Who Killed Kennedy*, Ishi Press, 2011

Television Documentaries

Capitol Records, EMI Records, *The Controversy: The Voices of President John F. Kennedy Warren Report*, produced by Lawrence Schiller, 1967

National Geographic Channel, *CIA Secret Experiments*, written, produced and directed by Tria Thalman, 2008

Rendezvous with Death, Wilfried Huismann, 2006, first aired on 6 January 2006 on German television station Westdeutscher Rundfunk

RFK

California State Archives, The Los Angeles Police Department Records of the Robert F. Kennedy Assassination Investigation. The 1969 Final Report (10-volume edition used by LAPD to indicate expurgated portions of the 1969 Report), approx. 1,500pp., courtesy of Nancy Zimmelman, Archivist, California State Archives, Reference Desk, 1020 O Street, Sacramento, CA 95814

FBI Records, 'Robert F Kennedy Assassination – (Summary)', 138pp. Report consisting of the Los Angeles County Board of Supervisors Independent Investigation by Special Counsel Thomas F. Kranz (Kranz Report), 1977

People v. Sirhan, 1972, 7 Cal.3d 710, 497 P.2d 1121, 102 Cal rprt. 385-Cal.06/16/1972.

Kirkham, James F., Levy, Sheldon and Crotty, William J., *Assassination And Political Violence: A Report to the National Commission on the Causes and Prevention of Violence*, US Government Printing Office, 1969

Foreign and Military Intelligence. Book I – Final Report of the Select Committee to Study Governmental Operations with Respect to Intelligence Activities, Section B, 2 The Rationale for Testing programmes, 1976

Books

Ayers, Bradley E., *The War That Never Was: An Insider's Account of CIA Covert Operations Against Cuba*, Bobbs-Merrill, 1976

—, *The Zenith Secret: A CIA Insider Exposes the Secret War Against Cuba and the Plot That Killed the Kennedy Brothers*, Vox Pop, 2006

Ayton, Mel, *The Forgotten Terrorist: Sirhan Sirhan and the Assassination of Robert F. Kennedy*, Potomac Books, 2007

Baden, Michael, *Unnatural Death: Confessions of a Forensic Pathologist*, Sphere Books, 1989

Baker, Robert Allen, *They Call it Hypnosis*, Prometheus Books, 1990

Bergman, Ronen, *Rise and Kill First – The Secret History of Israel's Targeted Assassinations*, Random House, 2018

Capote, Truman, *In Cold Blood*, Penguin Books, 1967

Denton, Sally and Morris, Roger, *The Money and the Power: The Making of Las Vegas and Its Hold on America, 1947–2000*, Alfred A. Knopf, 2001

Douglas, John and Olshaker, Mark, *Mindhunter: Inside the FBI Elite Serial Crime Unit*, Arrow Books, 1997

—, *The Anatomy of Motive*, Pocket Books, 1999

—, *The Cases that Haunt Us*, Pocket Books, 2000

Eppridge, Bill and Gorey, Hays, *Robert Kennedy – The Last Campaign*, Harcourt, 1993

Erikson, M.H., *The Nature of Hypnosis and Suggestion*, Irvington, 1980

Evans, Peter, *Nemesis: Aristotle Onassis, Jackie O., and the Love Triangle that Brought Down the Kennedys*, Regan Books, 2004

Faura, Fernando, *The Polka Dot File on the Robert F. Kennedy Killing: The Paris Peace Talks Connection*, Trine Day, 2016

Gates, Daryl F., *Chief: My Life in the LAPD*, Bantam Books, 1993

Hamburg, Eric, *JFK, Nixon, Oliver Stone & Me: An Idealist's Journey from Capitol Hill to Hollywood Hell*, Public Affairs, 2002

Heymann, C. David, *RFK: A Candid Biography*, William Heinemann, 1998

Houghton, Robert A., *Special Unit Senator: The Investigation of the Assassination of Senator Robert F. Kennedy*, Random House, 1970

Jansen, Godfrey H., *Why Robert Kennedy was Killed: The Story of Two Victims*, Third Press, 1970

Kaiser, Robert Blair, *RFK Must Die! A History of the Robert Kennedy Assassination and Its Aftermath*, 1st edn E.P. Dutton, 1970, 2nd edn Grove Press, 1970

—, *RFK Must Die! Chasing the Mystery of the Robert Kennedy Assassination*, 3rd edn, Overlook Press, 2008

Klaber, William and Melanson, Philip H., *Shadow Play: The Murder of Robert F. Kennedy, the Trial of Sirhan Sirhan and the Failure of American Justice*, St Martin's Press, 1997

Knight, Janet M. (ed.), *3 Assassinations: The Deaths of John & Robert Kennedy and Martin Luther King*, Facts on File, 1971

Marks, John, *The Search for the Manchurian Candidate: The CIA and Mind Control*, Norton, 1979

Mehdi, Mohammed Taki, *Kennedy and Sirhan: Why?*, New World Press, 1968

Melanson, Philip H., *The Robert F. Kennedy Assassination: New Revelations on the Conspiracy and Cover-up*, Shapolsky, 1991

—, *Who Killed Robert Kennedy?*, Odonian Press, 1993

Moldea, Dan E., *The Killing of Robert F. Kennedy: An Investigation of Motive, Means, and Opportunity*, W.W. Norton, 1995

Noguchi, Thomas T., *Coroner to the Stars*, Corgi, 1983

O'Sullivan, Shane, *Who Killed Bobby? The Unsolved Murder of Robert F. Kennedy*, Union Square Press, 2008

Parkin, Alan J., *Memory and Amnesia*, Psychology Press, 1997

Pease, Lisa, *A Lie Too Big to Fail: The Real History of the Assassination of Robert F. Kennedy*, Feral House, 2019

Pease, Lisa and DiEugenio, James (eds), *The Assassinations: Probe Magazine on JFK, MLK, RFK and Malcolm X*, Feral House, 2003

Roberts, Charles, *Tax-Haven Tales: Kooks, Crooks, and Con Men in the Offshore World*, Laissez Faire Books, 2012

Schacter, Daniel L., *Searching for Memory: The Brain, the Mind, the Past*, Basic Books, 1997

Seigenthaler, John, *A Search for Justice*, Aurora Publishers, 1971

Talbot, David, *Brothers: The Hidden History of the Kennedy Years*, Simon and Schuster, 2008

Tate, Tim and Johnson, Brad, *The Assassination of Robert F. Kennedy: Crime, Conspiracy and Cover-up – A New Investigation*, Thistle Publishing, Kindle Locations 2719-2721 3032, 2020

Turner, William W. and Christian, Jonn G., *The Assassination of Robert F. Kennedy: A Searching Look at the Conspiracy and Cover-up, 1968–1978*, Random House, 1978

Vorpagel, Russell, *Profiles in Murder: An FBI Legend Dissects Killers and Their Crimes*, Dell, 1998

Waldron, Lamar and Hartmann, Thom, *Ultimate Sacrifice: John and Robert Kennedy, the Plan for a Coup in Cuba, and the Murder of JFK*, Constable, 2005

Waterfield, Robin, *Hidden Depths: The Story of Hypnosis*, Macmillan, 2002

Witcover, Jules, *85 Days: The Last Campaign of Robert Kennedy*, Putnam, 1969

Audio and Video Recordings

The Assassination of Robert Kennedy, produced by Chris Plumley, Exposed Films
  Production for Channel 4 in association with the Arts and Entertainment Network,
  UK, 1992

RFK Must Die: The Assassination of Bobby Kennedy, written, directed and produced by
  Shane O'Sullivan, Soda Pictures, 2007

Personal Correspondence

Cardena, Dr Eyzel, letter to the author, 21 January 2004

Kenney, James W., letter to the author, 25 September 2003

Wagstaff, Graham, letter to the author, 15 March 2003

Index